# Building Resilience to Trauma

After a traumatic experience, survivors often experience a cascade of physical, emotional, cognitive, behavioral, and spiritual responses that leave them feeling unbalanced and threatened. *Building Resilience to Trauma* explains these common responses from a biological perspective, reframing the human experience from one of shame and pathology to one of hope and biology. It also presents alternative approaches, the Trauma Resiliency Model (TRM) and the Community Resiliency Model (CRM), which offer concrete and practical skills that resonate with what we know about the biology of trauma.

In programs co-sponsored by the World Health Organization, the Unitarian Universalist Service Committee, ADRA International, and the department of behavioral health of San Bernardino County, the TRM and the CRM have been used to reduce and in some cases eliminate the symptoms of trauma by helping survivors regain a sense of balance. Clinicians will find that they can use the models with almost anyone who has experienced or witnessed any event that was perceived as life threatening or posed a serious injury to themselves or to others. The models can also be used to treat symptoms of vicarious traumatization and compassion fatigue.

**Elaine Miller-Karas, LCSW,** is the executive director and co-founder of the Trauma Resource Institute and is adjunct faculty at Loma Linda University's School of Social Work and Social Ecology.

# Building Resilience to Trauma

## The Trauma and Community Resiliency Models

### Elaine Miller-Karas

Routledge
Taylor & Francis Group

NEW YORK AND LONDON

First published 2015
by Routledge
711 Third Avenue, New York, NY 10017

and by Routledge
27 Church Road, Hove, East Sussex BN3 2FA

*Routledge is an imprint of the Taylor & Francis Group, an informa business*

*Library of Congress Cataloging-in-Publication Data*
Miller-Karas, Elaine, author.
    Building resilience to trauma : the trauma and community resiliency
models / by Elaine Miller-Karas.
       p. ; cm.
    Includes bibliographical references and index.
    I. Title.
[DNLM: 1. Stress, Psychological—psychology.   2. Stress,
Psychological—therapy.   3. Community Mental Health Services.
4. Life Change Events.   5. Models, Psychological.   6. Resilience,
Psychological. WM 172.4]
    RC455
    362.19689—dc23
    2014038100

ISBN: 978-0-415-50063-0 (hbk)
ISBN: 978-0-415-82058-5 (pbk)
ISBN: 978-0-203-13411-5 (ebk)

Typeset in Perpetua
by Apex CoVantage, LLC

Printed and bound in the United States of America by
Edwards Brothers Malloy on sustainably sourced paper

This book is dedicated to:

My husband Jim Karas. His love, generosity, and encouragement have given me the strength to pursue my dreams. It is not easy to live with a wild woman with a calling! Thanks for staying on the planet on May 27, 2014!

and

My friend and colleague, Deborah Small, MD, for her dedication and support; for her vision and courage to support the mission and to do what is right and just, even at great cost to herself; and for her enduring care of the Trauma Resource Institute during its most difficult days. You are much more loved than you know.

# Contents

# Figures

# Tables

# About the Authors

**Elaine Miller-Karas,** LCSW, is the executive director and co-founder of the Trauma Resource Institute (TRI) and adjunct faculty at Loma Linda University's School of Social Work and Social Ecology. She has 30 years of experience in social work, education, and trauma therapy and has held leadership roles in international disaster-recovery projects in the Philippines, Haiti, Guatemala, China, Kenya, and Thailand. Her El Salvadoran ancestry fuels her commitment to create culturally sensitive interventions.

Miller-Karas managed the Community Resiliency Model (CRM) Innovation Project, which was designed to bring innovative mental health strategies to the underserved; the project was funded by the State of California's Mental Health Services Act from 2010 to 2013. She has presented at international conferences, including the Conference on World Affairs, Trauma and Resilience, International Society for Traumatic Stress Studies, National Association of Social Work, and the Psychotherapy Networker conference. She has also co-authored the *Trauma Resiliency Model Workbook* and *Community Resiliency Model* workbooks and authored a chapter in *To the Rescue: Stories of Healthcare Workers at the Scenes of Disaster.*

**Beverly J. Buckles,** MSW, DSW, is dean of the School of Behavioral Health at Loma Linda University (LLU). The founder and co-chair of LLU's International Behavioral Health Trauma Team, she is well known as an expert in mental health policies and services, and in international behavioral health response. She has received recognition regionally and nationally for promoting partnerships between academia and public mental health and for the delivery of mental health first aid and trauma resiliency methodologies in underdeveloped regions of the world to effectively assist governments, nongovernmental organizations (NGOs), and communities in preparing for and responding to natural and manmade disasters.

**Jennifer Burton,** LMFT, CEAT, CDWC, is a licensed psychotherapist in private practice in Encino, CA. She has worked with the TRI for the past nine years and is currently a master trainer for TRI. Ms. Burton was one of the lead trainers for the CRM Innovation Project. She has extensive experience using TRM skills in working with adults with chronic mental illness. She is trained in Eye Movement Desensitization Reprocessing, expressive arts therapy, and the Daring Way model.

**Jan Click,** LCSW, retired from the Veterans Administration in 2012 after 32 years of service. She has been a consultant to the TRI as a result of her vast experience in working with veterans and their families. She is a senior faculty member of the TRI as well as a CRM and TRM master trainer. Ms. Click coordinated the Veterans' Extension Project for TRI in San Bernardino County. She is an EMDR-approved consultant and has facilitated EMDR trainings for the Department of the Army. She is a renowned national expert in the area of innovative treatments, helping veterans and their families heal from the repercussions of combat zone and military trauma. Ms. Click currently has a psychotherapy practice in Valencia, CA, where she specializes in treating both military and civilian trauma patients.

**Kimberly R. Freeman,** MSW, PhD, is the executive associate chair and program director of the Masters of Social Work Program in the Department of Social Work and Social Ecology at LLU. She received her MSW and PhD from LLU and is both a social worker and a psychologist with a specialization in working with high-risk children. Her areas of research and academic focus include pediatric psychology, child trauma, and child behavioral health with an emphasis on recovery and global practice. Dr. Freeman has over 13 years of experience in working with high-risk child populations. She has also served on the LLU International Behavioral Health Trauma Team for eight years, where she has conducted numerous presentations/trainings on how to intervene and promote optimal development in high-risk children from a global perspective.

**Jeremy Hunter,** PhD, is assistant professor of practice at the Peter F. Drucker School of Management at Claremont Graduate University in Claremont, CA. Hunter challenges leaders to relentlessly transform themselves to face a complex and volatile world, while also retaining their humanity. He has been featured in the *Wall Street Journal, The Economist*, and National Public Radio's *Morning Edition*. His work is informed by living with a potentially terminal illness for 17 years. When Hunter was faced with the need for life-saving surgery, more than a dozen of his former students stepped forward as organ donors. Dr. Hunter received his PhD from University of Chicago, a Masters in Public Policy from the Kennedy School of Government at Harvard University, and a BA in East Asian studies from Wittenberg University.

**Dr. Michael Sapp,** PhD, is a clinical psychologist practicing in Claremont, CA, and is currently an adjunct professor of psychology at Azusa Pacific University. He received his MA in general psychology and his PhD in clinical psychology from the New School (formerly the New School for Social Research) in New York, NY. Dr. Sapp first learned about the TRM after consulting with Ms. Miller-Karas about a client. Surprised by the efficiency in which the skills effected lasting positive change in this client, with a particular respect for their roots in neuroscience, Dr. Sapp sought training through the TRI and is now a regular TRM facilitator and master trainer. In 2014, he accompanied Ms. Miller-Karas to Cebu City, where they trained leaders from various NGOs throughout the Philippines to teach CRM skills to members of their communities impacted by Typhoon Yolanda.

# Foreword

Trauma can happen in a moment, but its consequences ripple through time. The unhealed effects of overwhelming experiences can arise from historical or contemporary causes, such as war, disasters, accidents, and physical or emotional violence. These invisible weights shouldered by a person, family, or community are non-consciously and destructively transmitted throughout the human web of social relationships, poisoning wells of potential growth and thriving. Unresolved trauma inflicts great damage.

The costs of trauma have an impact on nearly every aspect of being human. Trauma impairs a person's ability to act effectively in the world, authentically relate to fellow human beings, or even feel safe in one's skin. The biological reality of trauma flies in the face of economic theories that assert people are rational and act in their own best interests. It is challenging to act in one's best interests when a built-in and overwhelmed biological alarm system sounds constant, immobilizing danger. Healing trauma and building resilience should be an essential part of economic and community development programs. However, until recently, it was difficult to discuss the reality of trauma, let alone explore methods for its repair. What this book offers is a hopeful, practical path towards a new future.

This work is significant for many reasons. First, it has strong roots. It draws upon the intellectual heritage of the University of Chicago's Eugene Gendlin. His pioneering studies of the transforming power of *focusing* and the *felt sense* reinforce the connection between body and mind. Focusing teaches a person to give affirming attention to sensations in the body. This process allows blocked places to resolve and release, resulting in insight, closure, and forward movement. Another major influence is the work of Peter Levine, who applied Gendlin's insights to the specific case of traumatic experience. Levine developed specialized tools for returning an over-activated nervous system to a sense of normalcy and safety. This creates the possibility for posttraumatic thriving. Elaine Miller-Karas has further raised the bar by making these practices available to communities that might not find themselves willing or able to lie on a therapist's couch for healing.

The book is important because it creates opportunities for a broad audience of first responders, disaster victims, veterans, and members of hardscrabble communities to heal and transform themselves. Furthermore, because of the way the information is presented, recipients of this knowledge are empowered to help and teach others. I recall the story of a Haitian schoolgirl beginning the post-earthquake, disaster relief resilience training. After participating, she returned to her school to heal her classmates, who in turn went home to heal their families. Like a holy fire, the power of this work spreads.

This book is powerful because it grounds the work in an easy-to-grasp biological framework. It makes sense to even unyielding skeptics who have undoubtedly experienced the reality of being "stuck" in hyperarousal and driven to act against their intentions and values. Who hasn't been there? The truth is self-evident.

The book is inspiring because it offers a vision in which people can direct their own growth and development. "Experts" are so willing to inform us that our lives are driven by genetic predispositions, social conditioning, and unconscious forces, leaving little to be self-determined and self-directed. This book delivers a heavy blow to the idea that our lives are out of our own control.

At the Peter F. Drucker School of Management, I teach executives the skills I have learned from Ms. Miller-Karas and her colleagues. These tools have helped talented and principled managers face challenging times with greater calm and intelligence. These methods have helped them heal the wounds that distort their efforts, resulting in clearer judgment and more compassionate action. This work has enabled leaders to step through the fear that kept them from moving forward with their lives and careers. The skills of grounding, tracking, and resourcing should be part of every decision-maker's tool kit.

The work you're holding in your hands is powerful. It offers time-tested ways for human beings to heal themselves and enhance their capacity for resilience and relationship. For a tired world facing simultaneous and seemingly insurmountable crises in ecology, economy, and society, the lessons of this book will be indispensable. The book gives us the tools to retain our humanity while facing great challenges. Instead of becoming debilitated, bitter, and broken, we can cultivate inner strength, growth, and love. This is a handbook for a livable tomorrow.

Jeremy Hunter
Peter F. Drucker School of Management
Claremont Graduate University
Claremont, California
July 2014

# Preface and Acknowledgments

My personal journey to conceptualizing the Trauma Resiliency Model (TRM) and the Community Resiliency Model (CRM) began at age 11 in El Salvador when I first witnessed suffering. I was visiting a small village, Atiquizaya, the birthplace of my mother, Elsy Pineda Miller. I was raised in the San Francisco Bay Area, and this was my first encounter with starving children. It was heart-wrenching and overwhelming. I remember one seminal moment when I gazed into the eyes of a baby, suffering from malnutrition, held tightly in her mother's gaunt arms. This moment is seared into my memory and it shaped how I would forevermore view the world. The alleviation of suffering would be my life's course, and my Latino roots would lay a foundation for the importance of community. My father, Arthur M. Miller, infused within me his Montana grittiness. This would lead me to many countries where I represented the Trauma Resource Institute (TRI) with a dedication to serve the world community as he did in the navy during World War II. He died too young when he was in a firm recovery from his alcoholism. He died a wise sage with a tremendous heart, and his love for me was foundational.

My perceptions of community evolved from being raised in a bicultural family. The concept of "familismo" meant primarily that the family was defined broadly, which included an extended family community with non-blood-related persons. When a tragedy or a celebration occurred, the family and extended family came together in large numbers. My mother, Elsy Pineda Miller, and my grandmother Eva Pineda McCauley, along with my sisters Donna Hester and Deenise Kosct, and my brother, Matthew (Bill) Miller, have guided and supported me, and I have a deep sense of gratitude to all three siblings and their spouses, Bob Hester, Mark Kosct, and Laura Miller. My husband Jim and my father-in-law Ken Karas, who recently turned 100, have been stalwart supporters of my work. My children Erik Karas and Jessica Karas Waterson and my goddaughter, Elisabeth Pellegrin, and their spouses Tanja Briechle Karas, John Waterson, and Pablo Liendro have inspired and humbled me. I am so proud of the world citizens they have become. We have held each other in laughter and tears through the joys and windstorms of life.

As a young woman, I was a Lamaze teacher and doula. The gentleness and power of the body was etched into every fiber of my being as I had the great honor of helping women give birth to their children. Marilyn Libresco taught me adult learning theory as part of my Lamaze training at the University of San Francisco in 1980. Her teachings are still with me and have given me the ability to craft teaching models that are simple and easy to learn. I learned from her that "less is more."

As a Lamaze teacher, the death of Andreas Gantert, the son of Jennifer Gantert, a mother in one of my first Lamaze classes, deeply affected me. As a result, I dove into learning how to support families after the death of a baby. This experience was transformational. It propelled me to start Helping after Neonatal Death of Santa Clara County, a support network for bereaved families. I hold in my heart the memory of each baby who was lost and their families who suffered greatly. Pamela Poetsch died in 2009 and was one of the dearest of friends and confidants since our early days as Lamaze teachers and co-directors of Helping after Neonatal Death. She was one of my biggest supporters and gave one of the first donations when I co-founded the TRI.

The international travel of my childhood and the bicultural lens of my upbringing imbued within me a global perspective and a desire to help heal the suffering of the disenfranchised in culturally relevant ways. As a social worker, I was drawn to Latino communities. While working in inner-city areas of San Bernardino and Santa Clara counties, I encountered a staggering and omnipresent breadth of individual and cumulative trauma from poverty, child abuse, inner-city violence, chronic illness, domestic violence, and migration stress. Simultaneously, I witnessed the resiliency and strength of people who, in spite of hardship and life circumstances, expressed life stories of hope and faith. Many of my most profound teachers have been my clients who could not speak English, who struggled for survival, and who met with unfathomable challenges. My work at Stanford University (my internship and later employment) under the leadership of Cecele Quaintance and Charlene Canger taught me about systems and advocacy for the underserved. No one in California at that time knew more than Cecele about the issues facing maternal child health. Her passion, humor, and guts were contagious.

My family moved to Southern California in 1992 and I worked as the associate director of Behavioral Medicine at Arrowhead Regional Medical Center, the large county hospital in San Bernardino, California. The catalyst for broadening the education of the biology of trauma was teaching the behavioral sciences to interns and residents in the Family Practice Residency Program at Arrowhead Regional Medical Center. Emily Ebert, MD, Elizabeth Richardson, MD, Ruth Stanhiser, MD, and Deborah Small, MD, encouraged me to continue incorporating this biological perspective into my teaching. They saw that it made a difference to patients when they (the patients) were able to understand their symptoms from a biological perspective. Many of the patients in our inner-city clinics were dealing with the worst kinds of trauma from poverty, violence, and racism. Our clinics were inundated with individuals presenting with symptoms related to their traumatic experiences. It was a revelation to the young physicians that most of the patients would never be seen by our mental health professionals—not only because of a lack of resources, but because neither their previous health providers nor the patients themselves had made the connection between their physiological symptoms and their traumatic experience.

I first started experimenting with teaching wellness skills (which have become known as the CRM wellness skills) to discover whether simple body-based interventions coupled with psychoeducation about the biology of traumatic symptoms could alter patients' perceptions of their physical symptoms. Patients started to feel better with simple interventions and began saying, "I feel like I am in control of my anxiety rather than my anxiety being in control of me."

I was profoundly affected by the work of Peter Levine. I was invited to go to Thailand by Peter Levine's organization, the Foundation for Human Enrichment, where my cultural lens was expanded. It was in Thailand where Geneie Everett and I merged our thinking to create the first derivation of an accessible biological model of intervention called Trauma First Aide (TFA). Somatic experiencing was inspirational for Geneie and me in the creation of TFA. Later, Laurie Leitch, Geneie Everett, and I joined forces and began conceptualizing how to bring TFA to a global community, including our veterans and active-duty service members, by starting the TRI in 2006. Geneie decided not to stay with the nonprofit, and she went on to start Trauma First Aide Associates in 2007. As Laurie Leitch and I began working together, we decided to change the name of Trauma First Aide to the Trauma Resiliency Model (TRM) to better reflect the model's efficacy for helping individuals not only with shock trauma, but with developmental trauma as well. Laurie Leitch's insights added another element to the TRM. Laurie Leitch resigned from TRI in 2012 to pursue other interests.

It certainly takes a village to actualize a vision into reality. Many people around the globe make up that village and there is not enough space to list them all. A few have given exceptional support to our international efforts. This amazing group of clinicians and community members includes Don Dorsey, Jennifer Burton, Brenda Williams, Ellen Elgart, Stephanie Citron, Mary Lynn Barrett, Corrie Marcellino, Jessica Klein, Nancy Sokolow, William Cross, Jessica Karas, Randy Imhoff, Marina Compean, Cynthia Costas Cohen, Martha Parra, Jan Click, Michael Sapp, Carol Michelson, Julie Porter, Dagmar Grefe, Gwen Morse, Toni Carreon, Satsuki Ina, Julia Gombos, Lois Clinton, Bill Moseley, Susanne Kulesa, Mariann Ruffalo, Deenise Kosct, Mark Dust, Beverly Buckles, Kim Freeman, Froylana Miller, Kim Cookson, Lovelyn Santos, Kirby Palmer, Michele Tae, Nobuko Hattori, Merdice Ellis, Daniel Bruce, Melissa Boley, Susan Rush, Wendy Svoboda, Joel Andres, Mary Zitkin, Wendy Flick, Atema Elcai, Martha Thompson, Debbie Small, Peggy Rowe

Ward, Price Marshal, Bryan Robinson, Nancy Barickman, Gloria Simoneaux, Dana Eisenberg, Daniel Merman, Paul Fugelsang, Nathan Bergeron, Rob Blinn, Soula Saad, Suzanne Snijder, Loree Sutton, Larry Shaw, Deborah Bateman, Carlos Rodriguez, Lois Bass, Sakti Rose, Jim Cowgill, Eva Nagel, Sherry Wheaton, Joyce Kirk Moore, Jeremy Hunter, Patricia Butler, Patti Giggans, Ellen Ledley, Beth Fitzpatrick, Bob Doppelt, Amanda Wirtz, Walt Johnson, Pam Riley, Garry Trudeau, Ruth Leibowitz, Anita Boling, Rocio Cuddy, Susan Reedy, Karen Chatt, Rainera Lucero, and Karen Banker. They have helped implement and/or support the TRM and the CRM in many locations around the world.

There are a group of individuals that I call "my posse." This group has been my council. They have supported the creation of the TRM and CRM and through their vision and relationship building have helped me create an infrastructure that has made it possible to bring the TRM and CRM forward to our world community. To each and every one of you, my heartfelt thanks. Thank you Brenda Williams, Ellen Elgart, Jan Click, Jennifer Burton, Stephanie Citron, Nancy Sokolow, Marina Compean, Cynthia Costas Cohen, Carol Michelson, and Kim Cookson.

This book could not have been written without the stalwart support, patience, and guidance of Margaret Nilsson. Margaret is my friend and editor, and I am eternally grateful to her for not "running to the hills" as we trudged through some of the difficulties of writing *Building Resilience to Trauma*. Her wisdom and encouragement have uplifted me many times.

Finally, the people who have shared their suffering and their resiliency with me have inspired me. You have touched my heart and soul to my core. Additionally, I have been deeply moved by my clients with dissociative "parts." Your courage and resilience can override the horror of your childhoods. I thank you for your trust. You all inspire me each day to keep working to bring our models to as many people as will listen and sense! You are all my teachers and my world has become so much smaller because my heart is now filled with each and every one of you. You have inspired me to write this book, which has not been easy. While I was teaching Lamaze, working as a doula, and helping families cope with the death of their babies, my beloved father died, and I helped him transition from this life to the next. At that time, I found a passage from a book I had read as a teenager in Atiquizaya, El Salvador—Leo Tolstoy's *Anna Karenina*. The main character, Levin, is witnessing the birth of his first child. His words resonated deeply with me and described the sentiment of being present to the deep wells of suffering and joy then and now. . . .

He only knew and felt that what was happening was similar to what had happened the year before in the hotel of the provincial town on the death-bed of his brother Nicholas. Only that was sorrow and this was joy. But that sorrow and this joy were equally beyond the usual conditions of life:

they were like openings in that usual life through which something higher became visible. And as in that case, what was now being accomplished came harshly, painfully, incomprehensibly; and while watching it, the soul soared, as then, to heights it had never known, before, at which reason could not keep up with it.[1]

## Note

1. Tolstoy, L. (1980). *Anna Karenina* (Louse & Aylmer Maude, Trans.). Oxford: Oxford University Press.

# 1  Resilience and Trauma Defined

*Elaine Miller-Karas*

Elpis was the spirit of hope. Along with the other spirits, she was trapped in a jar by Zeus and entrusted to the care of the first woman—Pandora. When Pandora opened the vessel, all of the spirits escaped except for Elpis (Hope), who alone remained to comfort mankind.

> *The young man had been hospitalized for nearly two years, recovering from injuries sustained in the Iraq War. He had lost a leg, suffered a traumatic brain injury, and severely injured the right side of his body. He wanted to learn new ways to heal his injuries, the obvious ones and the invisible ones. He learned about wellness skills and the importance of paying attention to sensations. He learned simple tracking, resourcing, and grounding skills. As he practiced, he slowing began tracking sensations connected to his well-being. As he paid attention, his hands came together with his fingertips gently touching one another. When he was invited to bring awareness to this movement, he suddenly stopped, and with a startled expression, said, "I feel whole again. For the first time since Iraq, I feel whole again!"*

This poignant story illustrates the hope and healing we have observed all over the world when people are gently reminded of the healing potential that exists within their bodies. In this book, we will show how "the elegant design of the nervous system" offers hope for those suffering from unresolved trauma. There is no question that trauma can wreak havoc on our lives, affecting us emotionally, physically, and spiritually. Human beings have a capacity to heal after experiencing traumatic events, and recovery can be achieved through the portal of the body—a system that is elegantly designed to return to balance. Our experience working with survivors of trauma throughout the world indicates that practitioners who learn a set of skills based on resetting the nervous system can help individuals heal from the trauma that has impaired their ability to live fully.

The Trauma Resiliency Model (TRM) guides the mental health practitioner to help clients reprocess traumatic experiences. Through this model the practitioner learns specific skills to help the client reset his nervous system. As the nervous system is reset, new meanings and beliefs emerge, and a new survival story emerges based on nervous system regulation. The Community Resiliency Model (CRM) is taught to community members as a set of wellness skills that return the nervous system to balance and can be used for self-care and shared with family members and a person's wider social network. The simple but powerful wellness skills of the TRM and CRM are accessible and effective across borders, cultures, and belief systems.

## Defining Trauma Simply

Trauma can be defined in many ways, but, most importantly, it is *an individual's perception of an event as threatening to oneself or others*. An event that results in trauma for one person may not be experienced by another individual as traumatic. Even if every member of a family experiences the same event, each may have a different perspective regarding the event.

Further, trauma doesn't have to be experienced firsthand. This is an important distinction because many people live in self-blame and self-criticism, wondering why they are having such a difficult time, when they, themselves, did not experience trauma. This vicarious trauma is experienced often by those in the helping professions, such as therapists, crisis counselors, firefighters, police officers, and medical professionals.

Dr. Francine Shapiro defines two types of trauma. She categorizes one as "large-T" and the second as "small-t" trauma (Shapiro, 1987). "Large-T" Trauma includes major events such as natural disasters, war, sexual assaults, child abuse, or acts of terrorism. Examples of "small-t" trauma could be a dental procedure, a dog bite, a routine surgery, a fall, or a minor car accident. "Small-t" traumas are labeled as such not because the person experienced them as a minor event. The individual involved may actually experience something as a "large-T" event; however, we may designate it as "small-t" because family members and the larger society deem the event as being of minor significance.

Cumulative trauma, or C-trauma was added to our conceptualization after a world leader in humanitarian efforts and restorative justice shared with us the lingering impact of colonialism on the people of her home country, Kenya. In addition, others shared the micro-aggressions of homophobia and racism, and Native American colleagues explained the collective trauma of losing one's culture and language as a result of genocide. Cumulative trauma, then, can be used to describe racism, poverty, and homophobia. Living with racism, for example—not knowing if you are accepted by others or even if your life could be in danger because of the color of your skin—can create a cascade of physical and emotional reactions that may be experienced daily.

Someone who experiences large-T Trauma may perceive his world as not being safe. Someone who experiences a small-t trauma may experience even a visit to the dentist as not being safe. And for those who have overarching cumulative trauma that impacts their lives on a daily basis, their wider world community is not safe. An individual can have experiences from all three categories at the same time. This "stacking effect" may be a tipping point for a person who has experienced a number of "large-T" and "C-traumas," so that when a "small-t trauma" such as a minor surgical procedure is experienced, the individual can have major traumatic stress reactions. Those who are simultaneously dealing with multiple types of trauma are at greater risk for psychological and physiological challenges.

Further, symptoms of traumatic stress can occur immediately following a traumatic event or it may be months or years before symptoms appear. Symptoms can wax and wane, plague people their entire lives, or appear suddenly.

According to the World Health Organization (WHO), "Traumatic events and loss are common in people's lives." In a WHO study of 21 countries (World Health Organization, 2013), more than 10% of respondents reported witnessing violence (21.8%) or experiencing interpersonal violence (18.8%), accidents (17.7%), exposure to war (16.2%), or vicarious trauma through a loved one (12.5%). An estimated 3.6% of the world's population suffered from posttraumatic stress disorder (PTSD) in the previous year, the study showed. The world's population is estimated at 7,222,547,911 as of 2014, so approximately 260 million people are suffering from posttraumatic stress symptoms.

A World Economic Forum report supplies comparisons across noncommunicable diseases that provide information about their global economic burden. Mental health costs are the largest single source—larger than cardiovascular disease, chronic respiratory disease, cancer, or diabetes. Mental illness alone will account for more than half of the projected total economic burden from non-communicable diseases over the next two decades and 35% of the global lost output (Bloom et al., 2011). Considering that those with mental health challenges are at high risk for developing cardiovascular disease, respiratory disease, and diabetes, the true costs of mental illness must be even higher. Rytwinski, Avena, Echiverri-Cohen, Zoellner, and Feeny (2014) reported that about one of every two people diagnosed with posttraumatic stress disorder (PTSD) also suffers symptoms of depression.

The WHO released new clinical protocols and guidelines in 2013 to promote effective mental health care for adults and children exposed to trauma and loss. According to a WHO report, "[M]ental disorders are common, disabling and usually untreated." The report recommends that primary health care providers provide mental health care support. It also mentions Cognitive Behavioral Therapy (CBT) and Eye Movement Desensitization and Reprocessing (EMDR) as two possible interventions. CBT and EMDR are both evidence-based practices that require a great deal of training on the part of the practitioner to become proficient. While we applaud WHO's report and its efforts to bring attention to the numbers of individuals affected worldwide by PTSD and depression, the sheer number of individuals who have experienced trauma would make it difficult, if not impossible, to train enough primary care providers worldwide to make a significant impact.

Through our work internationally and in the United States in areas where people live with the oppression of poverty and racism often in conjunction with the impact of natural and man-made disasters, we have seen there are not enough health professionals to help the number of people impacted by traumatic events. In addition, many individuals—because of their cultural perspectives, their spiritual beliefs, or an aversion to psychological interventions—do not seek the help of mental health practitioners. It is essential to think outside the box when considering how we can bring relief to large groups of trauma-affected people. The CRM provides interventions that can be taught by health professionals as well as lay people to help the wider community, with very simple, easy-to-learn skills that can stabilize the nervous system.

## Trauma and Stressor-Related Disorders

The *Diagnostic and Statistical Manual of Mental Disorders* (DSM-5) includes PTSD in a new category called "Trauma and Stressor-related Disorders." The diagnostic criteria for PTSD include a history of exposure to a traumatic event that meets specific stipulations and symptoms from each of four symptom clusters: intrusion, avoidance, negative alterations in cognitions and mood, and alterations in arousal and reactivity. Additional criteria concern duration of symptoms, assessment of functioning, and the stipulation that the symptoms are not attributable to a substance or co-occurring medical condition (American Psychiatric Association, 2013). As mental health practitioners, we need diagnostic criteria to help guide us in diagnosis and treatment. There is controversy over the new DSM-5 and time will tell how the DSM-5 will be incorporated into practice. Also, we have found that many of our clients prefer simple explanations that help them better understand their reactions to their life experiences. For more information on the DSM-5, go to http://www.dsm5.org/Documents/PTSD%20Fact%20Sheet.pdf.

## Trauma and the Impact on Health Care

Human beings throughout the world, regardless of ethnicity and culture, have common reactions to stressful and traumatic experiences. The TRM and CRM models recognize trauma as a *biological* reaction resulting from extraordinary life experiences. A joint study by Kaiser Permanente, in San Diego, California, and the Centers for Disease Control (CDC) highlights what we are learning about how trauma affects people physically and behaviorally. In the Adverse Childhood Experiences (ACE) Study, researchers noted that morbidly obese adults who were taking part in a weight management program at Kaiser Permanente were not successful in maintaining weight loss. In delving deeper into the background of these individuals, the researchers discovered that all had histories of trauma. As a follow-up, they decided to survey Kaiser patients to see how many had experienced childhood trauma.

Researchers identified the following 10 types of trauma: sexual, physical, and emotional abuse; physical and emotional neglect; and five types of family dysfunction including having a household member who treated the person violently, abused drugs or alcohol, was imprisoned, or had a diagnosis of mental illness, or having parents who were separated or divorced. Sixty-four percent of those surveyed had experienced one or more categories of adverse childhood events (Felitti et al., 1998).

Individuals were assigned one point if they had the experience, regardless of how many times they had the experience. Researchers wanted to see if there was a correlation between people's ACE score and their utilization of health care. *They found a strong link between adverse childhood experiences and adult onset of chronic illness.* Those with ACE scores of four or more had significantly higher rates of heart disease and diabetes than those with ACE scores of zero. In addition, in the group that scored four or higher, the incidence of chronic pulmonary disease increased by 390%, hepatitis: 240%; depression: 460%; and suicide attempts: 1,220%. Patients with ACE scores of six or more had a 4,600% increase in the likelihood of becoming an intravenous drug user, and they died nearly 20 years earlier on average than those with ACE scores of zero—they lived 60.6 years versus 79.1 years.

Researchers then conducted a more extensive psychosocial assessment of patients who came in to Kaiser, in which they followed up on the traumatic experiences individuals had gone through and asked them about how those experiences affected them in the present. The findings were impressive: In the year following this short intervention, there was a 35% reduction in primary care usage, an 11% reduction in emergency room visits, and a 3% reduction in hospitalizations of this group.

The results of the ACE Study support our belief that trauma affects individuals in a biological way. Since many people who have experienced trauma never seek therapy, we need more portals within the public health system to address the needs of those who have trauma-related symptoms. In addition, most psychological approaches are cognitively based. Cognitive models, while sometimes using relaxation exercises, focus on changing debilitating beliefs, providing insight, and developing problem-solving strategies. This is what is called a "top-down" approach and although it may lead to increased insight, it may not lead to nervous system stabilization.

Bryant, Creamer, O'Donnell, Silove, and McFarlane (2008) stated that acute physiological reactions measured during or immediately after a traumatic event have been shown to predict the later development of PTSD. Some individuals experience symptoms such as an elevated heart rate and respiration rate in the wake of a traumatic event. These symptoms may be able to be *sensed* away if the individual can learn to track his nervous system in order to intercept these sensations of distress and bring his attention to sensations of well-being. The nervous system can then return to balance and traumatic stress reactions can be reduced or eliminated.

In the Mind Your Heart Study, Cohen et al. (2013) studied 178 individuals who met the criteria for full PTSD and 18 who met the criteria for partial PTSD. The participants with PTSD scored significantly worse on processing speed, category fluency, verbal learning, and verbal recognition than those without PTSD. The authors concluded that patients with PTSD versus without had significantly poorer performance in several domains of cognitive function, particularly in tests involving processing speed and executive function. Thus, the parts of the brain responsible for verbal processing and introspection do not function at their best under stress or after a traumatic event.

There is a need for interventions that focus on the biological basis of threat, fear, and resiliency because neuroscience is illuminating that trauma can affect the parts of the brain responsible for verbal processing and cognitive functioning. The TRM and CRM focus on the body's innate ability to expand the sensations associated with resiliency in order to override the survival-based responses to threat and fear. The wellness skills, then, are aimed at nervous system stabilization. Although the symptoms from adverse childhood events may not be easily *talked* away, they can be *sensed* away.

## Resilience and the Hope for Healing

Human beings are resilient and have the capacity for healing after traumatic life experiences. We define resilience as the ability to identify and use individual and collective strengths to live fully in the present moment and to thrive while managing the tasks of daily living. We have seen that resilient people not only get back on their feet after a fall, they can create meaning from their struggles that transforms their lives and their communities. According to George Bonnano (2009), resilience is the most common reaction of those who experience trauma. We have traveled the world after man-made and natural disasters and have witnessed this capacity for resiliency.

Along with the common reaction of resiliency, a significant number of individuals experience long-lasting traumatic stress reactions. Our models aim to help individuals understand the biology of traumatic stress reactions and, most importantly, learn specific skills to return the body, mind, and spirit back to balance after experiencing traumatic events. Specifically, the models help individuals learn to distinguish between sensations of well-being and those of distress.

A large-scale study found that when individuals learned the wellness skills of the CRM and TRM, they experienced reductions in symptoms of depression, anxiety, hostility indicators, and body complaints (Citron, 2013). The following chapters lay out the key concepts and skills of the two models. In addition, we cover how to utilize these skills with certain specific populations, including children and veterans and service members.

*Maria survived Typhoon Yolanda of 2013 in the Philippines. She was stuck in the story of her traumatic experience. Her body began to shake before she even began telling her story. Maria was asked, "What helped you survive the experience?" She recounted that she and her friends had held hands in a circle, praying. When asked about her sensory experience as she recounted and emphasized this new element of the survival story, Maria took a deep breath and reported her heart rate was returning to normal. She suddenly gave new meaning to her experience. "I survived. I am okay!" she said, and she reported feeling the blood flow in her body as if she were finally really alive again. At the time of the storm, the fear of losing her life overrode the memory of what helped her get through. Maria was given time to notice the sensations connected to her survival story. As she recounted the story, her nervous system came back into balance. She shared that she could now remember that night as the night she survived, not the night that she almost lost her life.*

Both the TRM and CRM are clinical applications of current neuroscience and what has been an expanding area of knowledge over the past 20 years. Among discoveries in the field is a concept called "neuroplasticity." This is the knowledge that the brain is malleable—simply, the brain can change. If the brain can change, then so can our beliefs, feelings, and associated body sensations. Specifically, new pathways or connections between neurons can be created within the brain and body. The creation of new neuronal pathways can result in greater resilience. We think that when a person learns to stabilize his nervous system and can apply this knowledge in his activities of daily living, he is changing his brain. "Neuroplasticity refers to the lifelong capacity of the brain to change and rewire itself in response to the stimulation of learning and experience. Neuro-genesis is the ability to create new neurons and connections between neurons throughout a life-time" (Fernandez & Goldberg, 2009). Neuroplasticity is the "hope" of the nervous system.

*Maria had spent five months talking about the trauma of the typhoon without illuminating the survival elements of her experience. As she relayed the survival events, there was a corresponding sensory experience that was about Maria's resilience. As she sensed into the experience of well-being, she expressed that she felt relief in her body and mind. As Maria added new elements to her story, she created a new sensory experience, one that was connected to wellness and resulted in a new, more resiliency-focused narrative experience of the traumatic event.*

## Defining the Resilient Zone of the TRM and CRM

The "resilient zone" is an internal state of adaptability and flexibility. When we are in our resilient zones, we can navigate the challenges we encounter in our lives. The goal of both models is to help individuals become more aware of their resilient zones by learning to track sensations connected to their resilient zones. When a person learns to distinguish between sensations of distress and those of well-being, he develops a greater capacity to return to his resilient zone by intention. *Resiliency informed* means being aware of our ability to return to our resilient zone when we are bumped out.

Bonnano (2009) states that intervening with cognitive-based models during periods when an individual is in a state of recovery and/or resilience after a traumatic event can actually *increase* someone's traumatic stress reactions. This poses important questions about how we intervene after individuals have suffered traumatic events. Our view is that the sooner we intervene *with biological interventions* to help stabilize an individual's nervous system to return to one's resilient zone, the more likely traumatic stress reactions can be reduced or eliminated. In the immediate aftermath of natural and man-made disasters, it is difficult to assess who will be resilient and who will not. We believe wellness skills can greatly help those who have difficulty recovering from a traumatic event. For individuals who are naturally resilient, the wellness skills will be additional tools to enhance their resiliency.

Yet, there is much reason for hope, because the resilient zone—where we are neither stuck in the high or low zones—is a state that human beings are designed to achieve. The TRM and CRM provide easy and accessible skills that individuals can learn to help them recover from traumatic stress and cope with the ups and downs of daily living. Three thousand years ago, the ancient Greeks created the story of Pandora's box and the hope that was left for humankind to remind us all of this wisdom.

## References

American Psychiatric Association. (2013). *Diagnostic and statistical manual of mental disorders* (5th ed.). Arlington, VA: American Psychiatric Publishing.

Bloom, D. E., Cafiero, E. T., Jané-Llopis, E., Abrahams-Gessel, S., Bloom, L. R., Fathima, S., . . . Weinstein, C. (2011). *The global economic burden of non-communicable diseases.* Geneva, Switzerland: World Economic Forum.

Bonnano, G. (2009). *The other side of sadness: What the new science of bereavement tells us about life after a loss.* New York: Basic Books.

Bryant, R. A., Creamer, M., O'Donnell, M., Silove, D., & McFarlane, A. C. (2008). A multisite study of initial respiration rate and heart rate as predictors of posttraumatic stress disorder. *The Journal of Clinical Psychiatry, 69,* 1694–1701.

Citron, S. (2013). *Final CRM innovation evaluation report.* Claremont: Trauma Resource Institute

Cohen, B. E., Neylan, T. C., Yaffe, K., Samuelson, K. W., Li, Y., & Barnes, D. E. (2013). Posttraumatic stress disorder and cognitive function: Findings from the Mind Your Heart Study. *The Journal of Clinical Psychiatry, 74,* 1063–1070. doi:10.4088/JCP.12m08291

Felitti, V. J., Anda, R. F., Nordenberg, D., Williamson, D. F., Spitz, A. M., Edwards, V., . . . Marks, J. S. (1998). Relationship of childhood abuse and household dysfunction to many of the leading causes of death in adults: The Adverse Childhood Experiences (ACE) study. *American Journal of Preventive Medicine, 14,* 245–258. doi:10.1016/S0749–3797(98)00017–8

Fernandez, A., & Goldberg, E. (2009). *The SharpBrains guide to brain fitness: 18 interviews with scientists, practical advice, and product reviews, to keep your brain sharp.* San Francisco, CA: SharpBrains.

Rytwinski, N., Avena, J. S., Echiverri-Cohen, A. M., Zoellner, L. A., & Feeny, N. C. (2014). The relationships between posttraumatic stress disorder severity, depression severity and physical health. Journal of Health Psychology, 19, 509–520.

Shapiro, F. (1987). What is EMDR? www.emdr.com/general-information/what-is-emdr.html

World Health Organization. (2013). WHO releases guidance on mental health care after trauma (News report). http://www.who.int/mediacentre/news/releases/2013/trauma_mental_health_20130806/en/

# 2 The Nervous System, Memory, and Trauma

## Elaine Miller-Karas and Michael Sapp

The goal of the Trauma Resiliency Model (TRM) and the Community Resiliency Model (CRM) is to provide training in biologically based skills that increase resiliency and decrease the debilitating effects of traumatic stress. The models assume that responses to threats—real or imagined—are biologically based and primarily autonomic. Accordingly, the cognitive and psychological aspects of trauma are secondary to the biological response to fear.

That's not to say that the cognitive or psychological aspects of trauma are not important. They are. However, most traditional modalities of treatment focus on those two aspects as the entry points for alleviating the symptoms of traumatic reactions. In contrast, the TRM and CRM focuses on the biological responses themselves as the primary entry point—or portal—to promote healing. The reason is simple: Trauma's disruption of normal biological rhythms fuels the cognitive and psychological aspects of trauma.

Imagine someone who lives in a home with an electronic security system. Before she goes to bed, she sets the alarm, performs her nighttime rituals, and then finally climbs into bed to go to sleep. As she relaxes and drifts off to sleep, an intruder tries to break into the house and triggers the alarm. The alarm sounds, causing the intruder to leave. The alarm did its job; the threat has been averted. However, the sounding of that alarm also causes the homeowner to wake up out of a dead sleep—her heart pounding, her eyes searching the room for the intruder, her muscles tense and ready for action. In that moment, she would likely say she was "scared." Was the homeowner thinking or feeling or behaving in that way prior to the alarm sounding? No. The sound of the alarm fueled her thoughts and reactions.

Now imagine what it would be like for that homeowner in the subsequent few minutes. She doesn't know that the intruder has left, so the alarm continues to sound as she checks each room to make sure that her house is secure. Once she confirms that there is no intruder and that she is safe, what must she do next? She needs to shut off the alarm and reset it. Until that is done, trying to go back to sleep or read a book or do virtually anything would be extremely difficult. It's very hard to focus one's cognitive and psychological energies on anything else if an alarm is ringing.

In much the same way, traumatic events can set off a "biological alarm" that dysregulates normal biological rhythms in order to ready us for survival. TRM/CRM skills are designed to "reset" the biological alarm and restore the natural biological rhythms of the nervous system. As that happens, the cognitive and psychological aftermath of trauma will often self-correct.

Trauma has a major effect on our nervous systems. Learning about the nervous system and conveying brain science in simple terms helps clients understand the biology behind their symptoms. The brain is very complex, and speaking simply about the brain helps move individuals from perceptions of personal weakness to an understanding of biology. In the TRM/CRM, we highlight parts of the brain that can help us understand human symptoms and behaviors and, most importantly, pathways to healing.

Just as it would be helpful for the homeowner to understand the basics of her electronic security system, we find it helpful to have a basic understanding of our own internal, biological security system.

In the most basic sense, we interact with the world through our physical body. We take in information through our body's sensory receptors. We process that information and make decisions using our brain. We execute those decisions through our body's muscles and tissues. All of this is made possible through our body's nervous system. As you can imagine, the human nervous system is a very sophisticated and complex system. However, simplifying its processes so that we can communicate a basic understanding of it can provide us with immeasurable benefits.

Our nervous system has traditionally been conceptualized as having two main components: the **central nervous system (CNS)** and the **peripheral nervous system (PNS).** The CNS consists of the brain and spinal cord and can be thought of as the "decision maker" of the body. The PNS consists of all of the nerves that collect information from the body and transmit CNS decisions to the body. Please keep in mind that although we conceptualize them as if they are two separate systems, they are in fact inseparable. The mind and the body work as one. That being said, there are some specialized functions within the human nervous system that can aid us in understanding the effects of trauma and the ability of the body to adapt to a wide range of situations.

Let's focus on the peripheral nervous system first. The peripheral nervous system is considered to have two components: the somatic and the autonomic. The **somatic nervous system** includes all of the nerves that enable us to control our body's muscles. For example, you may notice that you have been sitting in the same position for some time now. The urge to shift your body to a more comfortable position is carried out when your somatic nervous system tells various muscles to actually move and reposition your body until it's comfortable.

The **autonomic nervous system** involves all of the nerves that control our glands and the muscles of our internal organs. For example, as you sit here reading, imagine a breeze carries in the smell of your favorite food. Your mind may drift off to thoughts of that particular food and you may notice your heartbeat quicken and perhaps feel a slight hunger pang. These changes are largely due to your autonomic nervous system telling your heart to pick up its pace and your digestion to turn on.

In this example, you didn't actively tell your digestion to turn on; it just happened. Accordingly, the autonomic nervous system is considered largely involuntary. In contrast, while there are times when the body's muscles respond reflexively and with little to no control, the somatic nervous system is considered largely voluntary. For example, under normal circumstances one could imagine being able to raise a hand or kick a ball by "telling" your body to do it. These biological actions are voluntary. However, "telling" your heart to race faster or getting your digestive system to turn on is another matter. These biological actions are largely involuntary.

The autonomic nervous system includes the sympathetic and parasympathetic nervous systems. During times of stress or challenge, the **sympathetic nervous system (SNS)** arouses and prepares the body for action. It directs the adrenal glands to release stress hormones (e.g., adrenaline and noradrenaline), readying the body to take action. The SNS causes the liver to provide extra sugar to the bloodstream in order to increase energy; it also increases breathing to provide added oxygen. The SNS diverts blood from the internal organs to the muscles, slowing digestion and suppressing the immune system. Along with increased heart rate and blood pressure, this gets the blood to the much-needed muscles, making it easier for the body to move and to move quickly. The SNS dilates the pupils, allowing in more light; it decreases salivation, but increases perspiration in order to cool down the activated body.

This is often called the "fight or flight" response and is a wonderfully adaptive process. When a threat is perceived, your SNS does all of these things without any conscious effort in order to make it easier for you to overcome the threat. If you were to imagine the last time you faced a particularly stressful event (e.g., giving a presentation, barely avoiding a car accident, etc.), how fast was your heart beating? Did you feel on edge? Did you have sweaty palms? Dry mouth? Your SNS was readying you for action. These biological processes are adaptive.

Just as a car needs both an accelerator and a brake, the body needs a counterpart to the SNS. That counterpart is the **parasympathetic nervous system (PSNS),** which calms the body and prepares it for rest. Once the "fight or flight" response is successful, the "rest and digest" response takes over. As the stress hormones slowly leave the bloodstream, the PSNS works to conserve energy and restore the body to a more balanced state. It slows breathing, lowers blood sugar, decreases heart rate and blood pressure, increases digestion and immune functioning, constricts the pupils, increases salivation, and decreases perspiration. As a result, the activated body becomes calm once again.

These two systems, the SNS and PSNS, work together to maintain a steady and balanced internal state within the body. The natural biological rhythm of charge (SNS) and release (PSNS) corresponds to the rhythm of the resilient zone. When we are in our resilient zone, our autonomic nervous system is in rhythm. When this rhythm is working properly, we are at our best in handling the challenges that we face. The accelerator and brake are being used appropriately. However, certain demands can be overwhelming and can cause a significant disruption in that rhythm.

Hans Selye (1936) defined **stress** as "the nonspecific response of the body to any demand." According to this definition, there can be stress that is caused by either desirable events (eustress) or undesirable events (distress). Regardless, both kinds of stress can tax a person's ability to cope. Babette Rothschild (2000) makes a useful distinction between stress and traumatic stress. She defines the most extreme form of stress as **traumatic stress.** Traumatic stress results when a traumatic event or crisis overwhelms or threatens to overwhelm a person's ability to cope. The normal rhythm of the autonomic nervous system becomes dysregulated. In TRM language, such events bump us out of our resilient zone.

In such cases, we might be bumped into a "high zone" in which we may experience something akin to SNS hyperarousal. Along with the normal sensations of SNS arousal, we may also feel edgy and irritable. We may get angry really easily (i.e., "short fuse"). We may experience panic or anxiety or pain. We often become hypervigilant and overly sensitive. Or, we might be bumped into a "low zone" in which we may experience something that looks like a hyper-PSNS response. We might feel numb, disconnected from others (i.e., isolated) or from ourselves (e.g., dissociative responses). We might experience sadness or a depressed mood. We often feel exhausted or tired. Or we might even oscillate between being stuck in the "high zone" and stuck in the "low zone." Some have reported feeling like they're stuck in both zones at the same time. Much like pressing on the accelerator and the brake at the same time, there is a seemingly paralyzed agitation.

TRM/CRM skills are designed to bring a dysregulated nervous system back into its natural rhythm, its resilient zone. When a person reenters his resilient zone, there is often an accompanying biological sensation of release. Nervous system **release** is a biological process that happens automatically when your body releases distressing sensations and comes back into balance. Sensations of release can include trembling, tingling, stomach gurgling and/or burping (as digestion comes back online), warmth, cooling down, throat clearing, shaking, itching, laughing, crying, and yawning. This is not an exhaustive list. However, just as it's important to know what biological sensations might accompany specific SNS or PSNS responses, it is equally important to know that there can be biological sensations that accompany a return to a more balanced state. In fact, inquiring about nervous system release and bringing the client's attention to the sensations often strengthens the release, bringing the body and mind back into the resilient zone.

Of particular note is recent research on a biological response that seems to be one of the most important mechanisms for regulating the survival-related behaviors in mammals—yawning. According to Anthony Newberg (2009), yawning may be the brain's attempt to eliminate symptoms by readjusting neural functioning. Numerous neurochemicals are involved in the yawning experience, including dopamine, which activates oxytocin production in the hypothalamus and hippocampus (areas essential for memory recall, voluntary control, and temperature regulation). Yawning may be a way to cool down the overly active cortex, especially in the region of the frontal lobe. Most vertebrates yawn, but so far it has only been found to be contagious among humans, great apes, macaque monkeys, and chimpanzees.

Now let's turn our attention to the central nervous system and specifically to the specialized functions of the brain as it relates to trauma. Keep in mind (no pun intended) that a thorough understanding of the intricate functioning of the brain as a whole is outside the scope of this book. Instead, our aim is a simple understanding of how the brain operates in response to stress, how it interacts with the body during those times, and how the brain might function better in times of resiliency. Being able to communicate this to clients is especially important and is generally met with great enthusiasm and appreciation by clients. The good news is you don't have to have an advanced degree in neuroscience to understand some of the basics.

The nervous system as a whole is made up of billions of microscopic nerve cells called **neurons.** According to some estimates, the brain has more than 100 billion nerve cells and over one trillion supporting cells (e.g., glia cells). Neurons are rather simple in functioning: They either fire or they don't. However, each neuron can have up to 10,000 connections to other nerve cells, resulting in estimates of over a quadrillion connections. The complexities of brain functioning lie in these intersecting connections.

Understanding the brain at the level of the neuron is helpful in understanding the concept of brain plasticity. Much like plastic that has a physical structure that is both structurally sound but moldable, the brain has a physical structure that is changeable. And like plastic, any change in the brain's shape often reflects a change in its function and vice versa. We refer to the brain's ability to change in structure and function, especially as a result of environmental influence, as **brain plasticity.** As with all things related to the brain, brain plasticity is highly complex and involves many different processes. However, for the sake of simplicity as it relates to therapeutic intervention, we can focus on at least two processes contributing to brain plasticity.

First, when neurons form strong connections with other neurons, they often develop into **neural networks,** or clusters of small workgroups. Essentially, neural networks form specialized functions based on the complex interactions among the individual neurons that make up that network. This is essentially the "neurons that fire together wire together" principle. Accordingly, changes in behavior or thinking do not necessarily involve the formation of new neurons, but rather a change in the connections that neurons make with each other. Furthermore, neural networks then form strong connections with other neural networks. Learning anything—e.g., riding a bike, memorizing a poem—involves the strengthening of complex interactions among multiple neural networks.

The principle that neurons that fire together wire together illustrates how various life experiences affect the actual architecture of the brain. For example, Kolb and Whishaw (1998) outlined many of the landmark studies dating back to the late 1940s about the effects of different environments on brain development in rats. They noted that in some of their own studies, which compared rats raised in impoverished environments (i.e., in a cage alone and without any playthings) to rats raised in enriched environments (i.e., in a cage with other rats and plenty of playthings), the rats raised in enriched environments showed significantly healthier brain development by day 60. Of particular note was the finding that rats from the enriched environments had estimates of up to 20% more neuronal connections in some parts of their brain than the rats from impoverished environments. Positive experiences can change the actual structure of the brain by increasing the number of connections between neurons.

In contrast, the second major process involved in brain development is called **pruning.** Neural connections that aren't used weaken and often disappear—the "use it or lose it" principle. This principle is often used as a possible explanation as to why infants lose their ability to tell the difference between certain sounds depending on what language they are exposed to. For example, infants younger than 6–8 months show the ability to distinguish between the sounds /r/ and /l/ regardless of culture. However, by 10–12 months, infants raised in cultures that do not discriminate between the sounds /r/ and /l/ (e.g., in Japan) show difficulty in discriminating between them. Werker and Tees (1999) noted that although these infants come preloaded with the ability to make such a distinction, their "subsequent experience functions to narrow, or 'prune,' their perceptual sensitivities." Whether this ability is irrevocably lost or not (see Rivera-Gaxiola, Silva-Pereyra, & Kuhl, 2005), these findings suggest that not only can one's experiences strengthen neuronal connections, but one's lack of experience may render some neural connections obsolete, resulting in a loss of functioning.

Imagine a field that people have to travel across to get to and from their destination. As people travel back and forth across the field, paths are formed. The paths that are used more frequently are broadened and become more permanent than the paths that have less frequent use. The paths that aren't used as frequently become less visible and are often lost. This is an important point that explains why the TRM/CRM emphasizes the repeated use of wellness skills.

Consider the well-worn paths of symptoms associated with traumatic stress. Perhaps a particular smell triggers intrusive thoughts, a sense of panic or dread, and avoidance behaviors. These pathways are well traveled and seem permanent to the client. The TRM/CRM model focuses on teaching skills that potentially strengthen healthier responses—i.e., healthier neural pathways. The more the skills are used, the more likely they are to develop into integrated neural networks of resilience. Likewise, the more time we spend "traveling" down paths of resilience, the less time we spend in the more well-worn, dysfunctional paths. And, if the "use it or lose it" principle holds, then the less we use those unhealthy paths, the more likely they will become obsolete (resulting in a reduction of symptoms). Therefore, according to Cozolino (2010), "From the perspective of neuroscience, psychotherapists are in the brain-rebuilding business."

Let's now zoom out from the level of the neuron, past the level of neural networks to focus on the various specialized functions of certain brain regions. The basic anatomy of the brain consists of two hemispheres, the right hemisphere and the left hemisphere. Regarding the specialized functioning of particular brain regions, it can be useful to think of the brain as a three-part system (MacLean, 1990), consisting of the cortex (i.e., the "thinking brain"), the limbic system (i.e., the "emotional brain"), and the brain stem (i.e., the "survival brain"). Of course, right now you might be horribly offended at the prospect of trying to boil down all of the complexity involved in a system that potentially has over a quadrillion connections to just three parts. You may be thinking that at the very least, it's a gross oversimplification. You're right. It is. That being said, it's a useful conceptualization to help therapists and clients better understand the brain without having to earn an advanced degree in neuroscience.

Working from the top down, the **cortex** or "thinking brain" is the outer bark of the brain. It contributes up to 85% of the brain's weight and each of its hemispheres can be divided into four lobes: the frontal lobe, the parietal lobe, the occipital lobe, and the temporal lobe. Visualize a boxing glove from the side and you can visualize these lobes. The "thumb of the glove" is the temporal lobe—located roughly right above the ears—and it houses the auditory cortex, which is generally responsible for processing auditory information. Just above the "wrist" of the glove is the occipital lobe—located at the back of the head—and it contains the visual cortex, which is generally responsible for processing visual information. From there up to the "knuckles" of the glove is the parietal lobe—located at the top-rear portion of the head—and it is known for its sensory cortex, which receives sensory information from the skin and from the movement of body parts. Finally, there is the portion of the glove where the "fingers" are. This is the frontal lobe—located just behind the forehead—and it is responsible for a lot of important and diverse functions.

Within the frontal lobe, there is the motor strip—roughly at the first set of "knuckles" in the glove—which is important in the planning, control, and execution of motor movements. Moving toward the "fingertips" of the glove, the area immediately adjacent to the motor strip is the premotor area, which involves the spatial and sensory guidance of movement. Clearly, both of these areas are important in the voluntary control of muscle movements.

Then there are the anterior cingulate cortex (ACC) and the insula. Activation of both of these areas has repeatedly been shown to be associated with empathy, especially when observing pain in others (Rameson, Morelli, & Lieberman, 2012). We often describe people who help those who are suffering as having "a big heart." It's probably more accurate to assume that their ACC and insula are highly active.

Regarding the insula, Paulus and Stein (2010) noted that it is responsible for our interoceptive awareness—i.e., the subjective sense of the inner body. The insula is the receiving zone that reads the physiological state of the entire body and then generates subjective feelings. The subjective sense of pain involves the activation of the insula, which likely explains its role in empathy. In addition, these subjective feelings can bring about actions that keep the body in a state of internal balance. The subjective sense of mind and body are integrated in a significant way in the insula.

According to a study on loving kindness meditation practiced by Tibetan monks and repeated prayer of Franciscan and Carmelite nuns, the insula was most active in those participants who reported experiencing the deepest level of empathy and compassion (Sternberg, 2009). Sternberg further comments that the areas that were activated in the praying nuns and meditating monks were the reward circuits and the prefrontal and parietal lobes. She goes on to emphasize that those parts of the brain are important in positive emotional responses and resilience. Once the nuns and monks reached a state of peace and love, the same regions of the brain became active that are responsible for passionate and compassionate love. The participants showed increased activation of the PSNS (i.e., the "rest and digest" system) and significantly thicker insulae compared to non-meditators/non-prayers. Considering the plasticity of the brain, it is hypothesized that perhaps TRM/CRM skills actually thicken the insula, which would result in a greater capacity to be in one's resilient zone.

Personal meanings about traumatic events can change. Individuals have reported that after a TRM/CRM session, they not only feel more compassion for themselves but also for others. A study was done on the effectiveness of TRM/CRM wellness skills with survivors of a genocide in the Ivory Coast. After learning the basic skills, many survivors reported feeling more compassion for their neighbors who had been responsible for the genocide.

Finally, there is the prefrontal cortex, which is largely considered the CEO of the brain because areas in this region help orchestrate our thoughts and actions.

When we refer to the cortex as the "thinking" brain, we are for the most part referring to the prefrontal cortex. Certain parts of the prefrontal cortex are active when we reason, strategize, and plan. Other areas of the prefrontal cortex along with the orbital-frontal cortex are active when we experience guilt and when we recognize inappropriate behaviors that may need to be corrected (see Jennings, 2013). In other words, this area plays a key role in moral judgment.

It is through experience and maturity that our prefrontal cortex learns to inhibit and control subcortical (e.g., limbic system) activation, which eventually allows us to regulate our emotional experiences. *In terms of neuroscience then, cognitive therapies essentially target changes in the prefrontal cortex.* Focusing on helping clients identify and change maladaptive ways of thinking (cortex) with the goal of better emotional regulation (limbic system), one can conceptualize this type of intervention as a "top-down" intervention, in which the goal is to strengthen the optimal functioning of the cortex so that it can better regulate the areas of the brain below it. Given the role of the prefrontal cortex in emotional regulation, one can also see why such therapies can be effective. But it's not a one-way street. There are bottom-up processes that can occur wherein the other two areas of the three-part model of the brain can hijack the "thinking" brain.

This brings us to the second section of the three-part model of the brain. The area just below the cortex as we move toward the spinal cord is referred to as the **limbic system,** or the "emotional" brain. In general, the limbic system plays an important role in the mediation and control of major activities like attachment, friendship, love, aggression, affection, and the expression of mood. This system is also very important in mediating the functions of self-preservation (i.e., fight, flight, or freeze). The limbic system is made up of multiple structures, but for the purposes of this book we will focus on just the hippocampus, the amygdala, and the hypothalamus.

The **hippocampus** is responsible for the processing of explicit memories (i.e., memories of facts and events). It is not a storage cabinet where we file such memories, but rather more like the desk we use to sort and sift them before moving them to where they will be stored. The hippocampus is also important in providing contextual cues to memories such as spatial and time information (e.g., Moser, Kropff, & Moser, 2008; Bonnici et al., 2012). We will discuss the importance of this later in the chapter.

The **amygdala** is a key component linked to aggression and fear, especially in the perception of these emotions. This part of the brain can be considered our danger appraisal system and operates much like a fire alarm. If danger is assessed, the amygdala sounds the alarm to initiate the biological sequences involved in our survival responses. The amygdala can even assess danger without our conscious awareness (Ohman, Carlsson, Lundqvist, & Ingvar, 2007), which might help explain why the "hairs on the back of our neck stand up" despite any obvious reason.

Finally, the **hypothalamus** helps to maintain a steady internal state of equilibrium by influencing maintenance activities related to hunger and thirst, body temperature, and sex. In addition, the hypothalamus also helps regulate the autonomic nervous system; in short, it helps govern the four "Fs": feeding, Fahrenheit, fornication, and fight/flight. The hypothalamus governs most of these functions by influencing the endocrine system (a system of glands that secrete hormones into the bloodstream) via the pituitary gland. As we will see later, the hypothalamus plays a key role in one of the major physiological responses experienced during times of crisis.

The third and final part of the three-part model of the brain is the **brainstem,** or "survival" brain, which begins where the spinal cord swells as it enters into the skull and is responsible for the exchange of information between the body and the brain. All information that travels from the body to the brain or vice versa goes through the brainstem. In addition, the brainstem is responsible for regulating our automatic survival functions such as breathing and heartbeat, pain sensitivity, alertness, awareness, and consciousness. Accordingly, the "survival brain" often goes into defensive responses (e.g., fainting, shock, etc.) automatically based on perceived threats.

Sitting on top of the brainstem is the **thalamus,** which acts as the brain's sensory switchboard. The thalamus receives information from all of the senses except smell and sends it on to the appropriate brain areas (mostly in the cortex) responsible for seeing, hearing, taste, and touch. (A quick side note: The sense of smell is processed by the olfactory bulb, which sits at the front of the brain just under the prefrontal cortex. Interestingly, the olfactory bulb has a direct connection to the amygdala and the hippocampus, underscoring the fast-track effect smells often have on emotion and memory.) Back to the brainstem: The **cerebellum** lies at the rear of the brainstem and is responsible for processing nonverbal implicit memory and helping coordinate voluntary movements.

All of the brainstem's functions occur without conscious thought. That is, they are still active whether we are awake or asleep. This is a remarkable design! Can you imagine having to stay awake in order to tell your heart to keep beating or your lungs to take in air? Have you ever woken up in the middle of the night to see your five-year-old staring at you? Did you ever wonder why you woke up? Because the thalamus—without your explicit permission—was still taking in sensory information (e.g., your child saying your name) and communicating to the areas of your brain that are responsible for waking you up. Ultimately, the brainstem responds to sensation and body memory and not to language and conscious thought.

Now that we have the basics down, let's turn to trauma's effects on the nervous system as a whole. Timothy Jennings (2013) provides a wonderful example of what happens when we are afraid:

Just as the school has a fire alarm, so, too, our brain has an alarm switch called the amygdala. . . . When the fire alarm is activated at the school, its job is twofold: first to grab the attention of everyone in the building, and second to alert the 911 operator. Like the fire alarm, the amygdala both releases attention-getting adrenaline from the adrenal glands to the brain, and it alerts a sort of 911 operator to send out an urgent call. The brain's 911 operator is the hypothalamus, which is connected to the "radio tower" of the pituitary gland. Instead of radio waves, the pituitary gland transmits hormonal signals calling for the body's emergency response, which comes from the adrenal glands; they're the stress steroids known as glucocorticoids [i.e., cortisol].

When emergency responders arrive at the school fire, there is a fire chief who assesses the extent of the blaze and how many responders are on the scene. When there are enough firefighters, the chief calls back to the 911 operator and reports that, even though the alarm is still going, the operator doesn't need to send any more.

Back in the brain, hippocampal neurons are the fire chief. They have glucocorticoid receptors that recognize the rise in stress hormones and signal back to the 911 operator (hypothalamus) saying, "Okay, you don't need to call any more responders (stress hormones)." Then after the alarm has sounded, the brain's administrator, which is [a specific portion of the] prefrontal cortex . . . acting much like the school principal, evaluates whether there is real danger or whether it was a false alarm. If the administrator determines there is real danger, the alarm gets louder. If the administrator determines that there's been a "false alarm," everything calms down.[1]

Imagine that you are the homeowner in the example from the beginning of this chapter. But this time, you are going about your nightly duties and you hear a noise right behind you. Immediately, the alarm in your brain (amygdala) fires and communicates directly to the adrenal glands telling them to release adrenaline, bringing you to attention. At the same time, it also calls your 911 operator (hypothalamus), which then radios (via the pituitary gland) for emergency responders to be dispatched (glucocorticoids). The adrenal glands dispatch the responders, flooding your system with cortisol. Along with the adrenaline already released, this causes your heart rate to rise, your blood pressure to elevate, and your digestion and immune systems to shut down, allowing for the blood to be sent to your muscles and glucose to flood your bloodstream, and you to start to sweat. Sound familiar? This is the sympathetic response. You are primed to fight or flee. This response system is also known as the hypothalamic-pituitary-adrenal (HPA) axis.

Now then, as you turn to orient to the sound, your body is primed to respond. But then you see your cat nonchalantly playing with the book he knocked off your desk. That's when your "administrator" (prefrontal cortex) kicks in and determines it to be a false alarm. Thinking and reasoning turn on as you immediately start to wonder why you ever bought that stupid cat! But beyond that, having determined that the once threatening noise was just your cat, you conclude that you are not in danger. The amygdala stops firing and that's when the parasympathetic nervous system comes online and your body starts to calm. Eventually, you may even remember how much you love your cat.

Imagine, however, that you turn around and don't see your cat. Instead you see a shadowy figure pass quickly out of sight. In this case, your "administrator" concludes that it isn't a false alarm. There is actual danger. In this case, your alarm (amygdala) may blare even louder, calling for more "responders" and causing even more adrenaline and cortisol to flood your body. And this is good. *Having our body's alarm system operating correctly helps us deal with all sorts of threats. It's when these systems don't work properly or when they don't turn off after the threat is gone that we start to observe the types of symptoms associated with a great number of emotional difficulties.*

Take, for example, the many studies focusing on the amygdala and its role in psychopathology. For example, an overactive amygdala has been linked to multiple anxiety disorders (Etkin & Wager, 2007; Nitschke et al., 2009), unipolar depression (Siegle, Steinhauer, Thase, Stenger, & Carter, 2002; Mandell, Siegle, Shutt, Feldmiller, & Thase, 2014), and borderline personality disorder (Domes, Schulze, & Herpertz, 2009). In contrast, individuals with psychopathy show reduced amygdala activity when exposed to stimuli that normally should trigger fear, resulting in a reduced autonomic nervous system response (see Blair, 2008).

Another common finding associated with compromised brain structures is that of reduced hippocampal volume. For example, Gilbertson et al. (2002) found that combat veterans with PTSD had smaller hippocampal volume than combat veterans without PTSD. What was particularly important about this study was that it involved identical twins (i.e., 100% genetically identical "clones" made naturally). The noncombat twin of the PTSD veteran had similar smaller hippocampal volume as his twin, while the noncombat twin of the non-PTSD veteran had similar larger hippocampal volume as his twin. This suggests that smaller hippocampal volume might make one more vulnerable to developing PTSD if exposed to traumatic stress. Remember, the hippocampal neurons act as the "fire chief" in recognizing and providing feedback about the rising levels of stress hormones when the amygdala is activated. Perhaps the smaller hippocampal volume compromises its ability to provide proper feedback to the hypothalamus, causing an exaggerated release of cortisol during times of stress, which then might make one vulnerable to the development of PTSD.

Of course, the causal factors behind the development of PTSD are much more complex than this, but such differences in brain anatomy and functioning highlight how important it is to understand the brain and its role in our response to stress. A basic understanding of memory and its function adds even more clarity to our experience of traumatic stress and can further help us move from perceptions of personal weakness to an understanding of biology. Memory is processed in some of the areas of the brain that we have already discussed (e.g., hippocampus, cerebellum, amygdala, etc.).

Memory essentially involves our ability to store and retrieve information over time. When we learn anything—a vocabulary word, our mother's voice, the smell of a rose, how to drive a car—we are forming memories. We are loading information into our brain, storing it, and then retrieving it. Sounds simple, but here's where it gets interesting. The mind generally operates on two tracks. We alluded to this earlier when discussing the brain. There are functions controlled by our brain that are voluntary (e.g., raising our hand) and functions that are involuntary (e.g., heartbeat). There are conscious functions and unconscious functions. In the same way, there are two types of memory: explicit memory and implicit memory.

**Explicit memory** is the conscious retention of information like facts and events. These memories are factual and autobiographical and have a sense of self and time (Cozolino, 2010). They are often the memories that we access intentionally. Language is necessary in order to store and retrieve such memories. Explicit memory is what we generally think of when we're asked if we have a good memory or not. If we can't remember the capital of El Salvador or the first name of the person we just met or what we did last Thursday, then we generally conclude that we have a poor memory. However, it might be more accurate to say that we are not very good at the conscious, intentional recall of some of our explicit memories. The fact is that if you can remember your name, the shape of a square, the town of your childhood, or the title of this book, then your explicit memory is pretty good.

**Implicit memory** is the unconscious retention of information. Implicit memories often involve information that is processed or accessed without intention. Unlike with explicit memories, language is not required for the storage or retrieval of implicit memories. Instead, they involve automatic procedures and internal states—thus the original use of the term *procedural memories* when referring to implicit memories. Unlike explicit memory, implicit memory does not have a sense of linear time or space, or a sense of self. Instead, these memories are often memories of skills and conditioned associations unfettered from the context in which they were learned. As such, mental models can be formed from experiences that entail somatic, sensory, motor, and emotional elements without our conscious awareness of forming them.

The example of riding a bike illustrates the differences between explicit and implicit memory. Perhaps you remember the day you first learned how to ride a bike. You may even remember the weather that day, or how many times you fell, or the color of the bike. These are explicit memories. However, staying balanced, pedaling, using the handlebars—these are implicit memories. You access these skills every time you get back on a bike. Therefore, you remember how to ride a bike (implicit memory) even though you may not remember the details of the day you learned (explicit memory). If I asked you to tell me about the last time you rode a bike (i.e., a narrative), you would be accessing explicit memories to do so. If I were to hand you a bike and tell you to ride it down the block, you would be accessing implicit memories. This illustrates an important principle about memory as it relates to trauma. Implicit memories and explicit memories do not always accompany each other. More on this later.

Further distinctions between these two types of memories are found in the corresponding areas of the brain that process them. Explicit memories are processed primarily by the hippocampus and the frontal lobes. The hippocampus helps put explicit memories in their proper perspective and place in our life's timeline. As we noted before, because of brain plasticity, the actual structure of the hippocampus can change in response to our experiences. For example, an interesting study found that the area of the hippocampus responsible for spatial memory was bigger in London taxi drivers the longer they spent driving taxis (Maguire et al., 2003).

Stress seems to negatively affect the functioning and structure of the hippocampus. It has been found that when the amygdala is highly active, the stress hormones (i.e., cortisol) released interfere with the proper functioning of the hippocampus. This may result in a traumatic experience not being explicitly remembered or being remembered in fragments (Van der Kolk & Fisler, 1995). Likewise, prolonged exposure to high levels of cortisol can result in significant hippocampal damage (Kim & Diamond, 2002).

Implicit memories are processed primarily by the cerebellum and the basal ganglia (i.e., brain structures near the thalamus involved in motor movements). The cerebellum is a key player in forming and storing memories created by classical conditioning. If your mouth starts to salivate when you smell your favorite food, that's an implicit memory that involves the cerebellum. The basal ganglia is involved in procedural memories for skills. Riding your bike down the block involves the basal ganglia. Knowing that the implicit memory system is processed differently and in a different area of the brain than the explicit memory system can help explain a lot of strange phenomena.

For example, both the cerebellum and basal ganglia are developed enough prior to birth to allow for implicit memories to form even before we take our first breath. At the same time, the hippocampus is one of the last brain structures to develop (around 18–24 months), resulting in few to no conscious (explicit) memories prior to the age of three—a phenomenon called infantile amnesia. Similarly, body memories processed by the cerebellum and basal ganglia can include sensations associated with traumatic experiences. Because they are processed separately from the hippocampus, bodily cues can trigger implicit memories without any explicit understanding.

One client who was sexually assaulted in her teens reported having a panic attack in her late 30s during a routine physical therapy session. The panic attack was "uncued," meaning that she reported no flashback or explicit memory that would have triggered her panic. As she put it, "It came out of the blue." While she was convinced that the panic attack had to be related to her assault as a teen, there was no conscious connection. Some of the TRM skills were employed to help her get back into her resilient zone, and a brief explanation about how the two different memory systems work was provided. It was emphasized that sometimes the body can take in sensory information outside of conscious awareness and store it as implicit associations related to the trauma.

Sure enough, as she recounted again some of the details regarding this particular physical therapy session, she noted a detail that wasn't obvious the first time she recalled it. She noted that an apparatus that was used to bind her ankles wasn't clasping correctly and the physical therapist had to use duct tape to secure it. It was the sound of the duct tape that triggered her panic attack. It was during this retelling of the episode that she remembered (explicitly) that her assailant had used duct tape to bind her ankles during her assault some twenty years prior. The implicit body and sensory memories of the event were triggered without the explicit memories of the event. She was so relieved to know that she wasn't "crazy," and knowing about the two types of memory helped her understand why she had the panic attack. This is just one way to help move individuals from perceptions of personal weakness to an understanding of biology.

But why duct tape? It's such a common item and yet, in this particular case under those particular circumstances, it signaled something more ominous. This is where emotion and memory intersect and we can thank the amygdala for it. As you may remember, the amygdala is our appraisal system—our fire alarm. If an event trips the alarm, the amygdala sends out its signal to release stress hormones. These in turn provoke the amygdala to initiate a memory trace in the frontal lobes (explicit memory) and the basal ganglia (implicit memory), causing particular memories to have a certain emotional signature (Buchanan, 2007). It is as if those memories are seared into our brain. Accordingly, templates from highly charged emotional memories are formed.

Some of these templates we call **flashbulb memories.** Where were you on 9/11? Do you remember your first kiss? For trauma survivors, vivid memories of the traumatic event often intrude again and again. These are emotionally charged memories that seem to be recalled with great clarity. They are seared into our memories. More often than not, we talk of emotionally charged explicit memories by focusing on the narrative of what happened. However, the amygdala can initiate a memory trace for implicit memories as well. In the example above, the original assault triggered the amygdala and various emotion-related memories were formed. The body memory of being bound at the ankles and the sound of the duct tape were implicit memories that retained the signature of amygdala activation. These bits of information were seared into memory just as much as the narrative of the event was. In fact, even when such details escaped the client's conscious recall initially, her "body" remembered and the amygdala was once again triggered.

Scaer (2007) refers to compartments of memory he terms **memory capsules**. These memory capsules hold explicit and implicit details of past traumas and can include defensive energy that has not been released. Accordingly, when a memory capsule of a traumatic event is triggered, one may experience a whole litany of uncomfortable outcomes such as pain, numbness, dizziness, trembling, paralysis, nausea, palpitations, anxiety, terror, shame, anger, rage, flashbacks, nightmares, or intrusive thoughts. When this happens, the trauma is perceived as being in the present.

Memory capsules can have external triggers such as visual stimuli (e.g., people, places, things), smells, sounds, and many more. Or they can have internal triggers—i.e., internal body sensations such as muscle tension, headache, stomach ache, elevated heart rate, and the like. This can help explain why some people who suffer from panic disorder often have panic attacks that are triggered by strenuous physical activities such as exercise. The elevated heart rate, shortness of breath, and sweating experienced during exercise can act as an internal trigger that pops the memory capsule of past panic attacks (the symptoms of which include elevated heart rate, shortness of breath, and sweating).

Again, there is an elegant design to how memory works. Ultimately, memory serves to help us make sense of our world, predict the future, and alert us to possible dangers. In economics, it's not wise to put all of your eggs in one basket. A similar principle is at play here. Within the brain are a variety of different systems capable of recording and storing information about life experiences. Some areas (hippocampus and frontal lobes) make memories by preserving records of experience to later allow conscious recollection of the past (explicit memories). Other areas (cerebellum and basal ganglia) process information implicitly. Sensory processing regions in the cortex store information about certain sensory experiences. Still other areas (motor cortex and cerebellum) allow learned movements to be stored. There is even a system involving the dorsolateral striatum that is necessary in forming habits—i.e., complex behavioral patterns that are learned and used in situations that routinely recur (Yin, Knowlton, & Balleine, 2004).

When an emotionally charged event happens, the amygdala fires, helping these brain systems to put an emotional trace on the narrative and body/sensory memory of the event as if to say, "Remember this! Beware the next time!" However, traumatic memories may or may not be remembered in a coherent explicit memory. Some traumatic memories may appear as fragments of images and sensations or may result in flashback memories (i.e., flashbulb memories of personally traumatic events). Some traumatic memories seem timeless: The entire multisensory implicit memory may be experienced as if the traumatic event is happening in the present moment. It's as if the explicit and implicit memories are no longer aligned, much like a video playback where the sound of the dialogue isn't quite lining up with the movement of the person's mouth. In fact, the multisensory implicit memory may be fully disconnected from a particular source memory, as in the example of the duct tape.

This can be incredibly frustrating for clients and therapists to work with, so why consider it a good thing? Joseph LeDoux (1996) told the story of a client who had damage to her hippocampus that prevented her from forming new explicit memories. Accordingly, she was unable to recognize her physician who, each day, would greet her by introducing himself and shaking her hand. One day, he tried an experiment. He put a tack in his hand. Just like every other day, he introduced himself and shook her hand. This time she pulled her hand back in pain. The next time he introduced himself the patient refused to shake his hand but couldn't explain why. A mean experiment, yes. But, an important one nonetheless. The explicit memory could not be accessed, but her implicit memory could. This allowed the patient to sense danger without knowing why. One structure of her brain (hippocampus) wasn't working properly anymore, but that didn't stop other structures (amygdala and cerebellum) from trying to keep her safe. That's an elegant design!

Now we can see how memory can affect how we respond to what happens around us. For example, when we are presented with sensory information from the outside world, we process it through one of two systems. The **slow system,** or **thinking response,** involves sensory input (i.e., sounds, imagery) being processed by the thalamus (i.e., the sensory switchboard). The information is then filtered through the amygdala. If the amygdala makes the appraisal that there is no threat, then the hippocampus and other cortical circuits provide further processing of the information. At this point the information is contextualized in time and space, assigned cognitive meaning, and then sent on to other areas of the cortex. The cortex is not blocked and the person can act with conscious thought and organized, complex survival behavior.

The **fast system,** or **unthinking response,** follows the same initial steps. Sensory information is processed by the thalamus and assessed by the amygdala. However, if the amygdala appraises the information as a threat—based on past experience—then the fear response is triggered (i.e., the HPA axis), flooding the cortex with chemicals that block slow thinking. The cortex is blocked and the person acts without conscious thought. This accounts for the common defensive responses of fight, flight, and freeze. These behaviors are often performed reflexively and without conscious thought.

A recent study by Ryan Herringa and colleagues (Herringa et al., 2013) illustrates how these systems can break down because of traumatic stress. According to the study, maltreatment in childhood seems to disrupt the regulatory capacity of the brain's fear circuit, leading to increased internalizing of symptoms by late adolescence. Brain scans showed that maltreatment predicted weaker prefrontal cortex-hippocampal connectivity in adolescent males and females, but lower prefrontal cortex-amygdala connectivity only in adolescent females. According to the researchers, for those with weaker prefrontal cortex-hippocampal connectivity, it's as if they have lost the ability to put a contextual limit on when they are going to be afraid. They seem to be afraid a lot and in situations that may not warrant fear. Furthermore, females with weaker prefrontal cortex-amygdala connectivity have difficulty even recognizing dangerous situations at all.

> When one or more neural networks necessary for optimal functioning remain underdeveloped, underregulated, or underintegrated with others, we experience the complaints and symptoms for which people seek therapy. We now assume that when psychotherapy results in symptom reduction or experiential change, the brain has, in some way, been altered. . . .
>
> (Cozolino, 2010)

The TRM focuses on reestablishing the natural rhythm of the nervous system through the portal of sensations. One could argue that when we are in our resilient zone, our neural networks are well-integrated, our memory systems are synchronized, and our mind and body are working as one. Helping clients manage stress—traumatic or otherwise—by increasing their ability to be in their resilient zones allows them to maximize their body's natural resilience, resulting in improved integration of the brain and body.

## Note

1. Taken from *The God-Shaped Brain* by Timothy R. Jennings. Copyright © 2013 by Timothy R. Jennings. Used by permission of InterVarsity Press, P.O. Box 1400, Downers Grove, IL 60515, USA. www.ivpress.com.

## References

Blair, R.J.R. (2008). The amygdala and ventromedial prefrontal cortex: Functional contributions and dysfunction in psychopathy. *Philosophical Transactions of the Royal Society, 363*(1503), 2557–2565.

Bonnici, H.M., Chadwick, M.J., Lutti, A., Hassabis, D., Weiskopf, N., & Maguire, E.A. (2012). Detecting representations of recent and remote autobiographical memories in vmPFC and hippocampus. *The Journal of Neuroscience, 32*(47), 16982–16991.

Buchanan, T.W. (2007). Retrieval of emotional memories. *Psychological Bulletin, 133*(5), 761–779.

Cozolino, L.J. (2010). *The neuroscience of psychotherapy: Healing the social brain* (2nd ed.). New York: W.W. Norton & Company.

Domes, G., Schulze, L., & Herpertz, S.C. (2009). Emotion recognition in borderline personality disorder—A review of the literature. *Journal of Personality Disorders, 23*(1), 6–19.

Etkin, A., & Wager, T.D. (2007). Functional neuroimaging of anxiety: A meta-analysis of emotional processing in PTSD, Social Anxiety Disorder, and Specific Phobia. *American Journal of Psychiatry, 164*(10), 1476–1488.

Gilbertson, M.W., Shenton, M.E., Ciszewski, A., Kasai, K., Lasko, N.B., Orr, S.P., & Pitman, R.K. (2002). Smaller hippocampal volume predicts pathologic vulnerability to psychological trauma. *Nature Neuroscience, 5*(11), 1242–1247.

Herringa, R.J., Birn, R.M., Ruttle, P.L., Burghy, C.A., Stodola, D.E., Davidson, R.J., & Essex, M.J. (2013). Childhood maltreatment is associated with altered fear circuitry and increased internalizing symptoms by late adolescence. *Proceedings of the National Academy of Sciences of the United States of America, 110*(47), 19119–19124.

Jennings, T.R. (2013). *The God-shaped brain: How changing your view of God transforms your life.* Downers Grove, IL: IVP Books.

Kim, J.J., & Diamond, D.M. (2002). The stressed hippocampus, synaptic plasticity and lost memories. *Nature Reviews Neuroscience, 3*(6), 453–462.

Kolb, B., & Whishaw, I.Q. (1998). Brain plasticity and behavior. *Annual Review of Psychology, 49*(1), 43–64.

LeDoux, J. (1996). *The emotional brain: The mysterious underpinnings of emotional life.* New York: Simon & Schuster.

MacLean, P.D. (1990). *The triune brain in evolution: Role in paleocerebral functions.* New York: Plenum Press.

Maguire, E.A., Spiers, H.J., Good, C.D., Hartley, T., Frackowiak, R.S., & Burgess, N. (2003). Navigation expertise and the human hippocampus: A structural brain imaging analysis. *Hippocampus, 13*(2), 250–259.

Mandell, D., Siegle, G.J., Shutt, L., Feldmiller, J., & Thase, M.E. (2014). Neural substrates of trait ruminations in depression. *Journal of Abnormal Psychology, 123*(1), 35–48.

Moll, J., Zahn, R., de Oliveira-Souza, R., Krueger, F., & Grafman, J. (2005). The neural basis of human moral cognition. *Nature Reviews Neuroscience, 6*(10), 799–809.

Moser, E.I., Kropff, E., & Moser, M. (2008). Place cells, grid cells, and the brain's spatial representation system. *Annual Review of Neuroscience, 31,* 69–89.

Newberg, A. (2009). *How God changes your brain.* New York: Ballantine Books.

Nitschke, J.B., Sarinopoulos, I., Oathes, D.J., Johnstone, T., Whalen, P.J., Davidson, R.J., & Kalin, N.H. (2009). Anticipatory activation in the amygdala and anterior cingulate in generalized anxiety disorder and prediction of treatment response. *American Journal of Psychiatry, 166*(3), 302–310.

Ohman, A., Carlsson, K., Lundqvist, D., & Ingvar, M. (2007). On the unconscious subcortical origin of human fear. *Physiology & Behavior, 92*(1–2), 180–185.

Paulus, M., & Stein, M.B. (2010). Interoception in anxiety and depression. *Brain Structure and Function, 214*(5–6), 451–463. doi:10.1007/s00429-010-0258-9

Rameson, L.T., Morelli, S.A., & Lieberman, M.D. (2012). The neural correlates of empathy: Experience, automaticity, and prosocial behavior. *Journal of Cognitive Neuroscience, 24*(1), 235–245.

Rivera-Gaxiola, M., Silva-Pereyra, J., & Kuhl, P. K. (2005). Brain potentials to native and non-native speech contrasts in 7- and 11-month-old American infants. *Developmental Science, 8*(2), 162–172.

Rothschild, B. (2000). *The body remembers: The psychophysiology of trauma and trauma treatment.* New York: W.W. Norton & Company.

Scaer, R. (2007). *The body bears the burden: Trauma, dissociation, and disease* (2nd ed.). Binghamton, NY: Haworth Medical Press.

Selye, H. (1936). A syndrome produced by diverse nocuous agents. *Nature, 138*(3479), 32. doi:10.1038/138032a0

Siegle, G. J., Steinhauer, S. R., Thase, M. E., Stenger, V. A., & Carter, C. S. (2002). Can't shake that feeling: Event-related fMRI assessment of sustained amygdala activity in response to emotional information in depressed individuals. *Biological Psychiatry, 51*(9), 693–707.

Sternberg, E. M. (2009). *Healing spaces: The science of place and well-being.* Cambridge, MA: Harvard University Press.

Van der Kolk, B. A., & Fisler, R. (1995). Dissociation and the fragmentary nature of traumatic memories: Overview and exploratory study. *Journal of Traumatic Stress, 8*(4), 505–525.

Werker, J. F., & Tees, R. C. (1999). Influences on infant speech processing: Toward a new synthesis. *Annual Review of Psychology, 50*, 509–535.

Yin, H. H., Knowlton, B. J., & Balleine, B. W. (2004). Lesions of dorsolateral striatum preserve outcome expectancy but disrupt habit formation in instrumental learning. *European Journal of Neuroscience, 19*(1), 181–189.

# 3 The Trauma Resiliency Model (TRM)

*Elaine Miller-Karas*

> Keep looking at the bandaged place. That is where the light enters you.
> —Rumi

The Trauma Resiliency Model (TRM) uses a set of nine skills to stabilize the nervous system and reduce or prevent the symptoms of traumatic stress. The TRM is a clinical intervention based on current research about the brain that reflects the knowledge that there is a biological response to stressful and traumatic events. The model provides a perspective that views the reactions experienced after traumatic events as common reactions, thereby depathologizing symptoms and shifting the paradigm from one of human weakness to one of biology. The first six skills of the TRM are called the Community Resiliency Model (CRM).

The TRM helps individuals learn to track their nervous systems and concentrate on sensations that are connected to well-being. As a person begins to pay attention to sensations of well-being, his nervous system can return to a state of balance. Clients are informed about the neurobiology of traumatic symptoms with simple explanations about the nervous system and the common responses to threat and fear. The six wellness skills, which will be explained in this chapter, can help a person learn to monitor his own sensations and begin to tell the difference between sensations of distress and those of well-being. Once his awareness expands, a person, through his own intention, can begin to bring his nervous system back into balance. When using the TRM to help an individual reprocess a traumatic experience, the clinician first helps the client learn the wellness skills for self-care. Once the client knows he can regulate his own nervous system during times of distress, the clinician can focus on helping the client reprocess traumatic experiences. There are three additional skills of the TRM that can be implemented by the clinician for reprocessing.

We stand on the shoulders of others who have come before with ideas and concepts that we have interwoven into the TRM. The TRM's foundation lies in the following topics.

## Lamaze Childbirth Education

As a Lamaze teacher in the early 1980s, I learned about the natural rhythms of the body that occur as women go through one of the most stressful biological events of their lives. The work was about attending and guiding; how we supported the laboring woman made all the difference in the world in relieving her suffering. As a doula, I monitored the sensations of the expectant mother and helped guide her as she gave birth. Being present during the birth process was not about directing but about "being with" the woman as she journeyed through the birth experience. Similarly, when helping individuals with the sensations connected to traumatic experiences, we are guiding them to pay attention to natural rhythms in their bodies. The natural rhythms of healing coexist with the haunting reactions connected to a traumatic experience. When the client learns she can bring her attention to the sensations of well-being, her nervous system begins to change, and traumatic sensations can lessen or dissipate altogether.

## Peter Levine's Somatic Experiencing (SE)

Dr. Levine studied many disciplines including stress physiology, psychology, ethology, biology, neuroscience, indigenous healing practices, and medical biophysics to create a model of intervention that focuses on releasing traumatic shock from the body so that an individual can heal from trauma. SE's concepts and methods are revolutionary. When creating the TRM, we incorporated some of the concepts from SE. There are, though, some differences in the models. In the TRM, we begin by teaching six wellness skills to the client as a self-regulation practice, and we use the paradigm of biology as a lens to view symptoms and design interventions. We stay "a half step behind" the client and guide based on observation. We do not lead. In the TRM, we ask for the client's interpretation and personal meaning and do not interpret the client's experience.

## Laws of Nature—The Elegant Design

In the natural world, there are the seasons, the cycles of the moon, the ebb and flow of the ocean's waves; there are bright, sunny days as well as torrential rains. Human beings are part of the natural design and there are rhythms within our bodies. We experience sensations of trauma as well as sensations of well-being. When we embrace the concept that we are also part of the elegant design of nature, there is hope that balance can return. We can learn to build shelters out of the storm; we can learn that the sensations connected to traumatic experiences can change like seasons change and that as human beings we can learn to pay attention to well-being. When we pay attention to our well-being, it expands. I use the analogy of my garden. If I water the weeds, they will grow and expand; however, I can choose to water the fruit trees, vegetables, and flowers. Even if a weed or two remains, paying attention to the abundance of the garden will override the existence of the weeds.

## Neuroscience

The concept that *the brain can change—it's malleable*—left an indelible mark when conceptualizing the TRM. Neuroscience not only helps us understand the biological underpinnings of the common human reactions to traumatic experience, but also provides us with the hope that human experience can change the brain and the body. Thus, human beings do not have to be trapped by the thoughts, feelings, beliefs, and sensations connected to past traumatic events. Diamond and Amso (2008) state that the brain is changeable at all developmental ages and that human experience plays a far larger role in shaping the mind and brain than previously conceived. The first six skills of the TRM are designed as a wellness practice. Clinicians help their clients learn the skills. As clients gain more experience with practicing self-regulation, the nervous system changes. The client is able to intercept the sensations of distress with sensations of well-being and this creates a new template of being in the present moment.

## Eugene Gendlin's Focusing

Gendlin coined the concept of the "felt sense," which he described as a person's internal bodily awareness. The "felt sense" is another portal of information. If a person begins focusing on the "felt sense" of an experience, ideas about resolution of problems will unfold. Gendlin also stated that the "felt sense" changes. In the TRM, we help people become aware of the "felt sense." We also help individuals differentiate between sensations of resiliency and those of distress. As people focus on sensations of well-being, sensations change in the body. As the sensations change, so do one's beliefs, feelings, and meanings about life experience. There is no need for clinical interpretation because as the clinician invites the client to become aware of sensation change, new meanings, beliefs, and feelings emerge spontaneously.

## Sensory Integration Theory: Jean Ayres, Williams, and Schellenberger

Ayres was a UCLA occupational therapist and a neuroscientist. Her work with children who had a problem with attending was inspirational and served as one of the foundational pieces of the TRM. She found that many of the children experienced the world as spinning around them. With very simple exercises that helped the children "ground" and experience safety within their bodies, they were able to learn better. When we think about how trauma can literally knock us off our feet, grounding methodologies are important in helping individuals be fully present in the here and now. In the book *How Does My Engine Run,* occupational therapists Williams and Schellenberger (1996) designed simple exercises to integrate sensory awareness into the home, school, and playground.

## Solution-Focused Psychotherapy (SFP)

SFP focuses on the present and holds the foundational concept that the client knows the best solutions for his own life's challenges. In the TRM, we hold the same belief and, as in SFP, the clinician does not make interpretations and does not confront. By having a non-directive stance of not knowing, the TRM clinician encourages the client's own curiosity about his internal sensory experience. As the client brings his attention to sensations of resiliency, solutions emerge that have greater meaning. The TRM is strength based, similar to SFP. The TRM clinician asks the client about a personal strength or resource and as the client describes the strength or resource, he is invited to notice the sensations. The TRM, like SFP, expands resiliency. In a similar way that an SFP clinician joins with the client by asking what is right about his life, a TRM clinician joins with the client by asking about what gives him joy, peace, or excitement in his life. The client begins to learn that there are pleasant or neutral experiences that can be sensed and focused upon that enhance resiliency.

## Resiliency-Informed Interventions

In the fields of psychology and social work, much attention is given to helping organizations and systems become trauma-informed. We believe that it is important to be not only trauma-sensitive, but also *resiliency-informed*. How do we create resiliency-informed individuals, systems, and communities? The first goal is an individual goal, and that is to deepen a person's ability to fully experience his resilient zone so he is better able to adapt to the stressors of life with flexibility and is able to maneuver in healthy ways through the ups and downs of life experiences.

## The Resilient Zone

The resilient zone represents the natural rhythm or flow within the nervous system. When we are in our resilient zones, we have our greatest capacity for balanced thinking and feeling. We can create the best solutions for our own lives, our families, and our wider community. The goal of the TRM is to help the client identify the sensations connected to his resilient zone. Further, when an individual is bumped out of his resilient zone into the high or low zones, TRM skills help the person monitor his sensations in order to bounce back and return to

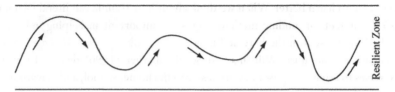

*Figure 3.1* The Resilient Zone

the resilient zone. All human beings can get bumped out of their resilient zones because of stressful or traumatic life experiences. Most of us have the capacity to return to the resilient zone on our own, but some of us need additional skills to help us get back into the resilient zone.

The resilient zone can be compared to Daniel Siegel's (2010) "window of tolerance"—an area of arousal in which we each can function. The window of tolerance pertains to any particular moment when we have more tolerance for some emotions and situations than others. Being outside of the window is chaos; one end of the window is hyperarousal and the other end is hypoarousal. HeartMath (2014) describes personal coherence "as psychophysiological coherence when there is a synchronization of our physical, mental and emotional systems. . . . It is a state of optimal clarity, perception and performance." In the TRM, we call this the resilient zone (Figure 3.1).

## The Nine Skills of the Trauma Resiliency Model

The TRM utilizes nine skills to reduce symptoms associated with stressful and/ or traumatic experiences. The first six skills can be used as a wellness practice and are taught to individuals to increase their capacity to manage sensations associated with trauma or stress. Some of the skills of the TRM were inspired by Peter Levine's SE method and are used by the mental health clinician to help the client reprocess his traumatic experience.

### Skill 1: Tracking

The first skill of the TRM is tracking. Tracking involves paying attention to sensations within the body. It is the foundation for helping stabilize the nervous system. The client learns to tell the difference between sensations of turmoil and upset and sensations of balance and well-being. Exploring sensations connected to well-being is key to helping a person feel better in mind, body, and spirit. Gendlin (2007) stated, "You can sense your living body directly underneath your thoughts and memories and under your familiar feelings." Tracking sensations gives us what Gendlin calls "a body-sense of meaning." Tracking can help clients bring to conscious awareness information about their life experiences using the portal of the body. The bodily sensations connected to thoughts and feelings can be an immense ocean of untapped information, which can help clients maneuver through their life experiences.

*Tracking: Step by Step*

1. The TRM clinician provides education about the autonomic nervous system and helps the client understand the importance of differentiating between sensations connected with the sympathetic nervous system and those connected with the parasympathetic nervous system. Tracking sensations is an additional portal of information for self-knowledge and empowerment. Every thought and feeling has a corresponding sensation—pleasant, unpleasant, or neutral. When one has experienced trauma, body sensations can be triggered by an array of multisensory reminders (i.e., smells, sounds, and images) that can derail well-being and present-moment awareness. When one learns to track and monitor those sensations, a person can, through intention, bring his awareness to sensations that are neutral or pleasant. The ultimate goal is that the client will become the best tracker of his nervous system. It is helpful to use the graphic below to explain how the nervous system affects the body. For example, if a person is

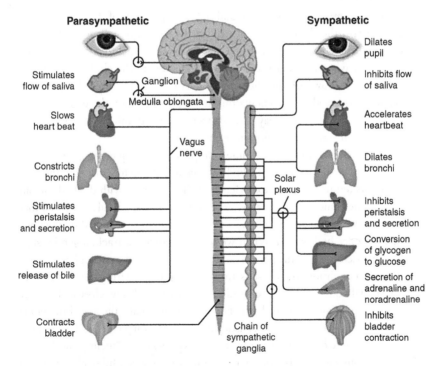

*Figure 3.2* The Autonomic Nervous System

Reprinted with permission from Kimball's Biology Pages, http://biology-pages.info.

anxious about giving a speech, his heart rate may be elevated and he may experience the sensation as unpleasant. When he thinks about his favorite place in nature that is calming, he will sense his heart rate and respiration slowing down. There may be pleasant experiences during which the heart rate is elevated, and the key is to differentiate those that are pleasant from those that are distressing. When the client learns to track his nervous system when he is upset and then shift his awareness to more pleasant or neutral sensations, he can live more fully in the present moment.

2. To teach the skill of tracking, the clinician must be able to track her own nervous system first. The better able the clinician is at returning to her resilient zone, the more she can help her client learn to be within his resilient zone. Thus, the therapeutic relationship is formed not only between two minds but two bodies (Schore, 2009).

The clinician draws attention to tracking her own body and staying grounded and resourced throughout the session. As empathic listeners, clinicians can be knocked out of their own resilient zones when witnessing the heart-wrenching stories of traumatic experiences. Learning to be fully present by self-tracking not only helps the client but can assist the clinician in reducing symptoms of vicarious trauma.

The clinician mirrors the gestures and the body postures of the client. As the clinician mirrors the client, the client will usually feel more supported. It can be helpful to let the client know that you may make the same gestures that occur spontaneously when a clinician is attuned to the client. The clinician monitors herself closely to stay with the client as the gestures and postures change as the trauma is reprocessed. Some clients find it off-putting when the clinician mirrors them. If that is the case, pay careful attention not to mirror the client. The clinician can still track but without movements and gestures.

Awareness of voice tone and volume is important when guiding an individual to experience the well-being of the body as well as helping to work with the sensations connected to traumatic experiences. When working with the body, it can be jarring if the clinician's voice is too crisp or too loud. As a doula, I learned that softening the voice and gently guiding a woman through labor would support her to work with her body's pain. When we help an individual track, a gentle, supportive approach can help the person deliver herself out of the pain of her trauma.

3. Bringing attention to body sensations. We begin by inviting the client to set his own spatial boundary. "Where would you like to sit?" "How close or far away do you want to position your chair?" For some individuals, the act of the clinician leaning forward can elicit a sensory experience connected with traumatic experiences. Some clients have never had the experience of "feeling safe." Thus, asking questions such as, "Is that safer for you?" can be a helpful qualifier. Judith Herman (1992) states that "establishing safety and stability in one's body" is one of the primary elements in helping individuals who have experienced trauma.

When tracking, the TRM clinician is not directive and stays "one half step behind" the client by inquiring about observed movements and sensations or ones that the client reports. The clinician does not interpret the client's experience, but rather asks open-ended questions and gently inquires of the client what's happening on the inside. While tracking, the practitioner asks invitational questions such as, "Is the sensation pleasant, unpleasant, or neutral?" Using open-ended questions such as, "What do you notice? What are you aware of now?" is essential. The client is the expert on his sensory experience. The clinician supports and encourages the client's exploration of the sensations connected to feelings, thoughts, and beliefs without judgment. Supportive statements like, "Sensations are not right or wrong. You are simply learning the importance of paying attention," can encourage curiosity and reduce a client's self-consciousness.

When tracking sensations, allow time for the client to respond. It takes time for sensations to develop and for the client to be aware of what is happening inside the body, especially when he is first learning to track. Taking time means taking enough time but not too much time. Some clients can feel like the clinician has abandoned them if the silence is too long. It may take a little time to build the right rhythm between the client and the clinician and to determine how long of a pause will help the client experience his sensation fully.

When learning how to track, some individuals have difficulty being observed, so begin with mind-body education to explain the rationale behind using a biological model. The clinician can also let the client know that she can observe sensations by not necessarily facing the client; the clinician can avert her eyes to the side—for some people it is too much for the clinician to observe their body posture or sensations straight on. If that is the case, the clinician can track her own body, and report sensation change to the client that may be mirroring the client's experience. For example, when the client is using the skill of resourcing and describes a beautiful place in nature, the clinician may take a deep breath mirroring the client's deeper breath. The clinician can say, "As you told me about your beautiful place, I took a deeper breath." This strategy can help the client begin to notice changes within his own nervous system without feeling observed by the clinician.

Use sensory language when helping an individual learn to track. Sensory language does not always come easily. It may take some time in terms of education and also experience for individuals to begin to tune into their internal climate. For some people, even sensing pleasant or neutral sensations may trigger unpleasant, even painful memories. If a client is experiencing too many unpleasant sensations, the clinician can bring him back to the present moment by using some of the strategies of the Help Now! skill discussed later in the chapter. It is important to honor where your client is because not every client is able to tolerate sensory awareness. If an individual is not able to sense pleasant or neutral sensations, discontinue the TRM and use your usual ways of engaging with your client. Not every method of intervention will be helpful to every client.

*Table 3.1* Sensations Chart

| Sight | Smell | Sound | Taste | Temperature | Touch |
|---|---|---|---|---|---|
| **Colors** Is there an object? | **(Describe the smell)** | **(Describe the sound)** | **(Describe the taste)** | **(Describe the temperature)** | **(Describe the feeling)** |
| **Shape** | Rancid | **Volume** | Sweet | Cool | Hard |
| Round | Fresh | Loud | Sour | Cold | Sharp |
| Triangular | Floral | Soft | Bitter | Icy | Rough |
| Oval | Fragrant | | Tasteless | Lukewarm | Pointed |
| Rectangular | | **Quality** | Spicy | Warm | Soft |
| Square | | Squeak | | Hot | Furry |
| | | Scream | | Neutral | |
| **Size** | | Grunt | | | |
| Small | | Cry | | | |
| Medium | | Laugh | | | |
| Large | | | | | |
| **Looks like** | | | | | |
| Flat | | | | | |
| Dark | | | | | |
| Curved | | | | | |
| Bright | | | | | |

When your client is learning the skill of tracking, the Sensations Chart (Table 3.1) can help describe what he or she is noticing inside. Through this practice, the client's sensory vocabulary can expand.

### Skill 2: Resourcing and Resource Intensification

Developing and expanding personal resources is the second skill. Resourcing is a strength-building skill. There are three types of resources that can be drawn upon to enhance nervous system reorganization: external resources, internal resources, and imagined resources. External resources can include the people, places, spiritual beliefs, skills, hobbies, and pets that have given us support and nurturance throughout life. Internal resources can include values and beliefs as well as positive character traits and body strengths that support and give meaning to life. Imagined resources are those we have not yet experienced but can imagine. Some individuals cannot identify external or internal resources. In this case, we can ask a client to bring to mind a resource he would like to have and imagine what his life would be like if that resource existed and encourage him to track the sensations connected to the imagined resource.

Developing resources builds internal resiliency and a renewed sense of one's own abilities and capacity and helps stabilize the nervous system. Individuals are often surprised by how many resources they have in their lives. If a person cannot identify a resource, the hope of creation of a resource can also bring about changes within the nervous system. As a client begins to sense positive, neutral, or less distressing sensations in the body connected to the identified resource, he begins to feel hope and possibility.

Initially, we want the client to learn that there is something else going on in his body besides unpleasant sensations. When guiding a client to track neutral and pleasant sensations, the clinician starts with helping the client identify pleasant memories from past experience. When asked to remember a resource, the client is bringing to present-moment awareness a multisensory experience connected to his past well-being. This is a positive implicit memory he is bringing to present-moment awareness by intention.

Resource intensification means asking more questions about the resource so the description is enhanced. When the clinician asks the client to notice the sensations connected to the more detailed description, the multisensory elements strengthen the resource experience. Hanson (2010) states that the amygdala uses about two-thirds of its neurons (brain cells) to look for bad news. Highly emotionally charged negative experiences are quickly stored in memory. This is what is called the "negativity bias" (Vaish et al., 2008). He elaborates that positive experiences need to be held in awareness for a dozen or more seconds to transfer from short-term memory buffers to long-term storage. Thus, in order to override the "negativity bias," it is important for the client to enhance the resource by describing it in greater deal. As he describes the resource in greater detail, the client is invited to notice the sensations. Noticing the sensations connected to the more descriptive resource creates a new template that the client can have more access to the more that he practices.

Learning to track by identifying a resource is of primary importance when being introduced to the skills of the TRM and CRM. As a client begins to describe a resource, we are accessing a positive implicit memory that is already within the body. Thus, when the clinician invites the client to be aware of the sensations connected to the resource, the client will most often describe a pleasant or neutral sensory experience.

Resources can have many qualities. When describing a resource, some clients can become sad or distressed because of the dual nature connected to many resources.

*For example, a client, when describing her grandmother, began to cry because her grandmother had died. The clinician does not have to ask for a different resource, but rather can first be present with the client's tears and sadness, asking her to notice the wetness of the tears; then after a pause, the clinician can gently ask the client to share some of the positive memories about the resource. As the client expands the positive memories, she is invited to bring awareness to parts of the body that feel more comfortable or neutral. Most often the person can learn to hold both parts of the resource and this can actually strengthen the resource. The same client was able to describe how her grandmother would make pancakes for her in the shapes of animals. She then smiled and took a deeper breath. The clinician invited her to notice the change. She then reported that the experience with resourcing was the first time she could talk about her grandmother without being overcome with grief. She was relieved to experience all the powerful sensations connected to the positive experiences she had had with her grandmother.*

Some questions that can be helpful to ask respectfully are as follows:

- Can you tell me some of your positive memories of her?
- What did you like to do together?
- What kind of words of encouragement would she say to you during difficult times?
- If she had known you would survive and she did not, what words of wisdom would she have said to you about going forward?

There may be instances when the client cannot shift awareness to more positive or neutral aspects of the resource. In this case, the clinician can ask whether a different resource might be preferable.

Resources can also initially be built around the traumatic experience. Some individuals have a great desire to tell their trauma story immediately to their clinician. Even though in the TRM we want to establish resources and grounding first, sometimes it is difficult to share the skills first because of the urgency of the presenting situation. Survival resource questions can be integrated into the assessment to help the client access other elements of the story:

- Can you remember the moment when you knew you were going to survive?
- Can you remember the moment when help arrived?
- Who else made it through?
- What gives you the strength to get through this now?
- When you have experienced other difficult times in your life, what or who helped you get through?
- Who is helping you the most now?

*In China after the Sichuan earthquake, an adolescent boy who survived the collapse of his middle school was brought to us for help. He had been unable to sleep since the quake. As we began to talk about his experience, he was asked to recount the moment that he knew he would survive the earthquake. He began to describe the moment he was walking away from the school and saw his mother. They ran to each other and cried. He reported feeling a great sense of relief and it was at that moment when he knew he had lived. He was able to smile and laugh. We went on to talk about other elements of his experience, often shifting attention back to his survival story when he had difficulty with other parts of his story. He reported feeling better knowing that there were good things that happened, too, like being closer to his mother.*

Helping clients identify resources in a myriad of formal and informal ways can help increase the bandwidth of the client's resilient zone. Some individuals because of temperament or life challenges may have a narrow resilient zone. Practicing the skills can help widen the resilient zone.

---

### Building Resources Exercise

- A resource can be anyone or anything that helps a person feel better.
- It can be something the person likes about him/herself, a positive memory, a person, a place, an animal, a spiritual guide, one's faith, or anything that provides comfort. It can also be an imagined resource.

Write down three resources.

1.
2.
3.

Circle one resource.

Write down three or more details about your resource that you circled.

1.
2.
3.

Now read to yourself the resource and the three details you have written down about your resource.

**Notice** what is happening inside as you think about the resource and notice the sensations that are pleasant to you or neutral. **Notice** what is happening to your breath . . . heart rate . . . muscle tension. Stay with that for a few moments.

   **Write** down the sensations that you notice on the inside that are pleasant.

1.
2.
3.

### Skill 3: Grounding

Grounding refers to the relationship between a person's body and the present moment. Gravitational security is the foundation upon which we build our interpersonal relationships, and grounding is essential to the sense of being present in the here and now (Ayres, 2005). If your relationship to the earth is not safe, your sense of safety needed for positive social engagement can be compromised. Grounding can be accomplished by sensing a part or the whole of your body in relationship to a surface. We have found that not everyone can ground sitting down, so providing options for grounding is paramount. You can ground standing, sitting, and lying down. You can also ground by being aware of your hands and feet making contact with a surface. A TRM practitioner, working with a client with quadriplegia, helped him ground through sensing his head making contact with his pillow. When working in the Philippines after Typhoon Yolanda, many individuals shared that they felt the most grounded when floating in the ocean. Thus, there are many ways to ground; therefore, the more invitational the clinician can be when helping the client learn the skill of grounding, the better, as there is so much variance in how a person grounds. The following script can be shared with your client to help him learn the skill of grounding:

- Find a comfortable position sitting, lying down, or standing.
- Notice how your back is making contact with the chair, sofa, floor, wall, bed, earth.
- If sitting, bring attention to your seat making contact with the sofa or chair . . . now notice your thighs . . . legs . . . and then your feet making

contact with a solid surface. Notice your feet making contact with the ground.

- Notice the sensations that are more pleasant to you or neutral within your body . . . take your time . . . notice your breathing, heart rate, your muscles relaxing.
- If you become aware of uncomfortable sensations, bring your attention to places that feel neutral or more comfortable.
- As you bring your attention to neutral or comfortable sensations, notice your breathing, heart rate, muscle relaxation.
- Take a few moments to bring your awareness to sensations that are pleasant and/or neutral.
- As we get ready to end, slowly scan your body and bring your attention to all sensations that are pleasant or neutral.

*Challenges with Grounding*

Take special care with individuals who are of shorter stature. Provide pillows, books, or a platform for shorter individuals so that they can sense their feet against a solid surface. Shorter individuals can be so accustomed to their feet not resting on the ground that they may not know it can have great value in how they perceive personal safety when their feet do rest on the ground.

For some individuals whose experience of trauma included the overriding sensations of their breath or their heart rate, drawing attention to the body in the present moment can trigger a traumatic flashback. The clinician may need to drop the grounding exercise altogether. However, once the client learns to bring more awareness to sensations of well-being through tracking with resourcing, the client can develop the ability to ground.

*An elderly man who came to one of our groups initially could not tolerate grounding. He had prostate cancer and degenerative disc disease. He was so accustomed to focusing on his chronic pain that any attention to his body and especially his heart rate was experienced negatively. Once he learned to use the skill of resourcing, he was able to learn grounding and after he was able to use all three skills to reduce his pain. He shared that he was now able to manage his pain better, as he could tell his doctor with greater clarity where he was experiencing the pain. Before learning resourcing and grounding, he would tell his doctor he felt pain everywhere. He shared that learning to be aware of parts of his body that felt neutral or pleasant increased his awareness of what was going right inside his body rather than what was not working.*

Grounding is helpful for individuals who dissociate. TRM clinicians help clients who dissociate track sensations that precede dissociation. When the client becomes aware, for example, of a sensation of floating away, the client can use grounding to return to an embodied present-moment awareness. Some clients who dissociate may need a physical sense of weight on their body. Weighted items like a heavy pillow, a beanbag, or a weighted blanket may be necessary for the client to sense his body. In addition, some clients may not be able to ground without the practitioner gently touching the person's hand or shoulder, or making contact with the feet. If the client is having trouble with dissociation, a simple but very helpful strategy is for the clinician to place her feet on the client's feet. Conversely, some clients will not be able to ground if the clinician is too physically close to the client. If this is the case, the clinician can ask the client, "How far away would you like me to be from your chair?" Sometimes, just the invitation will help the client ground. Clinician flexibility is imperative. Some clients can misinterpret supportive and respectful touch. The clinician who decides to use respectful touch in her practice needs to explain the uses of touch before using touch and let clients know they can always refuse touch. We recommend that clinicians use consent forms that include touch clauses if they integrate touch into their practice.

Grounding can be disquieting for some individuals, especially drawing attention to the client's feet and inviting the client to push his feet against the floor. The TRM/CRM clinician invites the client to notice how his feet are making contact with the floor rather than giving an instruction of "pushing feet into the ground." When working with individuals who have experienced high-impact shock trauma like those who have been in combat, introduce tracking with developing resources before introducing grounding. This is important because if a person was in a high-impact accident, pushing his feet into the ground can often be a traumatic trigger. Further, some individuals push their feet into the ground to brace themselves during other high-impact traumatic events. A woman in one of our workshops shared that when she was invited to push her feet against the floor, she was triggered into a traumatic memory of being in school with a stern teacher who would humiliate her in front of her classmates. We have learned that the clinician needs to proceed with caution with the skill of grounding.

Some clients will not share that the experience was disquieting, and may internalize that there must be something wrong with them because they don't experience grounding as comforting.

### Skill 4: Gesturing

Gesturing is the fourth wellness skill. Gestures emerge spontaneously and are usually below conscious awareness. Merriam-Webster Dictionary defines gesture as a "movement usually of the body or limbs that expresses or emphasizes an idea, sentiment, or attitude and the use of motions of the limbs or body as a means of expression." Kelly, Manning, and Rodak (2008) state that people of all ages, cultures, and backgrounds gesture when they speak. Kelly et al. further state that hand movements are so natural and pervasive that researchers across many fields from linguistics to psychology to neuroscience have claimed that speech and gestures form an integrated system of meaning during language production and comprehension. Further, gestures have a special meaning to the words that they accompany. In the TRM and CRM, it has been repeatedly observed that individuals all over the world, regardless of their culture and ethnicity, make gestures while they speak about healing experiences in their lives. In addition, there are also gestures that are inherently self-soothing that can be a part of an individual's repertoire for self-regulation. Clients will often share their self-soothing gesture with the clinician if asked.

The TRM/CRM clinician helps the client identify gestures that are self-soothing that can be brought into present-moment awareness to return the nervous system back into balance—back to the resilient zone. There are many types of self-soothing gestures and movements including the following:

- Self-calming gestures: movements that bring comfort and safety
- Gestures of release: movements that represent the body coming back into balance and a sensation of something distressing leaving the body
- Universal movements that represent wholeness, spiritual beliefs, or deep personal meaning
- Protective movements:
  - Hand, leg, and whole body movements

For some individuals, drawing attention to gestures can be intrusive. Having a rationale for why you are drawing attention to a gesture can be helpful to the client in understanding the value of intentionally bringing awareness to gestures. The clinician can say, for example:

"This model helps bring into awareness comforting or self-soothing gestures that are often just under conscious awareness. With your permission, from time to time, I will draw your attention to gestures that you make to help you learn about the gestures that may help you more easily return to your resilient zone." The clinician may add, "I may also at times suggest that you repeat a gesture slowly to help your nervous system come into greater balance."

While drawing attention to comforting gestures, it can be helpful to suggest slowing down the gesture as this can deepen the embodied sense of the gesture.

*Gesturing Exercise*

The following exercises can help the client sense the power of gestures:

- Take three seconds to think about a self-soothing gesture . . . count 1, 2, 3 and then make the gesture. As you do your gesture of self-soothing, notice what happens inside.
- Take three seconds to think about a gesture of confidence . . . count 1, 2, 3 and then make the gesture. As you do your gesture of confidence, notice what happens inside.
- Take three seconds to think about a gesture of joy . . . count 1, 2, 3 and then make the gesture. As you do your gesture of joy, notice what happens inside.

### Skill 5: Help Now!

This skill involves specific strategies to bring down activation within the nervous system when a person is stuck in either the high or low zone. The strategies help the client focus on something else besides the distress and the sense of being overwhelmed. The strategies activate other parts of the body and brain that help the person come back into balance. For example, slowly pushing again the wall, using the strength of your arms and legs and the large muscles of the body, helps to regulate the nervous system and bring it back into balance. Help Now! strategies can be shared with family and friends to help an individual get back to his resilient zone. The following represent 10 strategies. Not all the strategies will help each person. The clinician teaches the client about the importance of learning the Help Now! strategies and encourages him to use the strategies when needed.

1. Drink a glass of water, a cup of tea, or cup of juice.
2. Look around the room or wherever you are, paying attention to anything that catches your attention.
3. Name six colors you see in the room (or outside).
4. Open your eyes if they have a tendency to shut.
5. Count backwards from 10 as you walk around the room.
6. If you're inside, notice the furniture, and touch the surface of a couch or chair, noticing if it is hard, soft, or rough.

7. Notice the temperature in the room.
8. Notice the sounds within and outside the room.
9. Walk and pay attention to the movement in your arms and legs and how your feet are making contact with the ground.
10. Push your hands against the wall or door slowly and notice your muscles pushing.

*Help Now! Exercise*

1. Has there been a time in your life when you have needed the Help Now! strategies?
2. Is there a way you can remind yourself to use the strategies when you are out of your resilient zone?
3. If you are in situations where it may not occur to you to use the Help Now! strategies, to whom can you give the Help Now! information in order to help you when you get bumped out of your resilient zone?
4. When can you give the person(s) the Help Now! information?
5. Is there a person in your life with whom you could share the Help Now! strategies so that he can use them himself? If so, who?

### Skill 6: Shift and Stay

Shift and stay is the sixth and final wellness skill. Shift and stay integrates all five skills learned so far. This skill emphasizes that the client has the ability to shift awareness to one of the skills he has been practicing throughout his activities of daily living when trauma and/or stress-related reactions arise unexpectedly. There are many internal and external triggers that can create fear, anxiety, volatility, and isolation. When this occurs, the client can use the shift and stay skill to shift his attention from the distressing sensations in the body to a resource, to grounding, to a self-soothing gesture, to a Help Now! strategy, or simply to a place in the body that feels calmer or neutral. The client then stays with those sensations until stabilization has occurred. So, tracking is an elemental part of shift and stay. The therapist teaches this skill to the client to use in his daily life.

*Shift and Stay Practice Exercise*

As you think about a recurring, slightly annoying event, you can do one the following:

- bring your attention to a place in your body that is neutral, calmer, or has less unpleasant sensations; or
- notice how your body is making contact with the chair, sofa, floor, or bed and ground; or

- remember one of your internal or external resources, describing it to yourself; or
- remember a self-soothing, non-harming gesture; or
- remember one of the Help Now! strategies

As you select from the options above, notice what happens on the inside.

Bring your attention away from the distress to the sensations that are calmer, more comfortable, or neutral. Take your time.

Notice the changes in your heart rate, breathing, and muscle relaxation.

As you bring the shift and stay exercise to a close, slowly scan your body from head to toe, noticing all the positive or neutral changes. Stay with that for a few moments.

The six skills we have just described are the wellness skills of both the CRM and TRM. The next three skills are for the mental health professional to help a client in trauma reprocessing. These concepts were learned in SE and they have been adapted to the TRM as skills.

### Skill 7: Titration

Individuals who suffer posttraumatic stress injury can become stuck in the low zone or high zone. The sensations associated with being stuck in either zone can disconnect one from living fully in the present moment. The skill of titration adapted from Peter Levine's SE refers to becoming aware of smaller, more manageable sensations. The TRM clinician helps the client become aware of the sensations connected to the traumatic event. As the client describes the sensations, the clinician invites the client to concretize the sensation. Concretizing sensation helps the client learn to manage the sensations without becoming overwhelmed by them. The TRM clinician guides the client to sense a more manageable piece of the activation by asking about concrete details of the sensations. Invitational questions can include,

"What are you noticing now?"

"Is the sensation small, medium, or large?"

"Does the sensation have a shape or color?"

The client can also be asked to bring awareness to a smaller piece of the activation within the body.

"Can you just go to the edge of that distress?"

As a smaller part of the sensation is experienced, the nervous system releases some of the charge. As the TRM clinician tracks the client's nervous system, change is observed in deeper breaths, relaxed muscles, and the client's own report that his heart rate and breath have slowed. Titration follows the gentle nature of this model, as the client becomes increasingly aware that the traumatic sensations can be tolerated, managed, and released.

Some clients will have difficulty describing an image associated with the sensation of distress. If this is the case, you can ask if the sensation is small, medium, or large, and if the client can bring his attention to the edge of the uncomfortable sensation. The nervous system is designed for regulation, and when the clinician uses the skill of titration, the client often experiences an immediate relief as his sensations lessen in intensity or dissipate altogether.

### Skill 8: Pendulation

Pendulation—another method adapted from Peter Levine's SE—is the shifting back and forth between sensations of distress and sensations of greater well-being within the nervous system. Sensations of well-being are comfortable, neutral, or less uncomfortable sensations within the body. Sensations of distress can include pain, muscle tension, or autonomic nervous system dysregulation (being stuck in the high or low zone). When the client is experiencing distressing sensations, the TRM clinician uses the skill of pendulation by inviting the client to bring awareness to places within the body that are less tense, less painful, neutral, or pleasant. Ogden (2006) refers to a similar process as oscillation. She states that alternating back and forth is useful in helping clients shift their focus from traumatic activation to more resourced or present-time experience.

The skills of titration and pendulation are used together. When a sensation is titrated, a natural shifting occurs, bringing the nervous system back into balance. The client may notice the distressing sensation lessening as the nervous system returns to the resilient zone. The clinician invites the client to bring awareness to the change as the nervous system comes back into balance.

### Skill 9: Completion of Survival Responses

When human beings are threatened as explained in Chapter 2, there are four possible survival strategies: tend and befriend, fight, flight, and freeze. The elegant design of the human nervous system triggers survival responses when there is a perceived threat. Following a traumatic event that was existential, a person can be triggered by almost anything reminiscent of the event. Van der Hart (1997) identified the following triggers: sensory data; time-related stimuli; daily life events; events during the therapeutic session; emotional states; physiological states; stimuli recalling intimidations by perpetrators; and current trauma. In our work, we have discovered that almost anything can be a trigger. Thus, it is helpful to help clients understand that triggers can be anything that reminds the nervous system of a life-threatening event. This information can reduce the shame and self-blame that can be a constant bedfellow for those who are triggered frequently.

Peter Levine (1997) conceptualized that when a human being is threatened, massive amounts of energy are mobilized within the body for self-defense. If the person can complete the defensive response, there is a natural discharge of energy. The discharge sensations can include movements, such as shaking, trembling, and deep spontaneous breaths. Levine postulates that this discharge process resets the autonomic nervous system, restoring balance. What is problematic for human beings is that we place a brake on experiencing these sensations for many reasons, including the tendency to judge ourselves harshly. When we stop the natural release of these sensations, the energy meant for defensive responses becomes "stuck" in the body. The "stuck" energy leads to physical, behavioral, cognitive, and psychological symptoms. Levine's methodology helps the individual complete defensive responses that were blocked at the time of the traumatic event. The goal of SE is to release this blocked energy held in the body. When the energy is released, the nervous system can be reset and return to equilibrium. SE addresses three survival strategies of fight, flight, and freeze. We adapted some of these methods to the TRM.

The survival response continuum can help the clinician conceptualize interventions to reprocess the traumatic experience. As the client describes the traumatic event or as he is aware of the sensations connected to the traumatic experience, the clinician can begin to assess what phase was not able to be completed that led to the traumatic stress reactions.

*Phase 1: Orienting Response*

The orienting response refers to an automatic response in which a person reacts to new information from the environment that may or may not be threatening. The orienting response is protective and is designed to answer the questions, "What is that?" and "Am I safe?" The orienting response is an autonomic sensory motor reflex. It comes from the spinal chord and is pre-wired in the central nervous system. The orienting response emerged from Pavlov's (1927) studies of classical conditioning in dogs. Pavlov was inspired by the work of Sechenov (1863), who first described the orienting response.

*External Orienting*: The physical acts of turning the head and the body and focusing the eyes in the direction of the novelty is part of the orienting response when focused externally. For example, during the Asian tsunami, when the wave came, people naturally looked toward it because we are attracted to what threatens our survival. It was not only the visual image of the wave but the sound of the wave, which was described as deafening. During orienting, there is increased muscular tension as well as physiological changes including acceleration of heart rate and breathing. The orienting response happens automatically below conscious awareness. It is adaptive in helping people react quickly to events that call for immediate action. It is instinctual and important for people to increase their survival chances when faced with a threat.

*Internal Orienting*: Orienting can also be directed inward and there can be focused attention, for example, on sensations perceived as threatening. Some individuals become fixated upon their sensations.

As a result of a traumatic event, automatic preparatory movements can be overridden because the sudden impact of the traumatic event did not allow for time to respond, and the energy meant to respond to the threat is blocked (Levine, 1997).

*For example, a client's car was hit on the right side while he was driving on the freeway. He did not have enough time to orient to the right. It happened too fast. After this event, he was in two other accidents where he did not see a car changing lanes from the right side. He was not orienting to the right side. Until working with TRM skills, he had no idea he was not turning his head to the right. So the one accident led to diminished orienting. Thus, not being able to orient during a traumatic experience can leave a large imprint on a person's ability to orient directionally (right, left, up, and down).*

The person may also become hypersensitive to triggers that remind him of the traumatic event. In the Philippines, many individuals shared that since the catastrophic Typhoon Yolanda, rainy days triggered a fear response. Hypervigilance is an over-orientation towards a trigger. The response can be excessive to the external stimulus of a sound, smell, or visual image. There can often be an accompanying hypersensitivity to bodily changes and a misinterpretation of even benign changes in breathing as being potentially threatening. For example, as rapid breathing often occurs during a traumatic event, individuals can become afraid if their heart starts beating fast as a result of physical exercise. Additionally, a person may become less discerning and may not be able to distinguish whether an environmental cue is threating or not. Thus, the individual may unwittingly place himself into situations that are dangerous because his appraisal system is not interpreting the potential threat accurately. Some clients describe symptoms of disorientation, which may manifest as having problems with concentration, being "foggy," or experiencing the environment as being out of focus.

If a client has a blocked orienting response, the clinician can use TRM skills to help the client reestablish the orienting response in the present moment. Even though it did not happen in real life, implicit memory has no time and space. We can insert the time now, using TRM skills to accomplish this. When we take the client through reorienting strategies in present-moment awareness, the body can have the sense of orienting now. This can reset the nervous system and bring the person back to the resilient zone. The full orienting response can be reestablished.

*A Vietnam veteran described his combat experience while riding in a tank when it drove over a land mine and blew up. The tank was actually blown into the air and then crashed to the ground. The veteran was seriously injured and was still experiencing symptoms from those injuries. The veteran reported that he noticed that he was always looking down—so much so that he frequently hit his head on objects that were in front of him or above him. We discussed the concept of the orienting response. Because the ground became associated with danger, he was actually over-orienting to the ground and under-orienting to what was right above or in front of him. He already had resources well anchored in his body and was able to track his nervous system and ground himself. The session began by identifying a resource he wanted to use that day as well as remembering the moment he had survived. He reported that when he was taken by helicopter out of enemy fire was the moment he knew he was going to survive. He experienced heat and tingling, deeper breath, and other sensations of release as his awareness was brought to that moment. He was then invited to track what he noticed in his body when he looked straight ahead. He reported that this felt safer as he could see exactly what was in front of him. His attention was brought to the sense of feeling safer. The client was then asked to very slowly move his head downward. He was invited to move to the very edge of the activation and then move back to center. Slowly during the session, he gently moved his head back and forth between the downward orienting and looking straight ahead. We also shifted his attention between his resource and the survival memory. As we continued to work with the orienting response, the veteran noticed he had an urge to run.*

*He clarified that this didn't mean he would have run in that situation, because he said that would go against all of his training and he wouldn't leave his men. When he brought his attention to the desire to run, his body began shaking slightly, and he took a deeper breath. He reported that he felt as if something had changed from the inside out. He was again invited to sense the change. He spontaneously moved his head up and down, left to right and reported more flexibility in his movements. After this session, he reported that he no longer looked down and hit his head. His neck pain improved and he felt a great sense of relief.*

*Phase 2: Mobilization to Fight, Flight, or Tend and Befriend*

In response to a perceived threat, cortisol and adrenalin are released and the person feels a surge of energy to respond to the threat by fighting or fleeing. Many women and some men may tend and befriend. The release of oxytocin results in acts of affiliation and protection, and buffers the release of adrenalin to protect children and the social group.

Cannon (1915) first described the fight and flight response. He described that when an animal is strongly aroused, the sympathetic division of its autonomic nervous system combines with the hormone adrenaline to mobilize the animal for an emergency response of "flight or fight." He was the first to conceptualize that the autonomic nervous system stimulates changes in blood supply in order to gather the body's resources to produce what he called a "violent display of energy."

In the TRM, we have found the fourth survival strategy—"tend and befriend"—essential in working with women and some men. Taylor (2006, 2007) found that women not only have the capacity to flee or fight, but they have a capacity to "tend and befriend." Women release the hormone oxytocin, which is part of their stress response. Thus, oxytocin may override the fight or flight response and result in an individual tending to the children and affiliating with other women for protection. In addition, when an aggressor experiences a woman in this state, oxytocin may also be released in him, thereby increasing her chances of survival.

*Phase 3: Completion of Survival Responses*

In this phase, the person uses the heightened energy to fight or flee or the calming effect to tend and befriend. If the survival responses are completed, the nervous system returns to balance. If the person experiences extreme fear coupled with an inescapable attack, he may freeze and not be able to complete the response. The energy meant for fleeing, fighting, or tending and befriending is not released.

The freeze response or "tonic immobility" is characterized by profound motor inhibition and is triggered under inescapable threat in many species, including humans. When there is a predatory attack, some animals will freeze or "play dead." Tonic immobility may be the best option when the animal perceives little immediate chance of escaping or successfully fighting (Korte, Koolhaas, Wingfield, & McEwen, 2005). Tonic immobility can be useful when attacks may continue as a result of movement or when immobility may increase the chance of escaping, such as when a predator believes its prey to be dead and releases it. Humphreys, Sauder, Martin, and Marx (2010) stated that the experience of tonic immobility during childhood sexual assault may play an important role in the subsequent PTSD symptomatology in adulthood. Volchan et al. (2011) found that tonic immobility reports seemed more evident in PTSD than other mental health disorders, suggesting that for some individuals, tonic immobility may be elicited during reexperiencing episodes in daily life.

*Phase 4: Return to Resilient Zone*

As the survival responses are successfully completed, the nervous system returns to its equilibrium, back to the resilient zone. The person will experience nervous system releases that can include, shaking, trembling, burping, and yawning as equilibrium is restored. If the survival responses are not completed, the person is at risk for traumatic stress reactions.

**Completing Survival Responses Protocol**

*1. Education*

Be sure to educate during initial sessions and continue throughout therapeutic process:

- How trauma affects our nervous system
- Sympathetic and parasympathetic nervous system
- The survival responses
- Stuck in low/high zones concept
- The skills of the TRM
- The importance of learning the six wellness skills before starting trauma reprocessing
- Theory behind completing survival responses

## 2. Self-Regulation

Wellness skills are taught and the clinician assesses the client's readiness to be able to sense pleasant and/or neutral sensations before reprocessing a traumatic experience. Many sessions may be needed to frontload the wellness skills depending on the client's ability to self-regulate.

## 3. Identify the Target

In TRM, the client can relate the trauma story verbally or only through sensations as he thinks about the story. The client does not need to tell the story of the traumatic experience. The client can simply think about the traumatic experience and the clinician can help the client reprocess the experience by monitoring the sensations connected to the thought or image. The TRM clinician says, "You can tell me as little or as much about the experience as you would like."

In the TRM, if the client wants to tell the trauma story, the clinician will guide the client to share the story in a different way. At the time of the incident, as it was "too much too fast" or "too little for too long," it is critical for the client's nervous system to have a different sensory experience in the present moment as the story is shared. The clinician states that she will request to "pause" the recounting of the story from time to time if she notices the client becoming too distressed (high zone) or too disconnected (low zone). During the "resiliency pause," the practitioner shifts the client's awareness to one of the wellness skills to help the nervous system settle in the present moment before asking the client to continue. As the clinician monitors the sensations with the client, there is a point in the retelling when the clinician will ask if there is an impulse to complete a survival response. The energy in the story has to be of a survival quality in order to complete the survival response organically.

Counselors from Juarez, Mexico, reported that not sharing the story was very important with the survivors of the violence occurring in their city. Many individuals feared sharing stories of their trauma because of the threat of violence to themselves or their families by drug lords. Thus, being able to reprocess without telling the story becomes an important educational concept when working with individuals who fear retribution. It also provides hope that healing can be possible even without telling the story. This has been helpful when working with individuals who have experienced trauma from their service in the military. Individuals who serve in special forces, for example, may not be able to share their experiences yet suffer greatly with posttraumatic stress reactions. Many clients who seek out biological-based therapists do so as a result of having tried many other "talk therapies." They often report that they have more insight into what happened but that it has not changed the disruptive feelings they have when reminded of the event. When the clinician shares that the client does not have to talk about the details of his experience, there is often a great relief. If the client does not want to recount the story, the client is invited to think about components of the story while the clinician actively helps the client track sensations connected to the event and simply stays a half step behind as the body tells the story.

SPECIFIC SURVIVAL RESPONSES CONNECTED TO THE TARGET

**The Fight and Flight Response.** An individual with interrupted **fight** responses may be irritable, angry, and/or hypervigilant, and may display aggressive behaviors. The person may have a distorted lens with regard to how he reads experiences with others. He can misinterpret a person's glance and intentions as being threatening. The person may have a short fuse and overreact to benign situations. He also can display reactions conversely and feel depressed, apathetic, and hopeless.

When the client is completing a survival response, invite the client to slow down the movement so the movement can be fully sensed. At the time of the traumatic experience, the nervous system was overwhelmed. When the body is encouraged to do what it could not do at the time of the traumatic event, the person can experience in the present moment the completion of the survival response, and the nervous system can be reset and come back to the resilient zone. A new template can be made in the present moment in implicit memory that the person did complete the response biologically. Since we are working with implicit memory that has no sense of time or space, the nervous system can change, and symptoms connected to the traumatic experience can lessen, and in some cases, go away completely.

The clinician's tracking skills are a dynamic process when helping a client complete a survival response. Paying attention to micro-movements of the body and drawing the client's attention to the movements can help the client sense the energy necessary to complete a survival response. For example, the clinician tracks movements of the hands, legs, feet, mouth, jaw, and facial muscles. The clinician helps the client become aware of sensations connected to completing survival responses. The following invitational questions threaded into the intervention can assist with tracking the fight response. The questions are prompts that can help the practitioner in guiding the client.

"Do you have an impulse to do something? As you sense the impulse, which part of your body would like to move first? Notice what happens as you allow your body to move now."

"Is there a movement you would like to make now?"

"Sense the impulse to move and give your body all the time to organize the movement it wants to make and then notice what happens inside."

"Do your hands/arms/legs want to move in any direction? Allow the movement to *slowly* come through and then notice what happens inside."

"Repeat the movement as many times as feels right to you. If you can, slow down the movement, so that the movement can be fully sensed and registered by your body and mind."

Completing survival responses may also involve sounds and/or words that were not said at the time of the traumatic event. Perhaps the person was too frightened to say what he really wanted to say, or perhaps he was scared speechless. You may notice a tightening of his lips or a trembling in his chin. These are biological cues that tell the clinician there may be words that were left unsaid. Inviting the person to complete the words and/or sounds is another element to completing the survival response. Sometimes, people are surprised at the degree of their angry words and impulses. Reassuring the client that because he has an impulse does not mean he has become a violent person. Completing survival responses can challenge some clients' beliefs about their moral codes of conduct as they experience the desire to fight or flee. It is important to reassure the client that the responses are not about being violent or cowardly. We are helping the body complete the responses in a safe environment so that the nervous system can be reset and the traumatic stress reactions can diminish and in some cases remit altogether. We are working with normal biological responses and helping the body know through sensation that the traumatic experience is over. The following invitational questions can help the client: "Is there a sound you want to make or something else you want to say now or not? You can make the sound out loud or you can hear yourself saying it inside, in your mind's eye. As you do so, notice what happens inside." The clinician also suggests slowing down the words or sounds so that the client can fully sense the impact of saying what was unsaid.

*Mary had experienced sexual assaults from her stepfather for most of her childhood. When completing survival responses during trauma reprocessing, Mary found it helpful to push against the clinician's hands as if she were pushing her stepfather away. The clinician noticed that her chin was trembling. The clinician asked if there was something that she wanted to say. A tremendous amount of energy was observed by the clinician and Mary shouted, "Stay away from me! Get out of here!"*

*Then, the client had a tremendous amount of release in her jaw and extremities. She spontaneously said, "He will never hurt me again." She was again invited to track her sensations connected to the new meaning. She then described an image of herself as an adult cradling the little girl that she had been and telling her she would survive and live a meaningful life helping others. This personal meaning was the most powerful part of the session and she stated, "I feel like something has left me." The clinician asked her to notice the sensations connected to the new meanings. Mary took a deep breath and stated that her entire body and mind felt cleansed of him for the first time in her life.*

For some clients, it is not enough to just imagine completing the survival response. In this case, resistance can be helpful. The client may not know that the impulse to push against someone is appropriate in the therapeutic session. Thus, the clinician providing resistance options is part of helping the client complete the survival responses as it was for Mary. Some options are pushing against the therapist's hands, pushing against a pillow held tightly in the therapist's hands, or pushing against a wall. Some clients are so energetic that they may be afraid that they will be too physically powerful for the clinician to contain. It is important to use good posturing if you are to provide resistance in order not to be injured.

When working with survival responses, expanding or contracting the image of the experience can help bring down the activation. Guiding questions and statements can be integrated into the intervention, like: "You can move as far away as you need to from the image," or "Can you bring your awareness to just one part of the image?" This kind of invitation can also open up more options for the client as to how to respond to the threat. Statements like, "You have all the time you need now" support the client in taking time to explore survival options.

*Ken had been in a skydiving accident. He survived the fall but initially could not move. He had since regained his mobility. During reprocessing of the traumatic event, when he remembered lying in the field, he was focused on the lack of movement that he experienced in the immediate aftermath and the sense of being alone. He was first asked to describe the moment when he knew he would be able to walk again. He described the day as if he had won the Boston Marathon. The clinician encouraged Ken to notice the sensations connected to that moment. He reported feeling sensations of release as he experienced a light shaking in his legs. He was then asked if he wanted to continue with the story. He again described lying in the field and was asked to slow down and to look around the field he had fallen into. As he oriented to the field, his expanded lens was able to see people running toward him and to hear the sound of the paramedics and then to see the fire trucks arrive. As he was able to notice what else was true about this experience, his whole body relaxed and he reported experiencing sensations of release within his body. He then stated, "I wasn't alone. Help arrived sooner than I thought. I didn't know it then but I survived and I can walk." Wisdom about his survival cascaded out of Ken. Ken was invited to notice all the sensations connected to his expanded meaning of the event, and he could deeply sense the support he received after the fall and most importantly, sense into the words, "I survived and I can walk."*

People with incomplete **flight** response may have symptoms of anxiety, panic, and avoidance patterns and consistently have an urge to move away from any situation that is distressing or causes conflict. When they become distressed, the first impulse may be "I'm out of here." This attitude can make relationships challenging or cause avoidance patterns that lead to many unresolved life issues.

If movement during the time of the traumatic event would have meant injury or death, the client may be reluctant to move. So, you can expand their visual field by suggesting they insert protective allies into their image or suggesting they imagine running to something that represents safety. The following questions may help: "Can you imagine running with supportive friends, protective images, or even your older self?" or "Can you move in a direction that feels safer?" or "If you would like, see who or what you are running to" or "If you could imagine a safer place to run in the present moment, can you bring that image into your mind's eye and allow your body to sense the movement in your legs?"

*An Iraq War veteran was having difficulty with reintegration with his family. He had many close calls in Iraq and had survived an improvised explosive device (IED) explosion in his Humvee. When we worked with him to complete his survival responses, his first comment was that his impulse was to run;*

*however, he immediately edited himself by saying, "I would have never left my guys." We explained to him that we were giving his body the opportunity to do what it could not do in Iraq and assured him that it was about the biology of his body not knowing the event was over. He then stood up and he was able to monitor the immense energy in his body. His legs moved in place and he stated, "This is F!!!!!!ING WEIRD! I feel like I am really there and I am getting away this time!" He was invited to continue tracking the movement of running and he experienced release sensations. At the end of this, he said that it was the first time since being in Iraq that he felt like himself. As this new experience engulfed him, he was invited to sense what it was like to feel like himself again. He began to cry tears of gratitude.*

**Freeze Response.** If a person cannot tend and befriend, fight, or flee because of inescapable attack, the person may experience a freeze response. The freeze response is the most dysregulated of all the survival responses. When a person goes into a freeze response, it is like he is sitting in a car with the engine running, pushing down on the accelerator with the car in park. The engine is working at high capacity, but the car is not moving.

At times, as the client begins to explore sensations, the client may experience a part of the body that goes into a freeze response. This can be the result of a past physical or psychological injury. Reassure the client that this sometimes happens as people learn to pay attention to sensations. The clinician will then help the client come out of the freeze response by paying attention to movement within the nervous system. As the movement comes back, there will be release sensations. Tracking the release sensations helps rebalance the nervous system. The questions below can help an individual begin to move out of a freeze response.

"If your body could move just a little bit, how might it want to move first?"

"Is there any place in your body where you sense even the tiniest movement?"

"Notice what happens inside as you allow the movement."

"Would it be all right if I touched your hand to see if you can feel the warmth of my hand?"

"Can you see yourself moving in just the way you would like to move in your mind's eye?"

A respectful human touch, always with permission, may help the client's nervous system come back to the resilient zone. Conversely, if a person experienced intrusion into his personal space as a result of the traumatic experience, a touch can be more activating to the nervous system. The key is to ask permission and let the client know that he has a choice now. When a person has experienced trauma, his choice has been taken away. Thus, using invitational questions and giving choices is integral in creating safety. A helpful invitation could be, "Would it be alright for me to place my hand on yours or would you like me to move my chair further away from you? You can choose now."

The freeze response can be the most challenging for the client and the practitioner. When the client begins to come out of the freeze, the same terror and fear he experienced right before going into the freeze may again appear as he starts to sense his body. It is critical for the client to have a sound working knowledge of the CRM/TRM wellness skills prior to working with a traumatic experience that includes the freeze response. The clinician also must continue to track herself and if she is sensing her own distress because of the intensity of the client's experience, bringing her awareness to grounding and/or a resource can bring her back to her resilient zone quickly.

Clients who have symptoms of a freeze response need to be referred to a medical doctor so to rule out any untreated underlying physical conditions.

**Insertion of Protective Allies.** Some clients may need the sense of a protective ally in order to be able to experience enough energy within the body to complete a survival response. Many clients will spontaneously think of a protective ally, and the clinician can also ask, "Could a protective ally be helpful for you right now to help you do what your body wants to do?" A helpful ally can include superheroes, movie or television characters, supportive family and friends, or even the client's adult self. The "adult self" can be imagined protecting the client now. This can be a powerful, life-changing sensed experience for an individual to feel his power and strength in the here and now against a perpetrator whom he felt powerless against as a child or younger adult.

**Tend and Befriend Response.** If there were children or other important social affiliations involved in the traumatic experience, the adult caregiver may have a primal need to tend to the children and to draw social support together before completing a survival response of fight or flight for herself.

*A woman was in a car accident that resulted in serious injury to herself and her son. When the clinician tracked that there were movements of her hands and feet, she stated, "I can't take care of myself yet. I have to make sure my son is okay." During the accident, there were a few minutes when she did not know the whereabouts of her son as the paramedics took him out of the car. She was asked to notice her impulse and track her body to monitor what her body wanted to do. She said, "I need to hug my son and make sure he is safe." She saw herself (in her mind's eye) hugging her son and it resulted in release sensations. She then said, "He survived." She was able to cry for the first time. She stated, "I am relieved." The clinician invited her to notice the sensations of release. She was then able to focus on herself. We started the next session by using the spontaneous resource of her son's survival. As she remembered the moment that she knew her son had survived, her body settled and she could experience a parasympathetic response. We then continued to attend to the body's responses, and she stated, "I would have swerved to get out of the way if I would have seen the car coming on my left side." She was invited to do what her body wanted to do now, in the present moment. She was able to imagine orienting the car, something she was not able to do when the accident happened. When she oriented her body and head to the car, she was able to move her hands as if holding on to the steering wheel and move her car out of the way. She experienced an enormous breath and her hands and legs began to shake. The clinician brought her attention to the release sensations and her body continued to reset and return to the resilient zone. New meaning spontaneously emerged. She said, "My son not only survived but so did I." The clinician suggested that the client become aware of all the sensations connected to the statement. The client began to cry and she reported that the tears were different; the tears were of gratitude.*

If children or other important individuals were involved in the traumatic experience, posing questions that aid the client in completing survival strategies for them is essential before she can process her personal traumatic experience.

"If you could have, what would you have done first to protect your child and/or others?"

"As you see yourself taking action to protect, what do you notice on the inside?"

"As you know now in the present moment that your child and others you care about are safe, what happens on the inside?"

"What would have you wanted your child and others to know at the time, if anything?"

"Is there something you want to say to your child and others now or not?"

### 4. TRM Interweaves: Blending in Interweaves When Needed

If the client feels *frozen or collapsed*, it is important to help him sense movement in his system to proceed through feeling frozen or collapsed:

*   Invite the client to notice any place in his body that feels less frozen or collapsed.
*   Bring attention to any micro-movement made by the client.
*   When he reports movement, invite him to bring attention to it and notice what happens next.

If the client is *looping or stuck,* invite the client to notice what is happening inside as he is expressing a feeling of being stuck. The clinician can interject:

*   "When you say you feel stuck, what do you notice happening inside?"
*   "Is there a part of your body that feels less stuck than other parts?"
*   "As this thought keeps repeating, notice what is happening inside your body."
*   "Is there a movement in any direction that your body would like to make if it could?"

If the client begins *to dissociate,* the clinician can interject:

*   "Can you notice your back supported by the chair/sofa?"
*   If his eyes are closed, invite the client to open his eyes, or ask, "Can you bring your attention to the room and notice the paintings on the wall?" "What is yellow in the room?" What are three things that attract your attention?"
*   "Can you bring your attention to your feet and notice the sensation of your feet making contact with the ground?"
*   *With permission from the client,* help the client ground by placing your feet gently on the client's feet or at the edges of the client's feet or placing a heavy pillow on the client's feet so there is greater connection to the earth.

If the client has an *abreaction,* drop the content and work with sensation; the therapist can interject:

*   "Open your eyes."
*   "Sense the wetness of the tears."
*   "Notice the temperature of the tears."
*   "Notice a place in your body that feels less activation."
*   "Notice how the chair/sofa is supporting your body."

- "Bring attention to your feet resting on the floor."
- It may be helpful to touch the client respectfully and always with permission, or conversely you may move as far away from the client as he directs you until he feels less activated.
- Use any of the Help Now! strategies.

*5. Emergence of Meaning*

The client may spontaneously report new meanings, insights, feelings, and images. As this occurs, the clinician can bring the client's attention to his body so that he can track the internal changes associated with the new meanings, insights, feelings, and images. The clinician wants to link the entire sensory system to new, more integrated cognitions and feelings. Spiritual meanings often emerge. TRM clinicians often report that clients describe feeling more compassion for themselves and others; they often describe prioritizing their life in a different way and have an expanded ability to appreciate life and the people whom they love in their lives.

*6. Ending a Session*

Bring the client's attention to his whole body and invite the client to sense into all the neutral or positive changes that have occurred since beginning the session. If the session time is coming to a close, allow enough time for the client to come back to his resilient zone by using the wellness skills. This way the client can experience that he can work with difficult material in therapy and can come back to his resilient zone as he returns to his tasks of daily living.

This chapter has outlined the nine skills of the TRM. When using the nine skills, it is helpful to think about a TRM-skills scaffolding. A scaffolding is used to support people and hold materials that are used for construction or repair. Scaffolding promotes the safety of the workers and allows them access to areas that are difficult to reach. You can step up, down, or sideways on a scaffolding. The same is true for TRM skills. Sometimes you want to shift to a resource. At other times, you may suggest that a client complete a survival response. If the activation is too much for your client's nervous system, you can bring the client's attention back to grounding. As clinicians, we often want a succinct, step-by-step process. When working biologically, however, we do not use a "cookie-cutter" approach. Continuous monitoring of the client's sensations is paramount. The clinician can integrate any of the skills within the scaffolding that help the client stabilize his nervous system to come back to the resilient zone.

## References

Ayres, J. (2005). *Sensory integration and the child* (25th anniversary ed.). Los Angeles, CA: Western Psychological Services.

Cannon, W. B. (1915). *Bodily changes in pain, hunger, fear and rage.* New York: D. Appleton & Company.

Diamond, A., & Amso, A. (2008). Contributions of neuroscience to our understanding of cognitive development. *Current Directions in Psychological Science, 17*(2), 136–141.

Gendlin, E. (2007). *Focusing.* New York: Bantam Books.

Hanson, R. (2010, October 26). Confronting the negativity bias (Online newsletter). http://www.rickhanson.net/your-wise-brain/how-your-brain-makes-you-easily-intimidated

HeartMath. (2014). What is meant by personal and global coherence? (HeartMath FAQs). http://www.heartmath.org/faqs/heartmath-system/heartmath-system-faqs.html

Herman, J. (1992). *Trauma and recovery.* New York: Basic Books.

Humphreys, K. L., Sauder, C. L., Martin, E. K., & Marx, B. P. (2010). Tonic immobility in childhood sexual abuse survivors and its relationship to posttraumatic stress symptomatology. *Journal of Interpersonal Violence, 25*(2), 358–373.

Kelly, S. D., Manning, S. M., & Rodak, S. (2008). Gesture gives a hand to language and learning: Perspectives from cognitive neuroscience, developmental psychology and education. *Language and Linguistics Compass, 2*(4), 550–738. doi:10.1111/j.1749–818X.2008.00067.x

Korte, S. M., Koolhaas, J. M., Wingfield, J. C., & McEwen, B. S. (2005). The Darwinian concept of stress: Benefits of allostasis and costs of allostatic load and the trade-offs in health and disease. *Neuroscience & Biobehavioral Reviews, 29*(1), 3–38.

Levine, P. (1997). *Waking the tiger: Healing trauma.* Berkeley, CA: North Atlantic Books.

Levine, P. (2014). Somatic experiencing. www.traumahealing.com

Ogden, P. (2006). *Trauma and the body: A sensorimotor approach to psychotherapy.* New York: W.W. Norton & Company.

Pavlov, I. P. (1927). *Conditioned reflexes: An investigation of the physiological activity of the cerebral cortex.* Oxford, UK: Oxford University Press.

Rumi, J. a-D. (2004). *The Essential Rumi: New and Expanded Edition* (Coleman Berkes & John Moyne, trans). New York: HarperOne.

Schore, A. (2009). Working in the right brain: A regulation model of clinical expertise for treatment of attachment trauma (Slide presentation).

Sechenov, I. (1863). *Reflexes of the brain.* Cambridge, MA: The MIT Press.

Siegel, D. J. (2010). *The mindful therapist: A clinician's guide to mindsight and neural integration.* New York: W.W. Norton & Company.

Taylor, S. E. (2007). Social support. In H. S. Friedman & R. C. Silver (Eds.), *Foundations of health psychology.* New York: Oxford University Press.

Taylor, S. E., Gonzaga, G., Klein, L. C., Hu, P., Greendale, G. A., & Seeman, S. E. (2006). Relation of oxytocin to psychological stress responses and hypothalamic-pituitary-adrenocortical axis activity in older women. *Psychosomatic Medicine, 68*(2), 238–245.

Vaish, A., Grossmann, T., & Woodward, A. (2008). Not all emotions are created equal: The negativity bias in social-emotional development. *Psychological Bulletin, 134*(3), 383–403. doi:10.1037/0033–2909.134.3.383

Van der Hart, O. & Steel, K. (1997) Time Distortions in Dissociative Identity Disorder: Janetian Concepts and Treatment, *Dissociation,* 1997, *10*(2) 91–103.

Volchan, E., Souza, G. G., Franklin, C. M., Norte, C. E., Rocha-Rego, V., Oliveira, J. M., . . . Figueira, I. (2011). Is there tonic immobility in humans? Biological evidence from victims of traumatic stress. *Biological Psychology, 88*(1), 13–19. doi:10.1016/j.biopsycho.2011.06.002

Williams, M. S., & Shellenberger, S. (1996). *How does your engine run: A leader's guide to the Alert Program® for Self-Regulation.* Albuquerque, NM: Therapy Works.

# 4 Working with Children Who Have Experienced Trauma

## A Developmental Perspective

*Kimberly R. Freeman and Elaine Miller-Karas*

It is well understood that children and adolescents exposed to trauma are at risk for developing long-term behavioral, health, and social problems. Although clinicians have known this intuitively for years, it was empirically confirmed in the groundbreaking Adverse Childhood Experiences (ACE) Study, which found a direct link between the number of adverse experiences during childhood—such as abuse, neglect, and exposure to drugs/alcohol and domestic violence—and risk for a number of behavioral and physical health problems in adulthood (Felitti et al., 1998). Consistent with the above, research examining the effects of trauma on the brain found that during early development, childhood maltreatment can physically alter the biological structure and functioning of the brain, resulting in lasting behavioral and physical health problems across the lifespan (Teicher, 2000). These and related findings have led to the search for resiliency factors that mediate or even reverse the development of these adverse consequences (see Zolkoski & Bullock, 2012).

Resiliency, viewed early on as a fixed personality trait used to manage and adapt to stress and trauma, was once thought of as a characteristic that an individual was either born with or without (Asendorpf & van Aken, 1999; Hart, Hofmann, Edelstein, & Keller, 1997). Although this may be partly true in that resiliency has some innate biological influences, we now know that it also develops and is strengthened over time in the context of positive individual, environmental, and social supports. In support of this view, a recent meta-analysis found that enhancing protective factors such as self-efficacy, positive affect, and social support is effective in building resiliency within an individual (Lee et al., 2013). This perspective shift has led to more modern definitions of resiliency such as "an individual's and community's ability to identify and use individual and collective strengths to live fully in the present moment and thrive while managing the tasks of daily living" (Miller-Karas, 2013). By building on a child's "individual" and "collective" strengths, we build resiliency and change the trajectory of the child's life. There is also growing evidence to suggest that just as adverse events can reorganize brain functioning to respond in maladaptive ways, building resiliency in a child can "remodel" the brain to respond in more adaptive ways, and this remodeling can endure into adulthood (Sroufe, Egeland, Carlson, & Collins, 2005; Sroufe & Siegel, 2011).

It is this type of positive neurological change referenced above, aimed at restoring balance to the mind and body following trauma, that is a primary focus of both the Trauma Resiliency Model (TRM) and the Community Resiliency Model (CRM). These models specifically promote resiliency in that they focus on connecting with and intensifying specific positive memories or resources, while also attuning to body sensations in such a manner that allows the child's distress to be discharged. Within these models children are also taught to regulate their nervous systems by learning to recognize when they are bumped out of their resiliency zone and how to use the TRM and CRM wellness skills for coping with future stressors. In this respect, the models, which include a skills-based wellness program, are designed to be used by behavioral health professionals (TRM) to provide clinical treatment for trauma, and by any community member who is faced with stress (CRM).

## Prevention

Because of its focus on wellness, the TRM/CRM is an excellent approach for implementing primary, secondary, and tertiary prevention programs within the school and community settings where children spend a majority of their time. From a primary prevention perspective, the goal is to protect healthy people from developing or experiencing mental health issues. Because the CRM can be easily taught to individuals such as parents, teachers, and daycare workers within the community, specific educational programs can be designed to teach children about the biological effects of stress and trauma and the importance of skills such as resourcing, grounding, and tracking. When a person learns to read his nervous system, he can bounce back into his resilient zone when he gets bumped out. We believe that this ability can help prevent the impact of traumatic experiences.

*In one elementary school setting the CRM wellness skills were taught to a third-grade classroom as part of a wellness stress prevention program. Not long after the training there was one young boy who became mad and disruptive in the classroom. Recognizing that the child was activated, the teacher asked the class what they would do if they "were mad," and the students came up with several CRM resourcing and Help Now! skills, such as, "Think of your favorite thing to do; that's what helps me," "Go for a walk and get a drink of water," and "Count backwards from 100 and see if it gets better."*

The beauty of this example is that the suggestions came directly from the children themselves based on their knowledge of how the body responds to stress, and the children were able to help this young boy without ostracizing him. Once children understand the body's natural response to stress and learn what they can do about it, they are in a much better position to understand when someone is having a stress reaction and to use the skills to manage their own responses to stress.

When implementing secondary prevention, the focus is on helping a child who has been traumatized so that his symptoms are decreased or even eliminated. An example of the secondary prevention approach is demonstrated by one of our CRM-trained counselors in a school district.

> She indicated, "On Monday I sat on the floor in the hallway talking with a fourth-grade student who was deeply distressed. She had experienced a nighttime of wakefulness, hearing domestic violence down the hall and having to escape from a furious dad who chased them down the road as they tried to flee (to grandpa's where they arrived safely). She expressed fear and deep grief over the loss of her home and the relapse of her dad. She needed to tell some of the story, and it was easy to help her build a resource around the sense of safety she felt when she reached grandpa's house. She easily tracked her body—smiling, relaxing, and breathing slower—and told me that she's taught her mom about resourcing, too. After another round of becoming activated and resourcing again, she decided she'd like to try and make it through the school day and she thought she could if she could remember to resource. Yesterday I learned that she'd made it through the day." Because the teacher was trained in CRM, she was able to reach out to the student in need and reduce the risk of the student developing further trauma symptoms while also promoting resiliency. The importance of the skills to the child is reflected in her comment about teaching the resourcing skill to her mother and in her ability to continue on with her school day.

Tertiary prevention is aimed at helping people manage complicated, long-term mental health problems while maximizing overall quality of life.

*An example of tertiary prevention is seen in the treatment of a 13-year-old resistant adolescent who was being seen for self-harm, depression, and emotional dysregulation. She also had a number of risk factors including being financially disadvantaged, a father who was an alcoholic and emotionally unavailable, and a history of emotional abuse. In treatment, she was initially resistant as she anticipated being forced to talk about her problems. She demonstrated visible relief when told this would not be the case and when asked, she was open to noticing her physical sensations in the current moment and to discussing her resources, which centered on experiences with her best friend. By tracking her body sensations, utilizing resources, and pendulating from uncomfortable sensations to more pleasant or neutral sensations, this young teen gradually learned how to regulate her nervous system. She was subsequently able to deal more effectively with her daily stresses and she stopped self-harming very shortly into treatment.*

This non-invasive approach that does not require or force the client to retell the narrative of her traumatic experience is a key principle of the TRM/CRM and is ideal for working with adolescents, who are often distrustful of adults and do not like to talk about their problems. In this particular case, the adolescent did eventually want to share some of her trauma stories but did so on her own terms and in a manner that allowed her to work with small increments of arousal while interweaving the TRM skills. This approach allowed her to have a new and different experience in that she was able to share her experiences while releasing the defensive energy from the trauma that was stored in her body. Toward the end of her therapeutic work she stated, "I feel like I can deal with my family, like I'm in control of myself. . . . I am stronger and can use my skills whenever I need them. My mom is even trying to do them." As evidenced in the examples above, the TRM/CRM skills offer a powerful prevention tool for children and adolescents who experience typical daily stressors, who are at risk for developing mental health problems, and who have significant mental health issues.

Although the TRM is designed to be used by mental health professionals, the CRM shares six of the basic skills and can be used by individuals in the community. In this respect, the most important people in the child's life, such as parents and teachers, can reinforce the use of the skills with a child in multiple settings, across various situations. This is a feature that is missing in most other treatment approaches that require intensive professional training to implement. By increasing the child's use of the skills in this more generalized manner, his resilient zone is widened, thereby resulting in an improvement in the child's overall quality of life.

## Developmental Considerations

Although conceptually identical to the TRM/CRM for adults, there are a number of developmental factors and teaching adaptions that need to be considered when using these approaches with children. Of foremost importance and the overarching principle is the inclusion of the parents or caregivers in the skills learning process. When the skills are taught to both the parent and the child, the parent can model the skills and, when balanced, be more effective in helping the child. Further, by learning the skills, parents become more attuned to and are able to track their child's nervous system responses and redirect the child to a resource when they observe the child escalating or withdrawing. Focused attention on the parents or caregivers cannot be overemphasized, as research consistently shows that an important predictor of positive outcomes for children is the coping ability of significant adults (Gewirtz, Degarmo, & Medhanie, 2011; Silva et al., 2000). Additionally, other developmental factors that warrant attention and impact how a child responds to trauma include the role of memory, temperament, attachment, and the presentation of posttraumatic stress symptoms.

### The Role of Memory

Although brain functioning and memory are discussed in depth elsewhere in this book, child-specific information is presented here to highlight the effects of trauma on preverbal children, as it is often mistakenly thought that because young children may not have words to express their traumatic experiences that they are not affected by these events. Evidence of preverbal memories is demonstrated in what we now know about the development of implicit and explicit memory (Paley & Alpert, 2003). In contrast to explicit memory, which requires language and includes intentional, conscious learning and retention of information, implicit memory includes memory for things that we do not consciously try to remember. Examples include daily habits like riding a bike and brushing our teeth. Implicit memory develops before birth and does not have a sense of linear time, but rather is formed from somatic, sensory, motor, and emotional experiences. In the case of trauma, the body remembers and stores sensations associated with traumatic experiences even when memories cannot be verbally expressed. This is one reason why trauma-related cues sometimes trigger implicit memories and physiological reactions in the child even when no current threat exists.

With regard to trauma and memory, the literature is generally consistent in showing that young children do not maintain clear explicit memories for traumatic events over time. However, this is not the case for implicit memories. Tulving, Schacter, and Stark (1982) found that implicit memory tends to survive and even influence responses long after the ability to retrieve information explicitly. For most implicit memories this is a good thing as it allows us to engage in many routine activities automatically. With regard to trauma, though, these unwanted memories get "stuck" in the body, resulting in ongoing fear, dysphoria, anger, and/or dissociative responses that are difficult for children to manage and understand. In addressing this, the TRM intervention allows us to work with the body to slow down these reactions while at the same time teaching the body to respond in a different and more adaptive way to activating events.

To better understand the role of trauma and implicit memory in children, Paley and Alpert (2003) conducted a review of nine articles published between 1988 and 1999 that specifically examined memories of trauma that occurred during infancy or in very early childhood. They found that all nine studies reported *behavioral memories* or *behavioral reenactments* of trauma that occurred between birth and 24 months and in many cases prior to the development of verbal proficiency and explicit memory. Behavioral reenactments were defined by Burgess, Hartman, and Clements (1995) as "spontaneous expressions of trauma linked to behaviors in everyday activities" and included behaviors such as trauma-specific fears (e.g., fear of cars after a traumatic car accident), avoidance reactions (e.g., fear of being around someone associated with the trauma), posttraumatic play (e.g., acting out the trauma during play), and repetitive play (e.g., engaging in the same play over and over). Also included in the definition were personality changes such as mood swings, withdrawal, tantrums, behavioral regression, sadistic or sadomasochistic behaviors, and sexual or sexualized language or behaviors. An important clinical implication of this research is that children who have experienced trauma may not always "tell" you about a trauma in purely verbal terms but instead may "show" you their trauma histories. The fact that the TRM and CRM allow clinicians and trainers to work with the child's physiological responses and do not require a retelling or even verbal knowledge of the trauma highlights another reason why these models are so useful for helping traumatized children.

In addition to the above, other types of nonverbal memory were examined across the nine reviewed articles, such as visual memory and somatic-somatosensory memory. This latter type of memory is defined as "observations of physical symptoms or psychological arousal closely connected with trauma-specific experiences" (Burgess et al., 1995). Examples include automatic responses such as freezing or dissociating in response to direct trauma or to a traumatic trigger (e.g., a traumatized child vomiting or dissociating when walking into a school where she was bullied). Overall, the review of the nine studies indicated that nonverbal memories, generally expressed immediately following traumas, tend to be accurate and continue to be expressed well into adulthood in the form of behavioral, visual, and somatic-somatosensory memory presentations. Although visual and verbal memories were also present, they were found to fade and vary over time (Paley & Alpert, 2003).

Understanding the role of implicit memory in trauma reactions has been incorporated as a key principle of the TRM/CRM. Specifically, the models take into account an understanding of how preverbal children and individuals who cannot remember aspects of the trauma still experience reactions to the event. In order to effectively help someone who has been traumatized during childhood, it is necessary to process the associated implicit memory, which gets stored in the body's sensory, motor, and emotional memory. Although each of the TRM/CRM skills is aimed at helping the individual to bring his nervous system back into balance when triggered, the TRM skill of completing the survival response is specifically aimed at changing the intensity of the implicit memory by releasing the survival energy that is stored there so that the trauma memory can be relegated to the past and lose its hold on the individual.

### Child Temperament

Regardless of trauma history, children come into the world neurologically different in their adaptability and responsiveness to their environment. When asked, mothers will readily tell you just how different two children can be when they have one child who rarely cries and who eats and sleeps on a regular basis, and another child who seems to cry constantly, is irritable, and has unpredictable daily habits. These characteristic patterns in which children respond to and interact with their environment are referred to as temperament (Thomas & Chess, 1989). Temperament is thought to be mostly biologically determined and is believed by many to play a significant role in later personality development. In their original study, Thomas and Chess examined individuals from infancy through adulthood by rating them along nine different dimensions of temperament. Their results indicated that most children fit into one of three types of temperament patterns: the easy child, the slow-to-warm-up child, or the difficult child. Characteristics of the easy child, which made up 40% of children in the sample, included having regular, positive responses to new stimuli; easy adaption to changes in their environment; and generally positive moods and emotions. The slow-to-warm-up children constituted 15% of the sample and were described as having a low activity level, slow adaption to new situations, and a tendency to withdraw from new situations and people. Finally, 10% of the children in the sample were described as difficult in that they tended to be unpredictable in their daily habits, overly emotional, irritable, and fussy, with generally negative responses to new stimuli. Notable is that 70% of the difficult infants received psychiatric treatment as adults, whereas only 18% of the easy infants did so.

The above findings suggest the possibility that a child with a difficult temperament may present with more severe symptoms following a trauma than a child with an easy temperament. In this respect, the child's therapist should be aware of the child's developmental history and should make adaptions to the skills as necessary. For example, a highly reactive and sensory-sensitive (consistent with a difficult temperament) child who is reactive regardless of trauma history is likely to benefit from resourcing as opposed to grounding techniques, which may result in increased activation especially in the beginning of treatment before the skills are learned and practiced. Further, it is also important that these children learn to shift their attention away from the parts of their body that are activated to somewhere in the body that is more neutral or calm. This is likely to be a new experience for the child who has always been overly sensitive to his environment. Although the child's sensitivity to the environment is not likely to change because of the innate nature of temperament, how the child manages and responds to sensory information can be greatly enhanced through use of the TRM/CRM skills.

Knowing that children present with different temperament patterns provides one explanation for the variability in neurological reactions to trauma often seen in children despite their limited life experiences. As illustrated in the example above, there is substantial evidence to suggest that some children are naturally more sensitive to environmental stimuli and in some cases may be more prone to being bumped out of their resilient zones even when the stress is minor. In turn, the TRM/CRM approach is adaptive and sensitive to each child's unique presentation and allows the child to take the lead in determining the meaning and impact of a trauma. In this way, two children who experience the same trauma but who have different temperament styles may present very different symptom profiles such that a child who is considered highly reactive may have a much more intense reaction to a trauma as compared to a child who is moderately reactive. Also, the knowledge of temperament supports the need for a preventative approach for all children but especially for children with more difficult temperaments. As discussed previously, by frontloading these at-risk children with wellness skills, we can do much to reduce the potential effects of stress and trauma.

### Attachment and Trauma

"Attachment describes an emotional bond that serves to promote and preserve closeness between a young child and a small number of adult caregivers who are responsible for comforting, supporting, nurturing and protecting the child"

(Breidenstine, Bailey, Zeanah, & Larrieu, 2011). Bowlby (1980), the developer of attachment theory, believed that infants are *biologically* designed to form a close intimate relationship with a caregiver in order to ensure survival. As such, early on infants exhibit proximity-seeking behaviors such as crying, smiling, following, and clinging in order to attract the attention of their caregivers. The development of a healthy attachment occurs over several years and moves from seeking the attention of any potential caregiver (birth to 8 weeks), to showing a slight preference for his caregiver but still interacts freely with others (2 to 7 months), to showing a clear preference for familiar rather than unfamiliar adults with separation protests and stranger wariness (7 to 12 months), to showing a clear preference for his caregiver (12 to 18 months). At this point, the child begins to explore his environment while using the caregiver as a secure base to return to when frightened or distressed. In the final attachment phase (18 months and older), parents and children continually balance and adjust the need for autonomous functioning with the need for reliance on the caregiver (Boris, Aoki, & Zeanah, 1999).

In most situations, the caregiver is generally responsive to the child's needs and the attachment process results in a securely attached child who prefers the caregiver to strangers and seeks comfort from the caregiver when frightened. Further, when children are frightened they learn to rely on and trust that the caregiver will be responsive to their needs. However, when there are repeated failed episodes of seeking comfort from the caregiver (e.g., the caregiver is unresponsive, inconsistent, or abusive) one of three patterns of child insecure attachment develops, including avoidant, resistant/ambivalent, or disorganized. Children with an avoidant attachment pattern tend to adapt by avoiding close-ness and emotional connection with their caregiver, whereas ambivalent children never know what to expect from their parent so they tend to be anxious and insecure. Children with a disorganized attachment are often frightened by their parents and are often left feeling confused, traumatized, and overwhelmed. Each of these insecure attachment types is associated with a higher risk for child psychopathology, with the disorganized attachment pattern being the most severe (Ainsworth, Blehar, Waters, & Wall, 1978; Main & Solomon, 1990).

When working with a child who has an insecure attachment, it is important to remember that he is likely to experience fear and to be unresponsive in his interpersonal relationships. As such, it is critical that the TRM therapist create a safe environment by being fully present and attuned to the child's behavioral responses. One way this can be demonstrated is through tracking responses to let the child know that he has your full attention. Example responses may include, "I see you just took a deep breath," and "I noticed that you are smiling." When working with children, tracking responses should be used much more frequently than with adults in order to teach, model sensory language, and to show your attention. Also, adult TRM/CRM questions that require long verbal responses such as, "What do you notice?" should be limited with young children under 12, as they tend to reduce rapport and decrease participation. Better techniques include either providing them with verbal choices of likely responses or having a series of pictures or words that they can choose from. When the child experiences changes in his body from fear to safety within the context of a caring therapeutic relationship, the child's ability to function more fully in his social environment is strengthened in a manner that promotes resiliency, positive growth, and change.

Expanding Bowlby's attachment construct, Main, Kaplan, and Cassidy (1985) developed corresponding attachment patterns for adults, including the classifications of autonomous, dismissing, preoccupied, and unresolved. It has been found that the attachment status of the caregiver predicts the attachment status of his child to that caregiver with as high as 75% probability (van IJzendoorn, 1995). The table below describes infant and adult attachment patterns as well as associated adult caregiving behaviors and the relationship these have to the child's risk for psychopathology and social maladaptation.

The inherent reciprocal nature of the caregiver/child relationship highlights the need for intervention strategies that target both caregivers and the child when attachment problems occur. TRM therapists working with children need to be especially attuned to attachment patterns and the possibility that the child's problems are rooted in the parents' inability to form a caring, secure

*Table 4.1* Infant and Adult Attachment Patterns, Caregiving Behaviors, and Associated Risks

| Infant attachment patterns | Adult attachment patterns | Associated adult caregiving behavior | Links to child psychopathology and social maladaptation |
| --- | --- | --- | --- |
| Secure | Autonomous | Sensitive/responsive | Protective factor in high-risk samples |
| Avoidant | Dismissing | Emotionally distant; encouraging independence and discouraging neediness | Modest risk factor in high-risk samples |
| Resistant/ Dependent | Preoccupied | Inconsistent responsiveness | Modest risk factor in high-risk samples |
| Disorganized | Unresolved | Frightening or frightened behavior or disrupted affective communication (affective communication errors, role confusion, negative-intrusive behavior, disorientation, withdrawal) | Risk factor for externalizing disorders, dissociative disorders, internalizing disorders, social incompetence |

relationship with their infant. Too often parents bring their children to treatment expecting the therapist to fix the problem without realizing their own pivotal role in their child's progress. In fact, research shows that when parents have unresolved past traumatic experiences—as demonstrated by nonintegrated emotional reactions, disorientation, or dissociative-like responses—their children's attachment to them is likely to be disorganized (Breidenstine et al., 2011). This indicates that in some cases the parent needs to be a primary focus of treatment if relationship change is to be successful. Similarly, it makes theoretical sense that when the child, the caregiver, or both are continuously bumped out of their resilient zones, the attachment process is disrupted and the risk for developing an insecure attachment is increased. If the parent is able to process any past traumas with the TRM skills, she is better able to be present when other treatment components such as parenting skills and psychoeducation are being administered. Parents can also apply their knowledge of wellness skills such as tracking, resourcing, grounding, and Help Now! in working with their child and thereby provide the necessary level of attunement and emotional support to strengthen the relationship with their child.

### PTSD Symptoms in Children

Because trauma has such a profound impact on a child's physiological and environmental functioning, it is the contributing factor in the development of PTSD, particularly when the balance of risk factors for a child outweighs the number of protective factors (Blank, 2007). When a trauma reaction occurs, the child's nervous system reacts and prepares for life in a fearful world, and hormones and chemicals within the brain are released in defense of a perceived threat even when no apparent danger exists. In other words, the traumatic experience "re-sets" the child's baseline state of arousal such that even when no external threats or demands are present, he will be in a physiological state of persistent alarm. Even a relatively small stressor can instigate a state of fear or terror. This process also blocks the brain's ability to think rationally in a conscious and organized manner. Over time traumatized children can present as irritable, impulsive, hypervigilant, disconnected, numb, and/or fearful, and they generally function well outside of their resilient zones. Although a child can survive in this state, his nervous system is dysregulated and there is a high cost to the child's physical and mental well-being.

The fact that there can be multiple presentations and combinations of PTSD symptoms over time, and that PTSD can include unknown or unreported trauma, makes diagnosing PTSD in children challenging. Compounding this issue is the way in which PTSD symptoms overlap with symptoms from other childhood disorders such as Attention Deficit Hyperactivity Disorder (Perry, Pollard, Blakely, Baker, & Vigilante, 1995). Specifically, symptoms common in PTSD, such as difficulty concentrating, poor attention, exaggerated startle response, and hypervigilance can make the child appear hyperactive and/or inattentive. Misdiagnosing a child can have a negative impact on the child's ability to cope with the trauma, can lead to the use of inappropriate and/or ineffective treatments, and can result in unrealistic expectations for the child's behaviors given his trauma history. As such, clinicians are cautioned to assess for trauma history and to be aware of other risk factors that may increase the likelihood of being diagnosed with PTSD such as having a difficult temperament, a disorganized attachment, and/or behavioral reenactments of trauma.

The *Diagnostic and Statistical Manual of Mental Disorders* (DSM-5; American Psychiatric Association, 2013) was recently released and includes a number of changes in the PTSD diagnostic criteria. Most notably, the first criterion is more specific in what constitutes a traumatic event; the language specifying an individual's response to the traumatic event has been deleted; and there are now four symptom clusters as opposed to three—reexperiencing the event; heightened arousal; avoidance; and negative thoughts, mood, or feelings. Two subtypes were also added to allow for a PTSD Preschool Subtype for children six years and younger and a PTSD Dissociative Subtype. As PTSD criteria for adults, adolescents, and children older than six are discussed elsewhere in this book, the Preschool Subtype is presented in Table 4.2.

*Table 4.2* PTSD Preschool Subtype Diagnostic Criteria

A.  In children six years and younger, exposure to actual or threatened death, serious injury, or sexual violence in one (or more) of the following ways:
    1.  The child directly experiences the event.
    2.  The child witnessed the event (this does not include events that were seen on the television or other media).
    3.  The child learned about a traumatic event that happened to a caregiver.
B.  The presence of at least one of the following intrusive symptoms that are associated with the traumatic event and began after the event occurred:
    1.  Recurring, spontaneous, and intrusive upsetting memories of the traumatic event.
    2.  Recurring distressing dreams related to the event.
    3.  Dissociative reactions in which the child feels or acts as if the traumatic event(s) were recurring. Can include play reenactments.
    4.  Strong and long-lasting emotional distress after being reminded of the event or after encountering trauma-related cues.
    5.  Marked physical reactions to reminders of the traumatic event(s).
C.  One (or more) of the following symptoms, representing either persistent avoidance of stimuli associated with the traumatic event(s) or negative alterations in cognitions and mood associated with the traumatic event(s).

    Persistent Avoidance of Stimuli
    1.  Avoidance of or the attempted avoidance of activities, places, or reminders that bring up thoughts about the traumatic event.
    2.  Avoidance of or the attempted avoidance of people, conversations, or interpersonal situations that serve as reminders of the traumatic event.

*(Continued)*

*Table 4.2* (Continued)

---

Negative Alterations in Cognitions
3.   More frequent negative emotional states, such as fear, shame, or sadness.
4.   Markedly diminished interest or participation in significant activities, including constriction of play.
5.   Social withdrawal.
6.   Persistent reduction in the expression of positive emotions.
D.   Changes in arousal or reactivity associated with the traumatic event(s), beginning or worsened after the traumatic event(s) occurred, as evidenced by two (or more) of the following:
1.   Increased irritable behavior or angry outbursts. This may include extreme temper tantrums.
2.   Hypervigilance.
3.   Exaggerated startle response.
4.   Difficulties concentrating.
5.   Sleep disturbance.

In addition to the above criteria, the duration of the symptoms need to have lasted at least one month and result in considerable distress or difficulties in relationships or with school behavior. Finally, the symptoms cannot be better attributed to the physiological effects of a substance or to another medical condition.

---

In the DSM-5, PTSD is now listed under a class of diagnoses named *Trauma-and Stressor-Related Disorders* in which all included disorders require exposure to a stressful or traumatic event as a diagnostic criterion. In regard to diagnosing children, this includes PTSD, Acute Stress Disorder, Reactive Attachment Disorder, Disinhibited Social Engagement Disorder, and Adjustment Disorder.

## Using Wellness Skills with Infants, Children, and Teens

During times of distress, the needs of children often go answered. Too often adults believe that children are either unaware of and/or unaffected by trauma because children display their distress differently than adults. It is not uncommon to see a child who has experienced trauma happily playing one moment and tearful and irritable the next, as children tend to grieve in spurts. Children may also be reluctant to show their true feelings and thoughts about the trauma because they receive subtle cues from adults that the topic is uncomfortable or children try to protect their parents and other family members from being sad. Given that parents, family members, and teachers often underestimate children's reactions to traumatic events, teaching the wellness skills to children offers them valuable resources during times of stress. The section below provides age-sensitive techniques for teaching the six wellness skills (as developmentally appropriate) to infants, young children, and teens. The skills include tracking, resourcing, grounding, gesturing, Help Now!, and shift and stay.

*Wellness Skills for Infants*

When working with traumatized infants who are preverbal, the wellness skills of tracking, resourcing, and grounding can be utilized. Because infants remember and store traumatic events in their bodies, the wellness skills can offer specific techniques that caregivers can use to help the infant remain in or return to his resilient zone. The wellness skills are adapted to include what is known about infant development and can be utilized as a prevention program to promote infant wellness or as part of a larger therapeutic approach designed to assist families that have experienced trauma.

*Tracking*

Dr. Peter Wolff and Professor Heinz Prechtl found that infants have six different states of arousal or wakefulness that are associated with different behavioral responses (Shelov, Trubo, & Hannemann, 2004). These states include quiet sleep, active sleep, drowsiness, quiet alertness, active alertness, and crying. Trauma can affect the amount of time infants spend in the different states, but when a caregiver is able to track or pay attention to the subtle changes within her infant's nervous system, she is better able to meet the infant's needs, and is more likely to have a positive experience with her infant and strengthen the development of a secure bond and attachment.

The sleep states provide the infant and parent the opportunity to recharge and do not require response from the caregiver. However, if you watch an infant during the sleep state you will notice that he has two distinct sleep patterns. During quiet sleep, the infant will lie very still with a relaxed face and will demonstrate a steady heart and respiration rate. When an infant is in a state of active sleep, you will see rapid eye movements under the infant's eyelids along with arm and leg movement and facial expressions. During the drowsiness state, the infant is either waking up or falling asleep and may appear somewhat dazed. Picking up or talking softly to the infant will likely bump him up to the waking states (Shelov et al., 2004).

In the quiet, alert state, an infant is at his most responsive and this provides the best time for the parent and child to interact. In this state, the infant will look directly into the parent's eyes and will pay close attention to the parent's words and actions. The newborn only spends a few minutes each day in this state, but this period of interaction and play significantly expands each day. In the active, alert state the infant will begin to move his arms and legs and may look away from the caregiver, indicating that he has had enough. The activity that was fun in the quiet, alert state may now be overwhelming for the infant and indicate that the infant is hungry or fussy. Crying is the last state and is the infant's way of telling the caregiver that something is not right or is his way of releasing tension (Shelov et al., 2004).

By tracking an infant's states, the parent will know better how to respond to her infant. For example, if a parent attempts to play with the infant during the active, alert state, she is likely to push the infant into crying as the infant's nervous system is activated and in the high zone and is not able to take in the additional stimulation of the parent's play attempts. Nonverbal cues that the parent can track—indicating that the infant needs a "stimulation break" or is becoming stressed—include the infant looking away, yawning, coughing, sneezing, increased arm and leg movements, hiccups, and crying. In contrast to the above, if the infant is in the quiet, alert state or resilient zone and the parent does not engage, valuable interaction and bonding time is missed. Engagement cues that the parent can track—indicating it is time to play—include the infant making eye contact, cooing, smiling, and reaching. For most parents, learning to read their infant's cues comes naturally but for some parents, especially those who have experienced trauma themselves or who feel unprepared for parenthood, these skills will likely require practice and in some cases professional intervention. However, the benefits of intervening at this very young age cannot be underestimated. Tracking teaches parents how to read and respond to their infants' behaviors in a way that promotes parent/child connection, synchronicity, responsiveness, and attachment.

*Resourcing*

Infants are born with immature nervous systems that rapidly develop over the first few years of life. During this developmental period the most important resource or sense of comfort for the infant is the caregiver. Infants need help from their caregivers in regulating their nervous systems, as they have few self-coping mechanisms at this early age. Crying is the first way that infants communicate their needs, and most parents quickly learn to distinguish between different types of cries for hunger, fatigue, pain, boredom, or the need to discharge frustration. This latter type of crying typically occurs toward the end of the day and can last for several hours. It is often referred to as colic, which is characteristic of the first three to four months of life, and can be frustrating for parents who want to calm their baby (Brazelton & Sparrow, 2006).

Infants are also born with different types of responsiveness to their environment. The overall quality of a baby's cry and the ability of the newborn to be soothed offer insight into a baby's temperamental style and the amount of "work" the parent must do to bring the baby back into his resilient zone (Brazelton & Sparrow, 2006). For example, a non-sensitive baby may be able to take in much more stimuli (e.g., noise, light, and/or touch) and soothe himself when upset by sucking a thumb or fist or by turning away from the stimulation, whereas a very sensitive baby may become upset and overstimulated by too much sensory input and be very difficult to soothe. During times of infant distress, caregivers should keep the following principles in mind when resourcing or providing comfort to their child:

1.  Most caregivers do too much when an infant is crying. During these times of activation, less is more. Talking, rocking, and eye contact may be too

much. Crying usually calls for reduced stimulation and sensory input but can in some cases indicate under-stimulation as well.

2. Start with the less invasive forms of comforting in order to learn how much help the infant needs in order to be comforted. Parents or caregivers may want to give the infant a brief moment to see if the infant is able to self-soothe, but children should not be left to "cry it out."

3. A crying baby can easily bump a parent or caregiver into the high zone. As such, it is important that the parent work to be in her resilient zone when working with the infant.

To assist parents in managing their child's crying behaviors during the first four months of life, several techniques have been developed to help calm the infant. Some of the most useful approaches are described in Table 4.3. Before using these techniques, the parent should ensure that the infant's crying is not

*Table 4.3* Resourcing Techniques for Distressed Infants

1. Talk softly to the infant in a steady voice in a quiet area.

2. Allow the infant to have a pacifier or to suck his thumb. The sucking reflex has a calming effect on the nervous system.

3. Hold both of the infant's arms close to his body with your hand placed gently on the baby's chest. Because infants have limited control of their extremities, holding their arms steady calms the nervous system.

4. Hold the infant against your body (skin-on-skin) as touch and physical support can calm the infant.

5. Swaddle the infant: (1) lay a small blanket diagonally on a flat surface and turn down one of the corners; (2) place the infant's head on the turned-down corner; (3) hold the infant's right arm to his side and fold the left side of the blanket over the body and tuck it under the infant's left side; (4) pull the bottom of the blanket up, leaving room for leg movement; and (5) wrap the right corner across the infant's body and tuck the end toward the back. The blanket should be snug but not tight and never cover the infant's face. This technique provides containment and calms the nervous system. Infants should only be swaddled when fussy or sleeping.

6. Hold the infant in a rounded position with the infant's back against your chest and one hand on his chest and the other hand supporting his bottom. This simulates the womb and the rounded position calms the nervous system.

7. Use white noise to simulate the sounds in the womb. It should be played loud enough for the infant to hear it.

8. Use vertical rocking that involves a steady up and down motion. This is a very effective method of calming most infants. It is not currently known why it works.

9. Reduce the environmental stimulation by limiting noise (except white noise), dimming lighting, and turning the infant away from visual stimuli. Sometimes infants regulate by going to sleep during the day when there is too much activity and playing at night when things are quiet. The trick here is to create a calm environment during the day that is not overly stimulating.

10. For maximum support: Swaddle the infant and hold him in the rounded position with his back against your chest. At the same time, if used, hold the pacifier in the infant's mouth while facing the infant away from visual stimuli and while doing vertical rocking.

caused by hunger, needing to be changed, being too hot or too cold, or pain. If at any point it is believed that a medical condition exists, the child's pediatrician should be consulted.

Being able to comfort their infant is empowering for parents and promotes confidence in their parenting ability while also strengthening the connection between the parent and child. The infant also implicitly learns to trust that the parent will respond to his needs. From a developmental perspective, the formation of this trusting relationship builds resiliency and is a foundational task of infancy that can have lifelong implications for how the infant responds to and manages his social environment.

*Grounding*

Grounding techniques are likely to be helpful for traumatized infants who are highly activated and can include anything that helps provide physical support and helps regulate the infant's body. In this respect, many of the comforting techniques discussed in the above section such as swaddling and skin-to-skin contact with the caregiver can provide the infant with the support he needs when experiencing stress. During periods when the infant is not distressed, parents can promote a sense of grounding or connection to the environment by laying the infant on his back and moving his legs in a bicycle motion; allowing the infant playtime on the floor, as too often infants are kept in carriers for much of the day; and providing *child-safe* objects for the infant to hold in his hands and explore. As part of exploring, the infant is likely to look at the object and bring the object to his mouth. These types of sensory experiences are how infants learn about their world and should be allowed. Taken together, these techniques provide the infant with a sense of support and connection with his social and physical environment and therefore promote resiliency.

### Wellness Skills for Children

Play is the central activity for young children and is a necessary component in teaching children the wellness skills. By including drawing activities, games, storytelling, and music in the learning process, children become engaged with the treatment and are able learn through doing. In this respect, the TRM therapist and CRM trainer are "speaking the child's language."

The process of using the TRM/CRM wellness skills with children is to first teach the child about the different zones (e.g., the resilient zone, stuck in the high zone, and stuck in the low zone). Once this is established, the child's resource should be established and intensified prior to teaching the other skills. Tracking should be taught next, followed by the skills of grounding, gesturing, Help Now!, and shift and stay. In teaching the skills, the TRM therapist or CRM trainer guides the child in how to use the skills when activated. The goal is for children to learn to recognize body sensations associated with being in the high or low zones and to develop awareness that they can use the skills to get back into their resilient zones. When working with the child, the practitioner interweaves the wellness skills with periods of activation, which acts to reset the natural balance of the nervous system. For children needing therapy, the TRM offers additional therapeutic techniques aimed at reprocessing the traumatic experience so that the body learns to respond in a different and more adaptive way.

*Helping Children Understand the Zones*

The resilient zone includes a child's natural body rhythm where he feels at his best and is able to handle the ups and downs of daily life. Some children have a wide resilient zone and can manage many stressors, and some have a very narrow resilient zone and it only takes a small stressor to activate them. When a traumatic or stressful event occurs, the child often gets bumped out of the resilient zone and can get stuck in the high zone or in the low zone. He can also go back and forth between the two zones. When the child is in the high zone, he may appear edgy, irritable, angry, panicked, anxious, and/or hypervigilant. When in the low zone, the child may appear numb, sad, depressed, isolated, tired, and/or disconnected.

*Zones Activity:* The Cloth Game can assist in teaching about the zones and introducing the concept of tracking. In leading the Cloth Game, select a cloth size that is appropriate for the number of participants and have everyone stand around the cloth while holding onto the edge of the cloth with both hands. Ask the participants to very slowly move the cloth up and down together as a group. Once this is done, pause and ask sensory questions such as, "Is your heart beating fast or slow?" "Is your breathing fast or slow?" "Does your body have energy or is it calm?" If the children do not respond, the adult should model her own sensory responses, or if a child reports an emotion such as boredom, ask him to point to where in his body he feels bored. Older children may not require as much prompting and can simply be asked, "What do you notice inside?" Take time to explain how this can be like the low zone when our body sensations are very slow, but when we are in the low zone we might feel much worse. Give examples of the low zone (e.g., feeling sad, having no energy, crying).

Once everyone has been invited to share (children should not be required to share), have the group move the cloth quickly up and down together as a group. Once this is done several times, pause and ask the series of sensory questions again. Also explain how this can be like being in the high zone when our heart is beating fast and it is hard to listen, but in the high zone we might feel much worse. Provide examples of being in the high zone (e.g., can't sit still, feeling scared or angry). The goal is to have children notice their different body sensations and to teach them about the zones.

Finally, place a stuffed animal or similar object in the center of the cloth and ask the children to move the cloth together while being careful to keep the object on the cloth. Once again, pause and ask the series of sensory questions and explain that this is like being in the resilient zone when we are in control and our body is calm. Ask for and provide examples. At the end, have the group raise the cloth over their heads and say hello to the other participants as a way of ending the activity. This activity can be followed up with a "quizzing game" asking children about the zones (e.g., "If I am jumping up and down and not listening to my mom, what zone am I in?").

*Resourcing*

Resourcing is the most important skill in working with children and should be taught first. This skill provides a safe memory along with the associated positive physical sensations that the child is taught to rely on during times of stress. As such, TRM therapists or CRM trainers should spend sufficient time building and intensifying the child's resource and not rush this skill. A sample child-directed resource activity is provided below.

*Resource Activity:* Resourcing activities can be done with an individual child or with a small group. In teaching this skill, start by explaining to the child that a resource is something either real or pretend that makes our body feel good inside. Go on to explain that a resource can be a person, place, thing, activity, pet, faith, or something they like about themselves. Invite the child to pick one resource and to draw a picture of it. Once the child is done, ask him to tell you about the picture. Encourage the child to tell you more about his resource by using reflection. For example, if a child says, "It is my dog Sam," you would reflect this back by saying, "You drew a picture of your dog Sam." Reflection typically results in the child adding more to the story, but if not, follow up with at least two more questions such as, "Tell me about your favorite time with Sam," and "What do you like most about Sam?" As the child is telling you about his resource, you also want to track sensations by observation ("I notice that you are smiling as you talk about Sam.") and by asking him what he notices inside his body. Give prompts as needed. For example, "What happens with your heart rate, breathing, stomach, temperature when you talk about Sam?" Children should be told that anytime they feel bumped out of their resilient zones, they can go back to thinking about their resources.

*Tracking*

Tracking involves teaching children to pay attention to their sensations. For most children using sensory words will be a new experience and will require learning and practice. Taking the time to talk about the meaning of different sensory words and posting the words or meaningful pictures on the wall before doing the activities is very beneficial and ensures greater participation. Two sample tracking activities are listed below.

*Tracking Activity 1:* The Raisin or Candy Activity is a tracking activity that introduces children to sensory language. It can be played with a small group such as the TRM therapist or CRM trainer, child, and caregiver, or with a larger group of approximately eight children. It involves selecting either a raisin or a piece of candy to place in the individual's hand. General instructions include the following: (a) Hold the raisin in your hand; (b) As you hold the raisin in your hand, is it smooth, rough, scratchy, or soft? (c) As you look at the raisin, what do you notice in your body? (give examples if necessary); (d) If you smell the raisin, is it sour, sweet, smelly? (e) If you take a bite, is it juicy, tasty, sweet, or sour? and (f) As you take a bite, what happens with your stomach, heart rate, breathing?

*Tracking Activity 2:* The Tactile Box Game is another way to teach sensory language and can be done with individuals or with a small group of two to three children. The therapist should place six small objects of different textures inside a small box and stretch a large sock completely over the container. This will allow the child to put his hand in the sock to feel the object inside the container without seeing what is inside. If this is not possible, a paper bag can be used, but note that children will likely look in the bag or pull the object out before it is time to do so. Before the child starts the game, provide and review a list of sensory words. Next, tell the child the following rules: (1) He needs to pick one object to hold in his hand while keeping his hand in the sock; (2) He needs to describe the object using three sensory words from the list without guessing what the object is; (3) After this is done, he can try to guess what the object is and take it out of the box. If working with more than one child, have the children take turns. Sometimes the child wants the TRM therapist or CRM trainer to play as well.

## Grounding

Grounding involves the direct contact of an individual's body with the ground or with something that provides support to the body. These types of activities bring the child back to the present moment and to a safe environment.

*Grounding Activity 1:* The Grounding like a Tree activity is designed to help the child experience a sense of connection to his environment and to be fully present in the moment. It can be used individually or with a group. For this activity, the TRM therapist or CRM trainer invites children to stand and imagine that they are trees with roots. The following statements are then presented: (a) Stand tall like a tree; (b) Push in a little with your heels and bend your knees just a tiny bit; (c) Now, imagine tree roots growing down into the earth from your strong legs and feet; (d) Imagine what the strongest tree would look and feel like; (e) If you would like, move your arms slowly in the air and continue imagining yourself to be the strongest tree; (f) Imagine the wind blowing through the branches of your strong tree; (g) Bring attention to your feet as the wind blows your arms and notice how your feet are solid on the ground and the roots are holding you just right; and (h) Notice what happens on the inside (give prompts as needed: What happens with your heart rate, breathing, temperature?).

*Grounding Activity 2:* Activities that involve tactile and movement components can help a child feel grounded and can regulate the nervous system when the child is activated. When working with a child individually it is good to have items such as musical instruments, clay, Play-Doh, and a sand tray accessible in the treatment room. This allows the child the freedom to engage in these activities as needed throughout the session. It is important that tracking continues when engaged in a grounding activity to allow the child to notice his current sensations but also any differences experienced from before the activity. If the child notes a positive change, you want to take the opportunity to have the child really notice the change and sense the positive sensations. If working in the field with a group of children who may be dysregulated, having them sing a song from their culture and/or learn a new song is a great way to do group grounding. Adding movement to the song is even better. Although you may not be able to track each individual child, you can ask if anyone wants to share what he noticed inside his body when he was singing and moving.

*Gestures and Movements*

Gestures and movements are body movements used by children as a means of expression to portray an idea, sentiment, or attitude. These can be tracked and used by children to enhance positive sensations within the body.

*Gestures and Movement Activity 1:* Gestures and movements can be taught to an individual child or to a group of children. If working with an individual child, the TRM therapist or CRM trainer should do the activity with the child. In teaching gestures and movements, if needed, the TRM therapist or CRM trainer should explain what a gesture is (a body movement that means something—give an example of a wave hello). Once this is understood, invite the child to think of a gesture of happiness. Let the child know that you are going to count to three and you will both make your gesture of happiness after you say three. Once the gesture is made, track sensations using prompts as necessary (What happens with your heart rate, your breathing, your temperature?). Older children can be asked, "What do you notice?" Continue the above procedure using different gestures such as calming gestures, confident gestures, comforting gestures, and joyful gestures. Note that child should *not* be asked to make negative or self-harming gestures.

*Gestures and Movement Activity 2:* The Animal Game allows children to engage in large muscle movements and also connects positive characteristics such as strength with positive body sensations. In this simple game, take turns asking the children to pick and act like a fast animal, a slow animal, a strong animal, and a powerful animal. Spend time on each animal and track body sensations after a few moments of acting out the animal. The game can be enhanced by having children draw an animal that makes them feel strong, cut out holes for the eyes, and wear the animal mask while pretending to be the animal. Once again, track sensations.

*Help Now!*

Help Now! skills are taught to children and family members for use when the child is well outside of his resilient zone. They are designed to work when the child is in either stuck in the high zone or stuck in the low zone. In working with children it is important to practice the skills during the session so that using them becomes automatic. It is also good to ask the child which of the skills he likes best.

*Help Now! Activities*: When the child is highly dysregulated, the Help now! skills should be used. Specific activities include the following: (1) Asking the child to push against the wall or your hands with as much force as he can; (2) Having the child count backwards (if old enough) or to name all the colors he sees around him; (3) Taking a walk with the child outside; or (4) Giving the child a drink of water or juice. While doing any one of these alone or in combination, track the child's noticeable sensations. As the child begins to de-escalate, ask him to be aware of sensations that are more pleasant on the inside.

*Shift and Stay*: Shift and stay involves the child shifting his attention from sensations that are unpleasant to sensations that are neutral or pleasant and keeping the focus there. During a session with a child who has experienced trauma, it is likely that he will verbally reference or behaviorally act out his trauma history. When this occurs, the TRM therapist or CRM trainer needs to slow down the story/action and have the child notice the sensations inside his body (using prompts as needed: What do you notice about your heart rate, breathing, stomach, temperature?). If the child reports activation, or if you notice signs of activation, have the child shift his attention to a place in the body that feels positive or neutral, a soothing gesture, his resource, a grounding technique, or a Help Now! skill and stay there until the child is back in his resilient zone.

*Wellness Skills Specific to Teens*

While teens are generally able to participate in traditional adult TRM/CRM treatment, we present two resourcing adaptions that we have found to be beneficial in working with this age group. TRM therapists and CRM trainers should also use the teen skill methods as appropriate or for teens who present as less mature or regressed. Listed below are a few activities that are specific to working with teens (see the child section for descriptions of the treatment process and the skills).

*Resource Activity 1*

This resource activity can be done with an individual teen or with a small group. Begin by explaining to the teen that a resource is something either real or imaginary that brings about comfort or positive feelings. Go on to explain that a resource can be a person, place, thing, activity, pet, faith, or something they like about themselves. Invite the teen to think of one resource and give him the choice of telling you about it, writing a narrative about it, or drawing a picture of it. Once the teen is done, ask him to tell you about the resource. Encourage the teen to tell you more about his resource by saying, "Tell me more about . . ." Follow this up with three additional questions aimed at intensifying the resource through more details or through sensory experiences (e.g., ask the teen if there were any smells, what was the temperature, etc.). As the teen is telling you about his resource, you also want to track sensations by observation (I notice that you are smiling as you talk about . . .) and by asking the teen what he notices inside his body. Teens should be told that any time that they feel bumped out of their resilient zones they can go back to thinking about their resources.

*Resourcing Activity 2*

The Tree of Life Activity is a resourcing activity but does not take the place of establishing a specific resource for the teen. This activity was initially developed by Ncube (2006) as a narrative therapy technique for children who had lost a parent to AIDS. Adapted for TRM/CRM, it is aimed at helping children see their own abilities and strengths so that they can talk about their future in a way that offers hope and healing. For this activity, teens are given large (8½ by 14-inch) paper and crayons. Let the teens know that they are going to be drawing a tree in a step-by-step process. Instructions are as follows: (1) Draw the roots of the tree representing your family, culture, and country. If you want, write your name and the name of your village. Then, write the meaning of your name and your village to you. (2) Draw the ground representing things you like and what you do in everyday life. If you want, write what gives you pleasure and the things you do in everyday life; (3) Draw the trunk representing who you are or your essence. If you want, write who you are in the world; (4) Draw the branches representing your hopes, dreams, and wishes for the direction of your life in the future. If you want, write new direction you would like to take and your hopes and dreams; (5) Draw the leaves representing what you love most about yourself and what you are most proud of. If you want, write what you love about yourself; (6) Draw fruit that represents gifts you have been given, not necessarily material gifts (being cared for and loved, acts of kindness). If you want, write your major accomplishments, what gifts have people given you, and to whom you have given support; (7) Draw your fallen fruit, representing losses of any kind. If you want, write about your losses; (8) Draw your compost representing how you have transformed your losses into something positive. If you want, write about the transformation; and (9) Surround the tree, using any available space, with the names of those for whom you are most grateful.

## Conclusion

This chapter is intended to help therapists and community trainers understand how to use the TRM/CRM wellness skills with traumatized children within the context of developmental considerations. It also provides age-appropriate techniques and activities to aid in teaching the wellness skills to this population. While this chapter does not provide an exhaustive list of TRM/CRM adaptions needed for working with high-risk children, it does provide a valuable foundation for understanding how children can benefit from and be empowered by this strength-based approach.

In closing, the last 20 years of research demonstrate that there are many windows of opportunity to promote well-being in children (Lee et al., 2013; Zolkoski & Bullock, 2012). The TRM/CRM skills are grounded in our current understanding of how trauma is stored and processed in the body, and they can be used in different variations by therapists and community members, and as a prevention and self-care program. This adaptability makes the skills easy to teach to parents and teachers and to integrate into and use with other treatment approaches. Although research using comparative and randomized controlled trials is still ongoing, outcome research has demonstrated significant pre- and posttreatment improvements (Citron, 2013). Specifically, reductions in depression, hostility, anxiety, and somatic symptoms as well as increases in somatic well-being and friendly indicators were observed in a diverse group of high-risk youth and adults. These early findings along with overwhelmingly positive results from clinicians, trainers, child and adult clients, and community members around the world speak to the healing power of the TRM/CRM programs and suggest that they are powerful tools for helping children overcome trauma.

## References

Ainsworth, M.D.S., Blehar, M.C., Waters, E., & Wall, S. (1978). *Patterns of attachment: A psychological study of the strange situation*. Hillsdale, NJ: Erlbaum.

American Psychiatric Association. (2013). *Diagnostic and statistical manual of mental disorders* (5th ed.). Arlington, VA: American Psychiatric Publishing.

Asendorpf, J.B., & van Aken, M.A.G. (1999). Resilient, overcontrolled, and undercontrolled personality prototypes in childhood: Replicability, predictive power, and the trait-type issue. *Journal of Personality and Social Psychology, 77*(4), 815–832.

Blank, M. (2007). Posttraumatic stress disorder in infants, toddlers, and preschoolers. *BC Medical Journal, 49*(3), 133–138. doi:10.1016/j.burns.2009.06.033

Boris, N.W., Aoki, Y., & Zeanah, C.H. (1999). The development of infant-parent attachment: Considerations for assessment. *Infants and Young Children, 11*(4), 1.

Bowlby, J. (1980). *Attachment and loss*. New York: Basic Books.

Brazelton, T. B., & Sparrow, J. D. (2006). *Touchpoints birth–3: Your child's emotional and behavioral development* (2nd ed.). Cambridge, MA: Da Capo.

Breidenstine, A. S., Bailey, L. O., Zeanah, C. H., & Larrieu, J. A. (2011). Attachment and trauma in early childhood: A review. *Journal of Child and Adolescent Trauma, 4*(4), 279–290. doi:10.1080/19361521.2011.609155

Burgess, A. W., Hartman, C. R., & Clements, P. T., Jr. (1995). Biology of memory and childhood trauma. *Journal of Psychosocial Nursing and Mental Health Services, 33*(3), 16–26.

Citron, S. (2013). *Final CRM innovation evaluation report*. Claremont: Trauma Resource Institute.

Felitti, V. J., Anda, R. F., Nordenberg, D., Williamson, D. F., Spitz, A. M., Edwards, V., . . . Marks, J. S. (1998). Relationship of childhood abuse and household dysfunction to many of the leading causes of death in adults: The Adverse Childhood Experiences (ACE) Study. *American Journal of Preventive Medicine, 14*(4), 245–258. doi:10.1016/S0749-3797(98)00017-8

Gewirtz, A. H., Degarmo, D. S., & Medhanie, A. (2011). Effects of mother's parenting practices on child internalizing trajectories following partner violence. *Journal of Family Psychology, 25*(1), 29–38.

Hart, D., Hofmann, V., Edelstein, W., & Keller, M. (1997). The relation of childhood personality types to adolescent behavior and development: A longitudinal study of Icelandic children. *Developmental Psychology, 33*(2), 195–205. doi:10.1037/0012-1649.33.2.195

Lee, J. H., Nam, S. K., Kim, A., Kim, B., Lee, M. Y., & Lee, S. M. (2013). Resilience: A meta-analytic approach. *Journal of Counseling & Development, 91*(3), 269–279. doi:10.1002/j.1556-6676.2013.00095.x

Main, M., Kaplan, N., & Cassidy, J. (1985). Security in infancy, childhood, and adulthood: A move to the level of representation. *Monographs of the Society for Research in Child Development, 50*(1), 66–104. doi:10.2307/3333827

Main, M., & Solomon, J. (1990). Procedures for identifying infants as disorganized/disoriented during the Ainsworth Strange Situation. In M. T. Greenberg, D. Cicchetti, & E. M. Cummings (Eds.), *Attachment in the preschool years: Theory, research, and intervention* (pp. 121–160). Chicago, IL: University of Chicago Press.

Miller-Karas, E. (2013). The Community Resiliency Model 2014 edition (Powerpoint presentation).

Ncube, N. (2006). The tree of life project. *International Journal of Narrative Therapy & Community Work, 1,* 3–16.

Paley, J., & Alpert, J. (2003). Memory of infant trauma. *Psychoanalytic Psychology, 20*(2), 329–347. doi:10.1037/0736-9735.20.2.329

Perry, B. D., Pollard, R. A., Blakely, T. L., Baker, W. L., & Vigilante, D. (1995). Childhood trauma, the neurobiology of adaptation and "use-dependent" development of the brain: How "states" become "traits." *Infant Mental Health Journal, 16*(4), 271–291.

Shelov, S. P., Trubo, R., & Hannemann, R. (2004). *Caring for your baby and young child: Birth to age 5* (4th ed.). New York: Bantam Books.

Silva, R., Alpert, M., Munoz, D. M., Singh, S., Matzner, F., & Dummit, S. (2000). Stress and vulnerability to posttraumatic stress disorder in children and adolescents. *American Journal of Psychiatry, 157*(1), 1229–1235. doi:10.1176/appi.ajp.157.8.1229

Sroufe, L. A., Egeland, B., Carlson, E., & Collins, W. A. (2005). *The development of the person: The Minnesota study of risk and adaptation from birth to adulthood*. New York: Guilford Press.

Sroufe, L. A., & Siegel, D. J. (2011, March–April). The verdict is in: The case for attachment theory. *Psychotherapy Networker*. www.psychotherapynetworker.org/magazine/recentissues/1271-the-verdict-is-in

Teicher, M. H. (2000). Wounds that time won't heal: The neurobiology of child abuse. *Cerebrum: The Dana Forum on Brain Science, 2*(4), 50–67. doi:10.1038/scientificamerican0302-68

Thomas, A., & Chess, S. (1989). Temperament and personality. In G.A. Kohnstamm, J.E. Bates, & M.K. Rothbart (Eds.), *Temperament in childhood* (pp. 249–261). Oxford, England: John Wiley & Sons.

Tulving, E., Schacter, D.L., & Stark, H.A. (1982). Priming effects in word-fragment completion are independent of recognition memory. *Journal of Experimental Psychology: Learning, Memory, and Cognition, 8*(1), 336–342. doi:10.1037/0278-7393.8.4.336

van IJzendoorn, M. (1995). Adult attachment representations, parental responsiveness, and infant attachment: A meta-analysis on the predictive validity of the adult attachment interview. *Psychological Bulletin, 117*(3), 387–403. doi:10.1037/0033-2909.117.3.387

Zolkoski, S.M., & Bullock, L.M. (2012). Resilience in children and youth: A review. *Children and Youth Services Review, 34*(1), 2295–2303. doi:10.1016/j.childyouth.2012.08.009

# 5 Attachment Strategies and Adult Behavior

*Elaine Miller-Karas and Jennifer Burton*

This chapter discusses how attachment strategies learned in childhood influence adult behaviors. We also examine Stephen Porges's Polyvagal Theory to explain how the nervous system responds when developing secure, insecure, and disorganized attachment patterns. We explain how practitioners can integrate Trauma Resiliency Model (TRM) concepts and methods into their treatment of individuals who present with insecure and disorganized attachment strategies.

For infants, the major part development involves the relationship that forms between the child and his primary caregiver. The emotional bond that forms between child and caregiver early on in life—the attachment relationship—profoundly influences an individual's behaviors and the way he interacts with his environment throughout childhood, adolescence, and adulthood. The therapist's consideration of the client's attachment strategies learned in childhood can provide insight into how his nervous system responds when developing secure and insecure attachment patterns. Accordingly, integrating our understanding of the effects of attachment strategies on the nervous system with current TRM concepts and methods helps the practitioner learn new ways of integrating TRM methods into treatment, especially in helping clients with dissociative symptoms.

Attachment theory's primary tenet is that an infant needs to develop a relationship with at least one primary caregiver for social and emotional development to occur normally (Bowlby, 1973). Attachment behaviors are identified as attempts made by a child to gain proximity to his primary caretaker in times of stress. The theory suggests that the quality of the infant's attachment relationship can be classified according to specific observable attachment strategies and that these strategies form in response to the many interactions an infant has with his caregiver over time. The categories of observable attachment strategies are especially salient in the infant's behavior during periods of separation and reunion with his caregiver (Ainsworth, 1978). Furthermore, these patterns of attachment can create enduring templates that guide an individual in interactions with his environment throughout his life.

The basic patterns of attachment can be divided into secure and insecure attachment. The insecure attachment category can be further subdivided into insecure-avoidant and insecure-ambivalent. There are some who would add disorganized as a third category of insecure attachment. However, we argue that it is a stand-alone category because, unlike secure and insecure patterns that are marked by fairly consistent and organized patterns of behavior, the behaviors observed in individuals with disorganized attachment are inconsistent and unorganized—thus, the name of the category. The attachment strategies applied to adult behaviors—through the lens of the TRM—are as follows:

## Secure Attachment

People with secure attachment likely had primary caregivers who offered attuned, reciprocal somatic and verbal communication in response to their needs as a child. As such, they trust others, have lasting relationships, have high self-esteem, are comfortable sharing their feelings, and will seek out social support when in distress. Regulatory areas in their prefrontal cortex support social engagement and access to the resilient zone through the regulation of the autonomic nervous system, allowing them to accurately evaluate risk, danger, and life-threatening situations.

## Insecure-Ambivalent Attachment

People with insecure-ambivalent attachment likely had primary caregivers who were often inconsistent and had unpredictable responses (e.g., were either overly intrusive or non-responsive) to their needs as a child. As such, they may become overly preoccupied with and worried about interpersonal relationships. For example, the person may worry whether his partner loves him or whether his friendship networks accept him. These individuals seek social engagement but have difficulty being soothed or calmed within a relationship. There is simultaneously a desperate need for the other and a fear that one's needs will never be met. Ambivalently attached adults have difficulty self-soothing and have a tendency to be stuck in the high zone, with increased emotional reactivity.

## Insecure-Avoidant Attachment

Adults with avoidant attachment patterns likely had primary caregivers who actively blocked efforts to be physically close and/or appeared indifferent to their needs as a child. As such, while they may want social and/or romantic relationships, they invest little emotion in them. They have difficulty sharing thoughts and feelings with others as well as difficulty perceiving others. They may even have difficulty recalling their childhood. Thus, they are highly reliant on logic and tend to have reduced sensory awareness and reduced capacity to experience positive or negative affect. They may have a limited ability to experience pleasant and/or neutral sensations and may describe feeling numb; they are often stuck in the low zone. They may have learned to regulate their nervous system by engaging in solitary activities, given their primary caregiver's rejection of proximity.

## Disorganized Attachment

Individuals with a disorganized attachment pattern likely had a childhood marked by traumas including neglect, physical, and/or sexual abuse. It is likely that they were abused or neglected by their caregiver, which created a dilemma of the caregiver as both the source of fear and the source of reassurance. As such, by age one these individuals tend to display mixed avoidant and resistant behaviors that can continue into adulthood. The adult with this pattern can have significant difficulties with a coherent sense of self. Beebe et al. (2010) demonstrated that one year of disorganized attachment during infancy contributes to dissociative behavior. Schore (2009) stated that early abuse and neglect generate disorganized-disoriented attachment, which endures into adolescence and adulthood, and acts as a risk factor for later psychiatric disorders. He further elaborated that from a developmental neuroscience viewpoint, early abuse and neglect have immediate impact on critical growth periods that results in an immature right brain with a limited capacity to regulate intense affective states. In the most severe cases, the person can experience fragmentation or "tertiary structural dissociation," meaning that he develops multiple "parts" of his personality. The individual with parts may display erratic behaviors with fluctuations between low and high zones. He may not be aware of ever being within the resilient zone.

As one can imagine, secure attachment eventually helps establish a sense of "self" and the ability to experience safety in interpersonal relationships. In contrast, insecure attachments can have long-lasting repercussions resulting in challenges to one's sense of self and to forming healthy interpersonal relationships. However, these attachment patterns are not fixed. Though they may be resistant to change given their basis in enduring patterns of interpersonal interactions, they are not set in stone. They can change—for better or for worse.

Applying Polyvagal Theory to the attachment strategies can help us use the lens of neuroscience to create treatment plans that take into account the human being's elegant design and capacity to regulate the nervous system in order to change lifelong patterns.

## Polyvagal Theory

Stephen Porges's (1995) Polyvagal Theory poses that the autonomic nervous system is a complex and hierarchical system responding directly to environmental challenges. Polyvagal Theory describes three different subsystems:

1. Parasympathetic ventral vagal system (social engagement system)
2. Sympathetic system (in charge of fight/flight responses)
3. Parasympathetic dorsal vagal system (in charge of immobilization/shutdown and freeze/dissociative states)

This hierarchical system works in such a way that the most evolved response—social engagement—is utilized first. The social engagement system stimulates psychological states that promote social behavior, communication, and social bonding. This allows for flexibility and adaptability to the environment. Individuals with secure attachment patterns are able to socially engage to develop relationships with others and have a stronger sense of self. In the TRM, we call this being in the resilient zone.

Chitty (2013) states that if trauma and stress occur repeatedly in childhood, the individual as an adult may be unable to access the social engagement system when stressed and may instead respond from one of the other two systems. That is, if social engagement fails, the individual will proceed to the sympathetic system and finally to the most primitive—the parasympathetic dorsal vagal response. Thus, the insecure-avoidant, insecure-ambivalent, and disorganized attachment strategies likely develop as a response to the more primitive sympathetic system or the parasympathetic dorsal vagal system. In TRM language, trauma impacts the availability of the social engagement system, narrowing the bandwidth of the resilient zone. Without intervention, a person will exhibit difficulty self-regulating, often vacillating between being stuck in the high and low zones. This vacillation and becoming stuck in either zone can make it difficult to form lasting, healthy social relationships and to have a secure sense of "self."

Accordingly, a person with disorganized attachment primarily responds to his environment via his parasympathetic dorsal vagal system. When the dorsal vagal system is triggered by past trauma, an individual sees his world through the lens of past memories, resulting in a potentially inaccurate assessment of the current environment. This is evident particularly in reference to danger or safety. Porges (2011) calls this "faulty neuroception," which can result in a person perceiving danger in a safe situation, or conversely, perceiving safety in a dangerous situation.

Now for the good news: If someone has not experienced secure attachment in childhood, he can achieve and "learn" secure attachment through other relationships in which there is security, allowing for healthy attachment to develop, often referred to as "earned-security" (Roisman, Padrón, Sroufe, & Egeland, 2002). This capacity is part of the elegant design of the nervous system and is a testament to neuroplasticity and our ability to "rewire" our nervous systems. When individuals learn to become aware of pleasant and/or neutral sensations connected to attuned relationships, new neuronal pathways are created, and nervous system stabilization results. The person is less likely to be triggered into dysregulated states that lead to physical and emotional distress. New possibilities and hope abound that open up portals for greater self-awareness and compassion for self and others.

A multi-step approach will be utilized to highlight how to use TRM skills in the context of clients' attachment strategies. Nijenhuis et al. (2004) and van der Hart et al. (2006) support a multi-step approach. We have added a fourth step: family integration. The multi-step approach will be divided into two sections: A. Insecure-ambivalent and insecure-avoidant attachments and B. Disorganized attachment.

### Insecure-Ambivalent and Insecure-Avoidant Attachments: Step-by-Step

#### Step 1: Creating Safety

Creating safety by learning to experience sensations connected to attunement and pleasant and/or neutral experiences in the present moment is critical for those who have experienced insecure-ambivalent and insecure-avoidant attachments. Many individuals who seek treatment have had insecure attachments. When the practitioner assesses that secure attachment did not exist, stability and safety within the nervous system can be established through the relationship with an attuned therapist and through bringing the client's awareness to safer personal relationships with, for example, a teacher, spiritual leader, family member, friend, or co-worker. The clinician uses the skill of tracking to monitor the autonomic nervous system of the client, similar to the way an engaged parent monitors the reactions of an infant. Healthy attachment that was lacking in childhood can be created in the present moment, paving the way for increased connection and social engagement. The adult client is invited to sense the pleasant and/or neutral sensations connected to being safely socially engaged. There may be safer relationships within the client's social network, but the client's tendency to be stuck in the high zone or low zone may make the person unaware of those relationships. Tracking pleasant and/or neutral sensations connected to interpersonal relationships is a key element in helping the individual learn that there is a way to gain greater security. As the person becomes aware of sensations connected to an attuned presence, his nervous system can come into balance and he will be able to bounce back to his resilient zone more readily. For many, it is the attuned therapist who provides the gateway that can then be generalized to other relationships. Cognitive models of intervention can be useful in understanding how parental lack of attunement resulted in problematic behaviors for the client. However, this knowledge does not necessarily translate into changed behaviors and nervous system regulation. Integrating the vocabulary of sensation can begin to change long-held patterns as the client becomes aware of sensations connected to attunement, something that was missing in childhood.

*A client with a significant trauma history, including being abandoned as a baby and having traumatic experiences in his adoptive family, identified with being stuck in the low zone frequently, which he described as being "frozen" in public and social situations. In addition, he had trouble with his wife, feeling alternately disconnected and wishing for connection, which led to explosive arguments between them. Key concepts of the TRM were explained and he was introduced to tracking through resourcing. He was able to build resources fairly quickly and use them daily to assist with the "frozen" sensations. However, whenever he perceived a lack of attunement by the therapist, he would "move away" from treatment, missing sessions and feeling anger toward the therapist. Beginning with the therapy relationship and extending out to friendships, family, and ultimately his marriage, he could sense the urge to either pull away or fight (stuck in a fight/flight response). The therapist helped the client understand the attachment strategy that he used as a child to survive. In addition, the therapist, understanding this attachment dynamic, remained constant and continued to support the client with sensory awareness, education, and wellness skills. As the client learned to better track his sensations and distinguish between sensations of well-being and positive attachment versus those that bumped him out of his resilient zone, the bandwidth of his resilient zone expanded. He incorporated wellness skills into his activities of daily living. His prior adult attachment patterns fell away, his relationships deepened, and he reported increased awareness as well as an elimination of the sensations connected to freezing in social settings.*

*Step 2: Family Integration*

Integrating family therapy into the treatment plan can help untangle behavioral patterns that are causing distress within the family system. Without conscious awareness, individuals may choose a partner with similar characteristics to a parent's ambivalent or avoidant parenting patterns. When clients are educated about the autonomic nervous system and the survival brain being triggered by the amygdala, they can gain a biological perspective to behaviors that may not make logical sense. Helping individual family members learn to track their own nervous systems in order to learn to come back to their resilient zones when bumped out can reduce the stress experienced by other members of the family. As the ability to track one's own nervous system expands, family members can also help others in the family return to their resilient zones when they notice they are bumped out. Individuals within the family learn to change old patterns by tracking sensations connected to long-held beliefs, thoughts, and feelings, and by learning to track sensations connected to more adaptive ways of interacting.

*Katherine initiated therapy to work specifically on childhood trauma, but she presented with significant difficulty in her activities of daily living, including organizing her busy schedule with two young children as well as communicating with her husband. Prior to any trauma reprocessing, it was clear that Katherine would need to be educated about the six wellness skills as well as biological responses to trauma and stress. As she learned the wellness skills, she requested her husband be taught them as well to help them communicate. Once in the therapy room, it became evident that while Katherine had an insecure-ambivalent attachment style, her husband had an insecure-avoidant one, and this was at the core of their communication issues. She was more often stuck in the high zone when triggered, and he would become stuck in the low zone in response, causing her to feel abandoned. Both were educated in the wellness skills and encouraged to track their nervous systems and use skills of grounding and/or resourcing before engaging in important conversations. Subsequently, they reported that having the common language of the resilient zone reduced the criticism and blame in their interactions. This paved the way for them to learn about their attachment styles and find ways to meet one another's needs in more healthy ways, which in turn deepened the resilient zone of the whole family system.*

In addition, by using the lens of family relationships, the practitioner can help construct interventions that assist the client in reprocessing traumatic events. The follow case illustrates this:

Sarah came for therapy because of significant disturbances in her relationships with her children. As we explored her relationship history, it became clear that she had an insecure-ambivalent attachment style from her early relationship with her mother, who was alternately smothering and neglectful. Sarah was educated about the nervous system and taught the six wellness skills, which she regularly employed for self-regulation. She was also able to separate her daughter's dysregulated system from her own experience, use the wellness skills, and respond to her daughter from a more regulated place. Several months into the therapy, we began reprocessing early childhood traumas using the TRM, and one day Sarah reported that she had severe fear about dental work. Despite her awareness of times when her mother was part of the trauma of seeing the dentist as a child, those memories did not bring up the sensation of fear or suffocation that she reported. As TRM skills of titration and pendulation were used during session, Sarah was able to work with the sensation of suffocation and where the fear was located in her body. While she tracked her nervous system, a memory arose of the time she and her parents were fleeing Hungary during the revolution. She stated, "The Russians were shooting flares into the sky trying to catch people who were trying to escape. We were running through a field and had to lie down quickly. I was tired and scared and began to giggle and my mother put her hand over my mouth and nose whispering, 'They're going to catch us! They're going to kill us!' over and over again. By the time she removed her hand, I was gasping for air." As Sarah was guided to sense her body, she took a deep breath and shuddered and stated, "As I remember my mother's hand over my mouth I don't feel afraid anymore." Subsequently, Sarah was able to handle three- and four-hour dental procedures that she reported were "a piece of cake." Using TRM to uncouple the childhood somatic memory from the current stressor, the dental fears disappeared.

*Step 3: Reprocessing Trauma*

Some clients may not be able to identify anyone in their lives who has provided a sense of safety and may find it difficult to track their nervous systems. Their experience with adult caregivers was so inconsistent and lacking that tracking even pleasant sensations can trigger a numbness (stuck in the low zone) or agitation (stuck in the high zone). The practitioner can suggest identifying a nurturing and supportive resource from characters in books or movies, or from the client's imagination. The clinician can begin by asking the client to name the qualities of nurturing and supportive people. Once the client develops one or more nurturing resources, the clinician can gently suggest that the client notice the sensations connected to thinking about the resource and the qualities that are nurturing. This will intensify the resource, and the more that the client can bring his awareness to this presence in between sessions, the more he can begin to experience his resilient zone. The more time spent in the resilient zone, the more opportunities for social engagement that can begin to transform the client's interpersonal relationships. The client may need to insert an image of protective allies in order to complete survival responses. The client can then sense into the power of the nervous system to complete the survival response that can return the nervous system to balance. (See Chapter 3 for more information about completing survival responses.)

*A woman came to a group therapy program after being unable to work because of increasing depression and anxiety. A child of Holocaust survivors, she was often neglected in childhood and told she was the cause of her parents' suffering. As an adult, she married and divorced a man who perpetuated the idea that she was unworthy of love. Although now in a loving marriage, that relationship was not enough support to stave off the debilitating depression. As the therapist educated the group about core concepts of the TRM, including the neurobiology of trauma, the group began to be more cohesive, even tracking each other and exploring one another's resources. As the resilient zone of the group expanded, so did the woman's resilient zone. She was able to reprocess several childhood memories including a significant one where she was left alone at home at age four not knowing where anyone was or when they would return. She told the story with "resiliency pauses" (i.e., pauses in the telling of the story as activation increases), allowing for*

> *nervous system stabilization. With the therapist's gentle invitation, she ultimately chose to insert protective allies into her image. The protective allies helped her have the additional internal strength to create a new ending to the story. After treatment, she was ready to go back to work, reporting that she no longer thought of herself as "broken and unlovable."*

*Step 4: Wellness*

As the client reports an increased ability to manage his nervous system and intercept sensations connected to old patterns, the practitioner becomes more and more aware of the client's ability to integrate the new skills into his activities of daily living. The client can then be encouraged to experiment with weaving the wellness skills into new activities.

### Disorganized Attachment

The person with a disorganized attachment pattern can be incongruent—at times demonstrating excellent decision making and reasoning and at other times acting in ways that are in direct opposition to healthy functioning at home or in the workplace.

Affect regulation is also particularly difficult for individuals who have experienced disorganized attachment. Blizard (2003) states that disorganized attachment may result from several parental behaviors, including abuse; neglect; a frightening, intrusive, or insensitive manner; and disrupted affective communication. She goes on to state that according to longitudinal research, disorganized attachment in infancy predicts dissociation in childhood and adulthood. Liotti (2006) states that disorganized attachment is in itself a dissociative process, and predisposes the individual to respond with tertiary structural dissociation to later traumas and life stressors. In such cases, childhood traumas become stuck and are not integrated in the person's life narrative. As a result of the unprocessed childhood trauma, the personality becomes divided into "parts" that remain fixated on the traumatic experiences. (We will use "parts" to refer to the distinct, separate states that may exist within one person.) Therefore, one can argue that dissociation is part of the elegant design to protect children who have experienced the horrors of severe child maltreatment. As a result, some individuals develop distinct parts that each carry the memory of the traumas so that the individual can go forward in his life and attend school, work, make friends, and participate in life without having to live with the memory of the traumatic events.

We purposefully do not discuss the diagnostic criteria for dissociative identity disorder (DID) but highly recommend Brown (2011) for more diagnostic and therapeutic information about DID. While we realize and acknowledge the importance of accurate diagnosis and treatment planning, we have not found it clinically helpful to name dissociation as a "disorder." As alluded to above, we view dissociation as a "biological reaction" with ramifications in every aspect of human existence. We concur with Dell (2009) when he states that spontaneous, survival-related dissociation is part of a normal, evolution-selected, species-specific response; this dissociation is automatic and reflexive and is one part of a brief, time-limited, normal biological reaction that subsides as soon as the danger is over. However, for many people the dissociative process lingers and can steal away present-moment awareness.

Nijenhuis et al. (2004) elaborate on the definition of dissociation by discussing three types: primary, secondary, and tertiary structural dissociation. Their theory highlights the "apparently normal part" (ANP) and an "emotional part" (EP) of an individual. The ANP is a more organized part that conducts the functions of daily living and avoids the feelings, sensations, and information related to the traumas. EPs carry the memory of the traumas and often experience flashbacks or frightening body memories. As a result of the existential nature of the abuse these individuals may have experienced, some EPs may be focused on survival responses, always ready to fight or flee on one end of the spectrum or go into a state of immobility—the freeze state—on the other end. All three of these states are biological responses of the nervous system. EPs may or may not be outside of the conscious awareness of the ANP. An ANP may report losing time and/or being triggered into younger parts at times "out of the blue." He may often report sensations of numbness or feeling nothing. Even sensing what may be a neutral or pleasant sensation may quickly transform into a sensation connected to fear and terror and then disconnection. As one client shared, "My world is a landmine of triggers."

The three structural dissociation categories are explained below:

1.  Primary structural dissociation consists of an ANP and one EP. An example is a person with PTSD.
2.  Secondary structural dissociation consists of one ANP and at least two EPs. Individuals diagnosed with complex PTSD and conditions with characterological conditions (borderline) would be examples of this category.
3.  Tertiary structural dissociation applies to individuals with two or more ANPs and EPs. The parts can have individualized senses of self, including their own names, genders, and specific preferences.

Nijenhuis et al. (2004) also distinguish between narrative and traumatic memories: "Narrative memories are verbal, time-condensed, social and reconstructive in nature, [whereas] traumatic memories are often experienced as if the once overwhelming event were happening here and now. These . . . experiences consist of visual images, sensations, and motor actions, which engross the entire perceptual field."These traumatic memories are timeless and fixed. Thus, interventions that help individuals learn to track sensations and to complete motor actions that were blocked because of the traumatic experiences can reset the nervous system. Since the aftermath of disorganized attachment is a whole mind-body experience, biologically based models like the TRM offer compelling interventions for individuals who experience dissociation. The client can learn to shift awareness from the traumatic memory to present-moment awareness, thereby dampening the intensity of traumatic flashback. Each EP can learn how to regulate his nervous system. When the client has skills based on present-moment awareness, he can use the skills when not in session and learn that he has an internal locus of control. EPs can move out of the traumatic memory and learn new skills of self-regulation. This can be transformational for individuals who live with dissociative parts. This section covers using TRM skills to help individuals who experience secondary and tertiary structural dissociation.

*Step 1: Creating Safety*

Creating a therapeutic alliance with a person who has a fragmented sense of self can be challenging. One part may experience greater safety within the therapeutic relationship. Another part within the same person may be highly suspicious of anyone who demonstrates kindness or concern. The perceived kindness can be coupled with fear as the client's biographical history may have included a primary caretaker who at times gave him nurturance and also physically or emotionally abused or neglected him. The clinician may feel that a positive connection has been made with the client, and then the client may cancel and terminate further treatment. As one part senses connection, another part is fearful of the intrusion. This is an opportunity to contact the client with understanding and compassion and explore which part is discontinuing therapy. The therapist can acknowledge the client's need for more distance and support his need to seek safety. This approach can be a portal to greater understanding and a stronger therapeutic alliance. The clinician then modifies the TRM wellness skills depending on the developmental age of the part presenting. Providing stuffed animals, materials for drawing and sand play, and toys are essential in engaging younger parts to help create a greater sense of safety through play. See Chapter 4 for ideas about working with children to create safety. As many parts can exist within one person, each part can improve his own sense of greater safety by developing resources. As one part becomes aware of sensations of safety in the present moment, the whole system can begin to be helped. It is important to note that this process involves not only thinking about safer people or resources; the client must become aware of those sensations in the present moment.

*Mary presented with a highly volatile relationship with her husband. As therapy progressed and a therapeutic alliance developed, the clinician and Mary became more and more aware of Mary's lapses in time and the existence of parts. Mary had some co-consciousness with some of her parts and described a younger part that would direct Mary to toy stores to buy Barbie dolls and that often was afraid. Mary came to one session dressed differently: she wore shorts, her hair was in pigtails, and she was carrying a Barbie backpack. This was her first presentation as Trudy. Trudy stated in a high-pitched voice that she had been waiting to meet the clinician and wanted to show her the Barbie dolls. The clinician greeted Trudy and stated how happy she was to meet her and that she wanted to see her dolls. Trudy shared her Barbie dolls and as she did, her muscles relaxed, she breathed deeply, and she often smiled. The clinician in a gentle way suggested that Trudy pay attention to her body when she felt good talking about her Barbie dolls. Trudy appeared more and more relaxed and the clinician reminded Trudy that she could remember her dolls at times she felt scared or worried. Trudy closed her eyes and took a deep breath and smiled. Trudy suddenly shuddered and then Mary appeared, somewhat disoriented, not remembering the session. However, her body remembered and she stated she felt an unfamiliar sense of calm. When the clinician explained dissociation from a biological perspective, Mary began profoundly changing, as more parts made themselves known and expressed a desire to learn the wellness skills so they too could be aware of sensations of well-being.*

The wellness skills can be introduced to each part of the client, as the clinician keeps in mind that each part exists to create a greater sense of safety within the person. As each part learns the basic skills and how to become aware of distressing sensations and then to shift his awareness to sensations that are neutral and/or pleasant, the person can begin to feel that he is more in charge of his physical and mental health and not at the mercy of the endless triggers that knock him out of his resilient zone and into another part without warning. Each dissociative part, stuck in the trauma story, can learn that there is another way of being, a present moment, that can be accessed with greater awareness of the sensations connected to well-being.

Concurrently, as the client works with each part, the concept of collaboration between parts is introduced. The clinician explains to the client his ability to learn to collaborate with his parts and the importance of understanding the protective and survival strategies utilized by each part. As the client expands his awareness, each part can learn new ways to regulate the nervous system and old, fixated reactions can fall away and be replaced with healthier responses to the invariable triggers that have plagued the client's life. Increasing communication and coordination among parts is a fundamental goal of treatment. As the parts increase their individual ability to access the resilient zone, conflicts between parts can be resolved. Parts can learn greater appreciation for the positive qualities of other parts. As each part senses pleasant and/or neutral sensations connected to this increased understanding, an additional benefit is an expanded, embodied sense of safety. Clients learn that a positive side effect of collaboration is that one part can help another part who is bumped out of his resilient zone. Deanne Edwards, LMFT, a therapist who works with clients experiencing dissociation in San Bernardino County, calls this new learning "mixturing." "Mixturing" is the ability to bring two or more parts together to help a part that is knocked out of his resilient zone.

> *As a child the only time Tim got a break from the almost constant verbal abuse is when he would have an asthma attack. When that happened, his father and mother would take him to the hospital. Over time, it was discovered that one of his parts, Tommy, had asthma but another part, Jerry, did not. So, when Tommy could not breathe well and began to feel panicky, Tim started asking Jerry for help. When the "mixturing" occurred, Tommy's breathing normalized. When Tim learned that his parts could collaborate, this helped him physically and mentally. He began experimenting with asking for help from other parts when one part was distressed. Ultimately, Tim was able to have what he called a "well-oiled machine" in which each part was working together to make a healthier, more integrated whole.*

Step 1 can take an extended period of time. It is essential for the client to have an embodied sense of safety for as many of the parts as possible before doing trauma reprocessing. Some individuals will not be able to work with tracking their nervous systems. For some people who suffer from dissociation, paying attention to sensations can be too much and lead to sensations of distress. A primary tenet of working with clients who have been traumatized is also being respectful of some clients' desire not to engage in this kind of therapeutic intervention. In those cases, building the therapeutic relationship with more traditional talk therapies is the best way to begin to build safety.

*Step 2: Working with the Client's Family System*

(Steps 1 and 2 can be accomplished concurrently.)

Part of creating safety is helping the client's extended family or friendship networks who were *not* involved in the abuse understand dissociation and parts if they exist. For example, friends and family members can also learn the wellness skills and help the client with Help Now! strategies if he gets bumped out of his resilient zone and is having trouble getting back on his own. When we help family members understand the biology of traumatic experience and that dissociation is part of the elegant design of protection when life experience was too much for their family member, judgment can drop away and a new compassion and understanding can emerge. In addition, family members often feel helpless when parts are triggered and their family member is bumped into the high or low zones. Family members can use the wellness skills as self-help to regulate their own nervous systems and as concrete tools to bring their loved one out of the traumatic flashback to the present moment. If the client has parts, the family may not have been aware of the parts; however, they know about the attitude and affective changes that can be triggered in a flash. Family members are relieved to learn about the biology of trauma and most importantly, they learn that their loved one has new options to address the fluctuations in mood and behavior.

*Susan was often in conflict with her teenage daughter, Terry. Terry complained that her mother was unpredictable—one day being supportive and kind, and the next being authoritarian and rigid. Susan's husband, Ken, also was frustrated by Susan's chameleon nature. After working with Susan and helping her understand the biology of dissociation, the clinician decided to invite Susan's husband and then her daughter into session to help educate them about dissociation and to teach them the wellness skills that were very helpful to Susan's increased sense of internal safety. Terry learned in family therapy that her mother would give her different instructions depending on which part was "out" and learned that her mother's growing ability to collaborate with her parts could help resolve their conflicts. Terry and Susan learned that Susan's changeability was often fueled by fear that something bad would happen to Terry. Susan and Terry often fought about simple activities of living. Terry became very interested in learning about her mother's parts and enjoyed conversations with different parts. As Terry engaged her in conversations and Ken supported and nurtured her different parts, Susan's sense of safety expanded. She was able to sense more periods of calm and was able to ease up on Terry. Terry also felt that she could understand the shifts in her mother and the two of them worked together to negotiate their differences. Ken also began to be less judgmental as he understood the different parts. Susan worked diligently on her wellness skills and began to learn how to self-regulate and to "mixture" with other parts to help her come back to her resilient zone.*

Some clients may be reluctant to include their family in the therapeutic process. The clinician may have to develop a greater therapeutic alliance with the client before he is willing to think about discussing his tendency to dissociate with others. Many individuals with parts are undercover and have built a lifetime of disguise. Thus, for some people it can feel too exposing and unsafe to disclose. It is also valuable to talk about boundaries and safety with the client in terms of who within his social network he should share this information with. Although family members' education and understanding can have great benefits to the client and family system, there may be some family situations that are not safe and bringing the family in would be contraindicated. Even if the communication between family members is strained, the family can be educated about dissociation and how parts develop as a result of the client's traumatic childhood history. Family members as well as the client can learn better coping strategies.

*A woman came for therapy for childhood sexual abuse. In the beginning of treatment, she described herself as being in the low zone, feeling cut off from her body and emotions. She had trouble identifying resources and finding anything of value in herself. She reported that her four children also seemed disconnected, except one child, whom she identified as mainly in the high zone, like her spouse. She did not feel connected to her family. Over time, she was able to use TRM/CRM skills for stabilization, and she began sensing her resilient zone more often. She used the skills for herself frequently in front of her children, and she also used grounding and resourcing with her children with the help of iChill. In addition, she was able to reprocess*

> *her early trauma and complete survival responses in sessions, thus uncoupling the early trauma and lack of connection from her current family household. As her low zone shifted, and she sensed her resilient zone more, she was better equipped to notice her children's emotional states and to help them find more balance in their nervous systems. As such, the family's resilient zone deepened, and the woman reported more sense of "togetherness."*

The National Association of the Mentally Ill (NAMI) offers a family-to-family program that is an adjunct to family therapy, helping families understand concrete ways to help themselves and their family member who is suffering.

*Part 3: Reprocessing Trauma*

Learning to work with the freeze response is critical since it is a hallmark of disorganized attachment. As you introduce the concepts of the TRM, some clients will express fear at even the suggestion of beginning to sense neutral or pleasant sensations. In such cases, their bodies may have been the portal to an array of distressing sensations. If the client is amenable, the practitioner can introduce a container of items with different textures to bring up sensation in a safer way. Even different textures of the couch and pillows can be used for this purpose. Inviting the client to describe sensations outside of the body can be a beginning. For example, is the rock soft, smooth, rough? As the person begins to describe textures, you can gently inquire if he has an awareness of sensations inside the body. It can take time for clients to begin to sense the body. After introducing sensation in this way, the practitioner may be able to slowly transition to both the development and intensification of resources that can ultimately be brought to sensation.

Once the TRM practitioner assesses that the client's parts are learning to track sensations and can experience resourcing and grounding in the present moment, she can start working with the sensations connected to the client's traumatic experiences. Since survival responses are often blocked in these individuals, working on completing the survival responses is a major focus of intervention. Each part must be worked with in developmentally age-appropriate ways. Thus, strategies that help children need to be brought into the therapy session with adults. For example, having a client develop age-appropriate resources for each part, and using art exercises to reinforce and deepen the resources, can begin to build a "tool kit" of resources to be drawn upon before and during any processing of painful material.

*Justine had experienced sexual and physical abuse throughout her childhood, which was spent growing up in a cult. As a result, she developed many parts, some of whom were children, some adults, some men, and some women. Her clothing reflected which part awakened for the day first, as each part preferred different styles. Each holiday tended to trigger flashbacks for Justine because of ritual abuses in her past during these times. As one particular holiday approached, Justine reported that "the children" were all very frightened and were causing her to feel confused and unable to cope. Having already educated Justine about dissociative process and the wellness skills, the therapist combined resourcing with art. Justine took a large piece of paper and folded it several times, creating squares on the page. In each square, Justine created a developmentally appropriate resource for each of her child parts. She was then invited gently by the therapist to sense into each resource and notice what happened inside; if desired, she was also invited to touch each resource image while sensing into it. This process was repeated for each part. Justine reported that each child part experienced reduced anxiety and increased calm as a result. She then took the art home to remind the children of their resources until the frightening holiday passed, and she shared that this was the first holiday during which she didn't need to stay inside with all the doors locked and blinds drawn. The resources developed during that session were also employed in future sessions for further trauma reprocessing.*

Building competency in the six wellness skills will help the client help himself when not in session. Creating internal and external resources and finding neutral places within the body accesses and widens the resilient zone. As the person is able to track his nervous system (including identifying high zone and low zone states), he develops an increased sense of mastery and trust, thus increasing his sense of safety. The person can also learn to track sensations to alert him that he is beginning to dissociate. When he learns to intercede on this "hijacking" of the nervous system, he can learn to stay in the present moment by using the wellness skills of the TRM. In addition, as their sensory capacity expands, clients learn that the boundaries between the walls of the parts do not need to be so separate. The walls can be permeable. One client described her parts as being in a large apartment building with screen doors between apartments instead of solid steel doors. As she learned to sense each part, complete survival responses, and regulate disturbing sensations, the parts were able to see through the screens and visit one another's apartments. This was her form of "mixturing."

The client may require help in separating the need to be on alert and hypervigilant with being able to be calmer in order to enter his resilient zone. Many clients spend a lifetime expecting danger in every situation or, conversely, not reacting when danger exists. Their reactions to traumatic triggers may make no sense to them because there is no factual or autobiographical memory, only implicit memory. Brown (2011) reported that common somatoform symptoms in individuals with parts can include abdominal pain, pelvic pain, joint pain, face and head pain, a lump in the throat, back pain, non-epileptic seizures, and pseudo-asthma. Each part may hold different somatic symptoms. We contend that these symptoms are often connected to implicit memory releasing a "memory capsule" within the body that is experienced somatically, triggered by either internal or external triggers. The memory capsule holds all the sensory ingredients of the traumatic memory (Scaer, 2007). Psychoeducation about implicit memory and trauma can be very helpful. Gently helping the client sense even neutral sensations can be a beginning portal for him to be able to experience pleasant sensations.

When working with reprocessing traumatic experiences, clients will often report an array of somatic symptoms. When we bring a client's awareness to parts of the body that are less symptomatic or neutral, the somatic symptoms will often dissipate within a few moments. Paying close attention to gestures connected to self-soothing can also help the client alleviate the symptoms. The clinician can also shift the client's awareness to a resource, grounding, or one of the Help Now! strategies if the activation within the nervous system becomes too distressing. The clinician can also use the skills of titration and pendulation to ease somatic symptoms. For instance, she can titrate a strong physical sensation. If the client reports there is something stuck in his throat, the clinician can ask: "Is the sensation small, medium, or large? Does it have a shape? Can you sense an edge of the sensation in your throat?" As the client senses a small, more manageable piece, the sensation in his throat becomes smaller and the client's breathing becomes more even as he senses more room in his throat. The clinician invites the client to notice the changes and for most, the sensation in the throat will disappear altogether. As the clinician guides the client in using one or a combination of TRM skills, there is new hope and awareness that somatic symptoms can dissipate and/or be managed.

Parts exist to protect a person, help him survive, and regulate his distress. Helping each part with new sensory skills helps the whole system. When parts learn to complete a survival response and begin to sense this new embodied experience, the nervous system is reset. As the clinician works to help the client restore the survival responses, other parts may appear who are not presently known to the therapist or to the client. Some parts may appear for the first time and they may have an angry affect directed towards the practitioner for "messing" with the system (as one part of one of our clients suggested). Such parts will block further reprocessing until this conflict can be addressed. When this occurs, the therapist can thank the part for making himself known and suggest that the part share as little or as much as he would like to about the protection. The therapist can demonstrate gratitude to the part for his years of vigilance. This stance can be disarming, as the part usually achieves distance between himself and others by his angry stance. This may happen over a number of sessions, but this protective stance can be replaced with more adaptive ways of protection. The clinician may have to return to Step 1 strategies to create safety for the new part before proceeding with trauma reprocessing.

As the client comes out of a freeze response, he may have an impulse to complete a fight or flight response. When a client is completing a survival response, his understanding of collaboration among parts is critical. The person can learn that as he is able to collaborate, older or stronger parts can help younger parts and together they can organize their nervous system to have the strength and energy to complete a survival response. See Chapter 3 for an expanded explanation of completing survival responses.

*Jim was a survivor of ritualistic sexual abuse. He presented to therapy reporting difficulty with his wife and feeling like she did not understand his need to be autonomous. He often felt like he was being smothered. He loved her very much but at times disconnected from her and raged at her, demanding a divorce. The clinician suggested a joint session. When Jim's wife Carrie arrived, she shared that he was erratic, at times being peaceful and loving, at other times acting childlike and dependent, and at other times being full of rage and condemning. Carrie was exasperated. As Carrie began to talk about her husband's rage, Jim began to shake uncontrollably, almost falling off his chair. The clinician used grounding to bring Jim back into his body. At that moment, different parts of Jim cascaded out and he rapidly switched to different parts, to his wife's surprise. As Jim's nervous system calmed with grounding, he began talking in an English accent, sharing with his wife and the clinician that he had been waiting to talk to someone for years. The Englishman was the first part to make himself known to his wife in an explicit way. Over the course of many months, 16 different parts appeared. Carrie came to therapy intermittently to learn about and be introduced to new parts. Each part loved Carrie but some were frustrated by her interactions with them. Carrie realized that she had been aware of the parts without knowing what they were. With the clinician's guidance, Carrie began making friends with each part, realizing that each of Jim's parts had helped him survive a horrendous childhood. The clinician helped Carrie not pathologize the parts. Carrie was surprised that as she accepted each one, Jim's outbursts lessened. Jim was also able to learn about his parts and as he collaborated with each of them, he was able to experience more internal calm. Each part was introduced to the wellness skills in age-appropriate ways. Most parts loved the wellness skills and liked listening to the iChill app. Carrie was able to learn what triggered each part and that each part had different needs. Carrie loved Jim and learned over time to learn to love and accept his parts. The clinician worked with Jim and each of his parts to sense safety in the present moment, first in his relationship with the therapist, which was then generalized to his wife and other relationships. All TRM skills were used over the course of therapy with Jim depending on each part and his or her particular trauma and what needed to be processed. Jim had male and female parts and there were times when the male parts helped the female parts reprocess sexual trauma. The male parts "mixed" with the female parts to provide an embodied strength to help Jim complete the survival response. A recurring somatic symptom shared by most of the parts was an experience of being strangled, accompanied by sharp pain in the throat. The clinician helped Jim titrate the sensation in the throat with each part. Over a period of many months, he completed a survival response of pushing away the aggressor. This chronic pain symptom disappeared all together. Jim is now able to collaborate with his parts, which he describes as the Knights of the Round Table who have regular discussions about moving forward in positive ways as a collaborative whole, at the same time acknowledging the individual parts. He stated that the parts do not want to go away: "They want to survive to help me survive but now they work in synchrony, not in disharmony."*

*Step 4: Collaboration and Wellness*

Clients who have experienced disorganized attachment can wonder if there is hope for a different life. We have worked biologically with clients for years and have seen hope where there had been only despair. We have had the honor of witnessing a new collaboration of parts that have become a symphony, working as a well-practiced orchestra. There is beauty in witnessing a client's heightened ability to be creative, generative, and socially engaged with an expanded friendship network. We have seen individuals with parts who lived in dysregulated states begin to experience sensations of joy, happiness, and peace. We have borne witness to individuals learning to stop the dissociative process by tracking their sensations and bringing themselves back to the present moment. A person with this expanded ability to stay present in the moment has more choices to live dynamically with the ups and downs of life and has a greater aptitude for managing life stresses.

With an expanded knowledge of the various attachment styles and the utilization of TRM/CRM skills, people can experience greater wholeness and feel like they are in the "driver's seat" of their lives. They are able to deepen their resilient zones by regularly employing wellness skills in between sessions, and they experience getting bumped out less often. Over time, the clinician's role changes from holding weekly sessions to providing occasional tune-ups to address the windstorms of life that can happen to any one of us—with or without parts.

# References

Ainsworth, M.D.S., Blehar, M., Waters, E., & Walls, S. (1978). *Patterns of attachment.* Hillsdale, NJ: Erlbaum.

Beebe, B., Jaffe, J., Markese, S., Buck, K., Chen, H., Cohen, P., . . . Feldstein, S. (2010). The origins of 12-month attachment: A microanalysis of 4-month mother-infant interaction. *Attachment & Human Development, 12*(1–2), 3–141.

Blizard, R. (2003). Disorganized attachment, development of dissociated self states, and relational approach to treatment. *Journal of Trauma and Dissociation, 4*(3), 27–50.

Bowlby, J. (1973). *Attachment and loss, Vol. 2: Separation, anxiety and anger.* London: Hogarth Press.

Brown, L.S. (2011). Guidelines for treating dissociative identity disorder in adults: Third revision: A tour de force for the dissociation field. *Journal of Trauma and Dissociation, 12*(2), 115–187. doi:10.1080/15299732.2011.537247

Chitty, J. (2013). *Dancing with Yin and Yang: Ancient wisdom, modern psychotherapy and Randolph Stone's polarity therapy.* Boulder, CO: Polarity Press.

Dell, P.F. (2009). Understanding dissociation. In P.F. Dell & J.A. O'Neil (Eds.), *Dissociation and the dissociative disorders: DSM-V and beyond* (pp. 709–825). New York: Routledge.

Liotti, G. (2006). A model of dissociation based on attachment theory and research. *Journal of Trauma and Dissociation, 7*(4), 55–73.

Nijenhuis, E.R.S., van der Hart, O., & Steele, K. (2004, January). Trauma-related structural dissociation of the personality. Trauma Information Pages. http://www.trauma-pages.com/a/nijenhuis-2004.php

114 Elaine Miller-Karas and Jennifer Burton

Porges, S.W. (1995). Orienting in a defensive world: Mammalian modifications of our evolutionary heritage: A polyvagal theory. *Psychophysiology, 32*(4), 301–318.

Porges, S.W. (2011). *The polyvagal theory: Neurophysiological foundations of emotions, attachment, communication, self-regulation*. New York: W.W. Norton & Company.

Roisman, G.I., Padrón, E., Sroufe, L.A., & Egeland, B. (2002). Earned-secure attachment status in retrospect and prospect. *Child Development, 73*(4), 1204–1219.

Scaer, R. (2007). *The body bears the burden: Trauma, dissociation, and disease* (2nd ed.). Binghamton, NY: Haworth Medical Press.

Schore, A. (2009). Attachment trauma and the developing right brain: Origins of pathological dissociation. In P.F. Dell & J.A. O'Neil (Eds.), *Dissociation and the dissociative disorders: DSM-V and beyond*. New York: Routledge.

Van der Hart, O., Nijenhuis, E.R.S., & Steele, K. (2006). *The haunted self: Structural dissociation and the treatment of chronic traumatization*. New York: W.W. Norton & Company.

# 6  Veterans, Warriors, and Their Loved Ones

*Elaine Miller-Karas and Jan Click*

If I had learned these skills 40 years ago, how my life would have been different.

—Vietnam veteran

This chapter will focus on utilizing the Trauma Resiliency Model (TRM) and the Community Resiliency Model (CRM) with veterans and service members and their families. We will highlight important themes to be aware of when working with a military population that will help the clinician understand the culture. We will include case examples to illustrate the utilization of the skills in working with veterans, service members, and their families.

## Clinician Self-Awareness

Our veterans and returning warriors deserve the very best clinical care we can provide. Serving their mental health needs can be one of the most enriching experiences of a clinician's practice. The degree of human sacrifice and dedication to their battle buddies and their country can be life-affirming. Witnessing the tenderness of these men and women coupled with their courage and strength can touch a deeply spiritual core for many clinicians. However, bearing witness to stories of killing, horror, death, loss of innocence, betrayal, and inhumanity can be too much for some clinicians. Clinicians who want to work with a military population need to conduct a self-assessment about personal values and beliefs about military service. We have learned that working with combat trauma is not for every therapist. If the therapist has a value system that is in conflict with military service, it is important for her to evaluate whether or not she is in the best therapeutic position to provide support to the veteran or service member. Active-duty service members and veterans are very tuned in to the responses they receive from therapists. One special-ops veteran shared that he had started working with a civilian therapist who had not had much experience treating combat trauma. The veteran said, "I told her the 'least bad' thing I ever did, and she looked at me like I was a monster."

The following questions can help with the self-evaluation:

- What is your understanding of military culture?
- What are your attitudes about war and killing?
- Are you able to listen to graphic stories about war, combat, and "unspeakable horrors?"
- What is your attitude toward war crimes and atrocities?
- Are you comfortable working with high levels of activation and anger?
- Are you willing to increase your knowledge about military culture?
- Are you willing to work with individuals who worked in covert operations?

As you evaluate your responses to the questions, pay attention to your own sensations. Are you able to track your own nervous system? If you are sliding into your low zone or bumping up to your high zone, are you able to ground and resource yourself? If strong, negative responses come up for you, are you able to put them aside or would it be better for you not to work with this population? Veterans and service members are highly attuned to the responses of others and will pick up judgment and discomfort on the part of the provider. If you find you cannot support veterans, warriors, and their families, there are public and private mental health settings that serve this most deserving population.

Cultural competency with the military population and expertise with the TRM and CRM are essential for effectively working with veterans and service members. In preparation for working with this population you can do the following:

- Attend workshops and conferences about treating veterans, warriors, and their families.
- Develop an understanding of military culture and learn how to differentiate between branches of service.
- Become familiar with military structure, chain of command, and ranks.
- Learn about the unique role of women in the military including the special challenges they face such as military sexual harassment and sexual assault.
- Learn about how the "don't ask, don't tell" mentality impacted gays and lesbians serving in the military.
- Research unique issues related to combat trauma including PTSD.
- Participate in the CRM/TRM consultation group specially focused on this population.
- Obtain individual consultation from a TRM consultant with special expertise in working with service members and veterans.

## The Problem

There are thousands of veterans and active-duty service members who are suffering from mental health challenges originating from their military service. In addition, family members are affected by the mental and physical health of their loved ones. Some have become the caregivers for their family member who has been disabled because of his military service. The Department of Defense reported that from 2001 to 2013 there were 3,826,591 total deployments to Iraq and Afghanistan. Taking into account multiple deployments, the actual number of individuals deployed was 1,939,008. The Institute of Medicine (IOM, 2014) reported that between 2004 and 2012 the percentage of all active-duty service members with a diagnosis of PTSD increased from 1 to 5% and more than half a million veterans of all eras sought care for PTSD through the Veterans Administration (VA) in 2012. The report further stated that 53% of those who met criteria for PTSD had tried to get help but received minimal treatment. If PTSD becomes chronic and untreated, other conditions can arise, including depression, suicidal behavior, alcohol and drug abuse, and behaviors that result from being stuck in the high zone, including domestic violence and child maltreatment. The report further elucidates that spouses and partners of service members and veterans who have PTSD may experience PTSD symptoms themselves and can experience relationship distress in response to the service member's or veteran's PTSD symptoms. Military caregivers experience worse health, greater strains in family relationships, and more workplace problems than non-caregivers. Further, military caregivers are at higher risk for depression. The caregivers may be very young and may also be caring for children, which can amplify the strain on the caregivers.

Women veterans and service members have different challenges than their male counterparts. Many are mothers who have been away from their children for long periods. Other women may have been victims of military sexual trauma (MST). Mulhall (2009) stated that marriages of female troops fail at three times the rate of marriages of male service members. Women service members are more likely than men to experience a severe housing cost burden, placing them at significant risk for homelessness. Seelig et al. (2012) reported that deployed women who had combat experience had greater odds than non-deployed women of reporting symptoms of a mental health condition.

Our mental health system, charged with serving active-duty service members, veterans, and their families, is already stretched to the breaking point, even as many thousands are returning to civilian life. In a survey of members of the National Council for Community Behavioral Health Care, a not-for-for profit association of 1,600 behavioral health-care organizations, nearly two-thirds of the responders reported that veterans and their families, even those in crisis, experienced delays and excessive waits before getting in to see a mental health provider. It often takes warriors living in rural America as long as five hours to travel to the VA or military base for an appointment. Others do not have access to a vehicle or public transportation, or they have combat-related physical or mental limitations that prevent them from driving or taking public transportation. Civilian agencies take up some of the slack. On average, 22% of veterans who seek help, seek mental health care outside the VA system.

In addition to traditional professional mental health counseling, interventions must be created that are outside the usual delivery system of mental health services. The CRM trains peers and community members and will be discussed at length in Chapter 7. A safety net can be created to respond to this public health emergency in which individuals and communities are educated about the neurobiology of trauma and resiliency through peer support networks using the CRM. Many veterans and active-duty service members are not "psychologically oriented." We have found that many veterans are amenable to learning simple wellness skills that teach them about the biology of stress and trauma. The paradigm shift from "pathology or mental weakness to biology" can be a huge boost to a person's self-esteem. The wellness skills are not only helpful for the active-duty service member and veteran, but also for their family members, because the entire family system can learn to speak a common language. Learning the concretized resiliency skills can reduce the symptoms of traumatic stress and contribute to greater resiliency (Citron, 2013). Once the veteran or warrior can learn to regulate his nervous system, he can then be ready to reprocess the traumatic experience with a TRM mental health practitioner.

## Special Nature of Warfare

Since the terrorist attacks of September 11, 2001, the United States has initiated four military operations:

Operation Noble Eagle (ONE) refers to a Department of Defense-wide enterprise and, for the U.S. Air Force, to the service's operations related to homeland security (e.g., combat air patrols over U.S. cities); its actions to ensure force protection; and its support to federal, state, and local agencies after the 9/11 attacks, such as recovery operations undertaken and disaster assistance provided in New York City and at the Pentagon.

Operation Enduring Freedom (OEF) (2001–projected December 2014) is the official named used by the United States for the war in Afghanistan.

Operation Iraqi Freedom (OIF) (2003–2010) is the official name used by the United States for the war in Iraq.

During Operation New Dawn (ODW) (2010–present), U.S. service members serving in Iraq are conducting stability operations, which focus on advising, assisting, and training Iraqi Security Forces (ISF). Operation New Dawn also represents a shift from a predominantly military U.S. presence to one that is predominantly civilian, as the U.S. Department of Defense and Department of State work together with governmental and non-governmental agencies to help build Iraq's civil capacity.

U.S. military operations over the last decade have resulted in special challenges for our service members, veterans, and their family members along with injuries that men and women have faced in all wars. This section will highlight some of the elements that make these wars different from past conflicts—including the lack of a "front line," advances in military medicine, lack of adequate dwell-time, a greater presence of women serving in every branch of the military, and the aftermath of injuries to body and mind—as well as some of the similarities such as exposure to horrific images. Knowledge of these differences and similarities will help the clinician make better assessments. In addition, by knowing which military operations the veteran or service member was involved with, the clinician will have a better understanding about the degree and intensity of combat exposure.

The military value system sets service members apart from civilians. The core mantra of every service member is this: "No soldier, sailor, airman, or Marine will be left on the battle field." Disregarding their own safety, these warriors will do everything in their power to retrieve the remains of fallen comrades. They learn that there is no greater bond than the one they share with people "to their left and to their right." In life-or-death situations, they will pull their fallen comrades through; they will come for them if they are wounded or killed, fighting right by their side (Halvorson, 2010). This mantra can also be difficult when a service member feels betrayed by his battle buddies, for example, in combat or because of MST. This betrayal can destruct the very core of the service member's belief and value system and magnify the deleterious psychological impact.

In previous wars, such as World War I and World War II, there was a clear front line. Those in the back were safe from enemy fire and could carry on their assignments without fear of attack. However, in these most recent conflicts, there is no "front line." A service member is potentially in danger "inside of the wire" as well as "outside of the wire." He can be standing in the chow line waiting to eat one minute and the next minute be under attack. This results in service members needing to stay at a high level of arousal and tactical readiness, which can create havoc on the nervous system. The combat zone can be an intense place where troops deal with having to move very quickly and make split-second decisions that involve life and death, as well as standing down and waiting for long periods. This "hurry up and wait" is a clear reality in these war zones. Many vets have described the contrast of intense fear and terror followed by long periods of incredible boredom. There can be significant physical challenges with being sleep deprived, enduring extreme temperatures of hot and cold, and transporting and carrying heavy packs weighing 60–80 pounds.

Troops in the combat zone can face traumatic losses, grief, and guilt. They can be involved in an intense firefight in which they lose buddies. The images of the loss are searing (body parts, blood, guts), but there is not time for the troops to process the experience lest they compromise their tactical readiness. They may be charged to collect the body parts of their buddy whom they just saw in the chow line. McCarroll, Ursano, and Fullerton (1995) found higher levels of PTSD symptoms in veterans who had handled human remains compared to those who had not. These troops may have to make decisions that impact their spiritual and moral beliefs. Life-and-death acts that are black and white in the civilian world are not so clear-cut in combat where one may have to choose between killing a potentially innocent civilian and protecting one's entire unit (Halvorson, 2010).

Multiple deployments and the lack of "dwell time" increase the service member's risk of developing mental health conditions. Service members have an increased risk with each additional deployment. A report from the U.S. Army Surgeon General (2008) indicated that 27% of soldiers on their third deployment reported serious combat stress or depression symptoms, compared to 19% on their second, and 12% on their first deployment. Dwell time is the time between the end of one deployment and a redeployment. Hoge et al. (2008) found that dwell time has an important impact on PTSD. Iraq and Afghanistan veterans did not have adequate dwell time between deployments. A service member deployed for a year should have at least two years of dwell time before being redeployed. Evidence suggests that 12 months is insufficient time to "reset" the mental health of soldiers after a combat tour of over a year (U.S. Army Surgeon General, 2008).

Lew et al. (2009) reported that advances in battlefield medicine and protective armor for the torso have led to a higher percentage of soldiers surviving physical injuries that would have been fatal in prior conflicts. Polytrauma refers to the many injuries that may have occurred to a service member. According to the VA, polytrauma is "two or more injuries to physical regions or organ systems, one of which may be life threatening, resulting in physical, cognitive, psychological, or psycho-social impairments and functional disability." Lew et al. (2009) described polytrauma as a clinical triad of chronic pain, PTSD, and traumatic brain injury (TBI). They further reported that the most common pain symptoms described by OIF and OEF veterans have been back pain and headache. TBI occurs when a sudden trauma causes damage to the brain. The differences between PTSD and TBI can be difficult to discern and the conditions can co-occur. Hoge et al. (2008) indicated that people with TBI are more likely to develop PTSD than those who have not sustained brain injury. The military estimates that one-fifth of troops with mild TBI injuries will have prolonged—and for some lifelong—symptoms requiring continuing care (U.S. Army Surgeon General, 2008). Thus, young men and women in the prime years of their lives may be coming home with physical and emotional pain that derails their goals and personal dreams.

At the end of World War II, there was a long ship ride back to the United States during which service members had an opportunity to debrief with their battle buddies and have space between war and home. Many service members from the current wars reported that in one day they were in the combat zone and, hours later, they were back at home sitting at the kitchen table. Many service members find the express return challenging and disorienting. Some may isolate themselves and not want to interact with loved ones. They may bring the horrors of war home and be triggered into a traumatic flashback by sounds or smells, or by watching television. One service member reported he would have to have his girlfriend fill up his car with gas because the smell of gasoline was too disorienting and took him back to combat where he lost five of his buddies.

In addition, in previous conflicts communication could take a considerable period of time, with several weeks between when a letter was sent, received by a loved one, and a reply sent back to the service member. If he received an upsetting letter while deployed, there was time to process the information with battle buddies before having a live conversation with the family member. With the advent of technology, a service member can be arguing with a spouse about money on a live video call one minute, and the next minute, be on a mission outside the wire in a potential combat situation. This back and forth can be very disorienting and can create dangerous distractions for the service member, which can result in increased risk to his safety as well as the safety of those in his unit.

## Women in the Military

The wars in Iraq and Afghanistan have cultivated a new generation of women with a warrior's ethos—and combat experience—that for millennia was almost exclusively the preserve of men (Myers, 2009). Women have served side-by-side with men in many situations where they engaged the enemy, and a changing war environment with no front lines required women to be placed in harm's way along with male service members.

> As soldiers in the Iraq and Afghanistan wars, women have done nearly as much in battle as their male counterparts: patrolled streets with machine guns, served as gunners on vehicles, disposed of explosives, and driven trucks down bomb-ridden roads. They have proved indispensable in their ability to interact with and search Iraqi and Afghan women for weapons, a job men cannot do for cultural reasons. The Marine Corps has created revolving units—"lionesses"—dedicated to just this task. A small number of women have even conducted raids, engaging the enemy directly in total disregard of existing policies.
>
> (Alvarez, 2009)

With the resulting changing role of women in the armed forces, the military has had to make adjustments in their living arrangements, privacy, and medical care. Men and women have also been co-located in bases throughout combat theaters. MST has been a reality for many of the women serving. Although some women respond to this primarily male environment by being extra strong, men usually have more physical strength, which can make women vulnerable to sexual assault. Having at times to live with the enemy outside the wire and an enemy within the wire because of sexual assault has made the psychological impact of serving in a war zone more difficult for women. There can also be practical issues like using the bathroom. One soldier recalled kicking her men out of the truck so she could pee in a cut-off water bottle. Another reported the difficulty of taking off her equipment to pull down her pants and worrying that the time it took could put herself and her buddies in danger. Eventually, the military began supplying a device called the feminine urinary director that enables women to pee standing up (Myers, 2009).

When creating treatment plans for this population, clinicians must keep in mind Lew's polytrauma clinical triad concept, which may be present in the service member and veteran, and whenever possible work as part of a multidisciplinary team providing care. In addition, it is helpful to include the family as part of treatment to increase their understanding of the complexity of the effects of military service and, most importantly, to help the family system with resiliency skills.

## Suicide Risk

There have been alarming increases in the suicide rates among active-duty service members and veterans. The Army Study to Assess Risk and Resilience in Servicemembers (Army STARRS) is the largest study of mental health risk and resilience ever conducted among military personnel, and research about suicide risk from the study has recently been published in the *Journal of the American Medical Association*. Schoenbaum et al. (2013) found that:

> the rise in suicide deaths from 2004 to 2009 occurred not only in currently and previously deployed soldiers, but also among soldiers never deployed; nearly half of soldiers who reported suicide attempts indicated their first attempt was prior to enlistment; and soldiers reported higher rates of certain mental disorders than civilians, including attention deficit hyperactivity disorder (ADHD), intermittent explosive disorder (recurrent episodes of extreme anger or violence), and substance use disorder.

Nock et al. (2014) reported that soldiers attempting suicide appeared to be lower-ranking, enlisted, female, and previously deployed. He also found that pre-enlistment mental disorders, including panic disorder and PTSD, were linked to increased rates of suicide attempts after joining the Army. Sixty percent of first suicide attempts in the army could be associated with pre- and post-enlistment mental disorders. Kessler et al. (2014) found that 85% of those who self-identified as having had a mental health disorder reported that the problem began prior to joining the Army. As we look at these recent findings, it is evident that we need to screen for PTSD, ADHD, intermittent explosive disorder, and panic and substance use disorders when working with military populations and to screen for suicidal ideation and plan.

## Military Sexual Trauma (MST)

The Department of Defense defines MST as rape, sexual assault, and sexual harassment (Stalsburg, n.d.). As larger numbers of women enter the military and live in close proximity to men, incidents of sexual assault have increased significantly. For fiscal year 2013, the Department of Defense identified 5,061 reports of sexual assault (Department of Defense, 2014). Both men and women may experience MST.

Although the military has a strict "no tolerance policy" for sexual harassment and assault, many incidents go unreported for a variety of reasons. A victim may not want to cause trouble; some fear retaliation from the perpetrator or perpetrator's friends. She may be uncomfortable reporting the incident or believe that nothing will be done about it if it is reported (Halvorson, 2010). Perpetrators of MST often wield control over the victim, especially since perpetrators are likely to outrank the victims. If the perpetrator is in the victim's chain of command, reporting the incident can seem impossible. Victims of MST often feel that they need to make a choice between their military careers and seeking justice for their trauma" (Stalsburg, n.d.).

It's important to note that sexual assault and harassment of military members by others in the military violate the values and ethics upon which service in the military is based. The psychological and emotional effects are multiplied when the perpetrator is someone in the individual's chain of command and someone whom he or she must rely upon for safety and well-being. One of the core values of the military is "having the back" of other service members. Sexual assault, then, becomes a double betrayal because not only is the service member not protecting the victim, he has in fact become the perpetrator. "MST triggers an intense feeling of betrayal in survivors as it upsets deeply-held belief systems about loyalty to fellow service members and respect for chain of command. In this way, MST is similar to incest, as perpetrators and victims are akin to family members" (Stalsburg, n.d.). The nervous system can be stuck in the high or low zones from combat but also from sexual assault, where the survivor is literally living with the enemy.

Although the Department of Defense has made great strides in bringing awareness to this problem and making reporting easier, changes in policies may not change the culture. Victims can be subject to retaliation by the perpetrator. Commanders often fail to protect those who report MST. Commanders and other service members may blame the victim for ruining "a good soldier's" reputation. They may try to convince her that it is not worth reporting as it will cause a rift and conflict in the unit. Men and women who suffer sexual trauma have a greater likelihood of developing emotional and psychological problems and many develop PTSD. In a review of the literature over a 20-year period (1990–2010), researchers identified sexual trauma, pre-military sexual trauma, combat exposure, substance misuse, and gender difference in the development of PTSD in women veterans (Middleton & Craig, 2012).

## Clinical Application of TRM and CRM

Chapter 3 went into detail about the skills of the TRM and CRM. The following sections highlight psychoeducation, the skills, and their application to specific common themes in the treatment of veterans, warriors, and their families.

### Importance of Psychoeducation and Biology Versus Mental Weakness

For those who have served in the military, being able to persevere and get through any situation is an essential ingredient to being a successful warrior, as are completing one's mission and helping one's buddies survive. The idea of asking for help or entering into therapy may mean to them that they are weak and that something is wrong with them. Biologically based models like the TRM and CRM, with their focus on skill-building, are much more acceptable to many service members and veterans versus traditional therapy where the focus may be on pathology. When we discuss with a veteran or warrior that it is his nervous system that is dysregulated based upon many months of being on high alert during deployment and it is not about his being "screwed up or crazy," we can begin to see a significant shift in his perception of the situation. We explain that even though his nervous system is currently dysregulated, he can learn the wellness skills to help the nervous system begin to reset and experience longer periods in his resilient zone. This concept is particularly important when teaching these wellness skills in a group setting (see Chapter 9).

### The Tasks of Daily Living

Part of the psychoeducation involves talking with service members and veterans about their resilient zones. As veterans learn the wellness skills, they begin to notice that they are experiencing more time in their resilient zones. Over and over as we teach this concept to veterans, they describe the shift they experience as they walk through their activities of daily living and are better able to manage difficult situations as they learn the skills.

*One veteran shared a story that beautifully illustrates the difference in his life when he was increasingly able to be in his resilient zone. He described going into a building supply store to purchase some items and when he got to the checkout line, he asked the clerk for his veteran's discount. She replied that he could only get the discount on Veterans Day. This vet replied that the discount was supposed to be every day. As the clerk continued to insist that he was not eligible for a discount, the vet was tracking his nervous system. He realized that he was getting angry and moving out of his resilient zone. He put his hand on the counter to ground himself and then thought about his daughter, who is an important resource for him. The veteran then felt himself come back into his resilient zone and he calmly asked to speak with the manager. Not only did he end up getting the discount for himself that day, he eventually had an opportunity to speak with the corporate office of this company and advocate for other veterans to receive the discount every day. He said that in the past, he would have gotten so angry that he would have left the store without purchasing his items, and that this was a huge shift for him.*

### Military Families

Military families make significant sacrifices along with the service members. They are frequently required to move every three to five years, necessitating changing living arrangements, schools, and employment. Moving may mean leaving behind friends and other support systems and starting over in a new environment. Deployment poses special challenges upon every member of the family. Learning about the various deployment phases can help the clinician understand the challenges faced by military families. The phases are pre-deployment, deployment, sustainment, redeployment, and post-deployment (Pincus, House, Christenson, & Alder, 2010).

During the pre-deployment phase, which begins upon notification of being deployed, service members and their families may suffer anxiety in anticipation of the deployment. This is a time of planning for the service member's departure. This phase can also be a time when the service member is preoccupied with his impending deployment and spending many hours away from home preparing for deployment. The spouse/partner may feel emotionally abandoned even though the service member is physically present.

The deployment and sustainment phases cover the period from deployment to demobilization when the service member is physically absent from the family. There can be great tension and apprehension as roles and responsibilities are redefined. In addition, there can be a tremendous amount of worry for the well-being of the service member, which can amplify the distress within the family system. Family members may live on an emotional rollercoaster as advances in communication can lead to amplified worries at home for the family and in theater for the deployed service member. In addition, the family is adjusting to their new roles and responsibilities, all of which happens without the help and support of the deployed family member.

The redeployment phase is the month before the service member returns home. This stage is full of excitement, anticipation, and apprehension as the family gets ready for the service member's return. There can also be concern about whether he will return a different person because of his service. Because the roles and responsibilities of family members may have changed since the deployment, there can be anticipation about how such roles will change upon the family member's return.

The post-deployment phase lasts three to six months after deployment. There can be an initial "honeymoon" period. However, the realities soon are apparent as the entire functioning of the family is renegotiated as the service member resumes his role within the family. A spouse may get used to handling things on the home front and functioning independently. When the deployed spouse returns home, it may be challenging for the service member to reintegrate into the family. The children may be used to taking direction from the parent at home and resist being parented by the returning service member. The oldest child may have taken on more of a parenting role and can resent the returning parent for resuming the responsibilities of father or mother.

Pincus et al. (2010) reported that there can be challenges with the children through every phase of deployment depending on the developmental age of the children and their ability to comprehend deployment. He states, "Babies less than 1 year old may not know the soldier and cry when held. Toddlers (1–3 years) may be slow to warm up. Preschoolers (3–6 years) may feel guilty and scared over the separation. School age children (6–12 years) may want a lot of attention. Teenagers (13–18 years) may be moody and may not appear to care." In addition, children are not familiar with the parenting style of their returning parent. They may have difficulty adjusting to the co-parenting being initiated by both parents.

Multiple and prolonged deployments are associated with increased anxiety and depression in the spouses of service members. Mansfield et al. (2010) surveyed over 250,000 medical records of active-duty U.S. Army soldiers and found that the rates of psychopathology in soldiers' wives correlated with deployment length—the longer the deployment, the greater the risk of depression. Reising

(2013) states that having a depressed parent can put children and adolescents at increased risk for internalizing and externalizing symptoms of psychopathology. She goes on to say that "depression in a parent creates chronic stress for children and adolescents through exposure to parental negative cognitions, impaired parent-child communication, stressful parent-child interactions, and elevated levels of stressors associated with depression in their environment" (Reising, 2013).

The values of discipline and order can also impact family relationships. In combat, if one's equipment is not in working order and ready to go, it could be a matter of life and death.

> *One Vietnam veteran complained that his wife was messy in the kitchen and it would frustrate him to no end when he would be looking for a spice or something in the kitchen and could not find it. The practitioner asked him, "Is someone going to die if you cannot find the salt?" A look of amazement came over his face and he laughed and said, "No. No one is going to die if I cannot find the salt." That led to a whole discussion about untangling what was necessary in combat from the normal routine of civilian life. The veteran was able to use his CRM wellness skills of tracking, grounding, and resourcing when this happened in the future and did not get into arguments with his wife about the neatness of the pantry. In fact, he later reported, "I gave her a shelf in the pantry! It is hard for me to see that shelf be messy, but I know no one is going to die if it's messy. My wife says thank you for the shelf!"*

Thus, although many families cope well with deployments and military service, others do not. A "family systems" view of deployment is essential. As we metaphorically toss the pebble in the stream and watch the ripple effect, we observe how the same can be true of deployment and how the entire family system may suffer as a result. If the service member returns with posttraumatic stress injury, he may be more reactive and stuck in either the high or low zone. If stuck in the high zone, he may be more irritable in ordinary family situations, responding in anger or even violence. On the other end of the spectrum, if he is stuck in the low zone, he may isolate himself and avoid interactions with other family members. Others vacillate between the high and low zones. Their behavior may be unpredictable towards their family members. Thus, the partner and the children may be on high alert, stuck in the high zone, trying to determine how the service member will react. The whole family may be living in dysregulated autonomic states themselves, vacillating between the high and low zones.

Helping each family member in age-appropriate ways learn about the nervous system can greatly alleviate the stress placed on the family. The biology versus mental weakness paradigm helps each family member understand the biology of symptoms and most importantly, how to move into the resilient zone when bumped out. The skills can be easily learned and can become a different way of communicating that does not involve shame. Family members can begin to track each other's nervous systems and when someone is bumped out of his zone can ask, "Honey, are you in your resilient zone?" The skills can be practiced together to help the entire family begin to have wider resilient zones.

*A veteran reported that after learning the skill of grounding, he went home and showed his wife the workbook we were using in the group and taught her the grounding exercise. He reported that before learning these skills, when he and his wife had any financial matters to address, they would get into a big argument. He says that after teaching his wife the grounding skill, they would practice it together before talking about finances and they did not have arguments anymore. The wife learned how to track her husband's nervous system and when he got bumped out of his resilient zone, his wife would place a hand on his shoulder and he would immediately begin to calm down.*

If someone is really amped up, it can be difficult for him to get back into the resilient zone. When a family member knows the Help Now! strategies, she can use this skill to help the person get back into his resilient zone. The Help Now! strategies can be particularly useful when someone in the family is stuck in the high or low zone. Pushing against the wall or walking can help release the stuck energy. The movement of the major muscle groups such as arms and legs seems to help individuals get back into their resilient zones more quickly.

The games that have been developed for children can be taught to the younger members of the family. They can be a playful way for children to learn how to track their nervous systems and widen their resilient zones. Chapter 4 has many strategies to help children using the TRM/CRM skills.

### Different Perceptions of Life and Death

Individuals who have been in combat may have very different perceptions of life and death than those in the civilian world. In order to survive combat, many experience emotional numbing. They may seem to be callous and indifferent to the pain of others.

*One marine shared that shortly after he returned from Iraq, his wife had a miscarriage with twins. She understandably was very emotional and devastated. The veteran reported that he did not feel anything. His wife accused him of not loving her or the twins. The concept of emotional numbing was explained as a survival response to help him get through the rigors of war. The upside of emotional numbing is that he did not feel the pain and the downside is that he did not feel the joy. Many veterans have a restricted range of affect. Gradually, as the man began to use the wellness skills of tracking, resourcing, and grounding, he was able to experience more enjoyment in his life, and as his resilient zone began to widen, he was able to experience greater closeness with his wife and children.*

### Discipline and Order and Traumatic Coupling

Discipline and order are essential components in military and combat operations. They can save lives in combat; however, the civilian versus military mindset can create challenges for the service member or veteran attempting to reintegrate into civilian life. For example, many individuals return to school after discharge from the military. They have been shot at, watched buddies die, and lived in 130-degree heat.

*One veteran who enrolled in school became frustrated with the civilians in his classes who complained about insignificant issues. He had low tolerance for "whiners" and the lack of respect he saw some students exhibit. It was helpful for the veteran to realize that his classmates' behavior was triggering because in a war zone, the lack of discipline could result in someone dying. He knew this cognitively. However, simply telling himself to stop reacting that way did not change the reactivity of his nervous system. Because of traumatic coupling, the veteran was reacting to those transgressions as if they were a life-and-death situation. Further, the veteran would sit in the back of the classroom, against the wall, scanning the room for signs of trouble. Uncoupling these reactions was an essential part of the therapeutic process. The TRM practitioner also taught the veteran the wellness skills to help him self-regulate when faced with distressing situations.*

In the above example, the veteran learned to differentiate between "a forest fire and a match," and he became able to intercept the distressing sensations and bring his nervous system back into balance.

*An Iraq War veteran was driving to Disneyland when he spotted something on the side of the road. He immediately turned his minivan away from what was garbage on the roadside, almost causing an accident. The sight of garbage on the roadside was coupled with his convoy having been blown up by an impro- vised explosive device (IED) in Iraq where he had almost been killed. After learning the wellness skills and how to track his nervous system, he was able to identify the beginning sensa- tions of fear, immediately resource and ground while driving, and shift his nervous system to the present moment, back to his resilient zone. The veteran felt empowered that he could reclaim his body and mind and not be tormented by the daily triggers that had accompanied him while driving in Los Ange- les. Truly, he was learning to biologically pay attention and dis- tinguish between the match and the forest fire!*

### Deconstruction of the Soul

Ed Tick (2005), in his book *War and the Soul,* writes about the impact that war can have on the soul. He states that becoming an effective warrior may mean violating one's own moral code and deconstructing one's soul to survive. One Vietnam veteran, a captain in the Marine Corps, described the gut-wrenching experience of having to violate his own moral code on multiple occasions in order to save his men. He said, "[T]o help keep my men alive and do my duty as their leader meant violating my own moral code." Some of the most challenging work that he did in his healing process was coming to terms with that internal conflict. The person he thought that he was had to be put aside in order for him to be a good leader and help keep his men alive.

For every thought about combat, there is a corresponding sensation. In TRM/ CRM, we work with the sensations that emerge, helping the veteran learn to track sensations. As he is more able to resource, ground, and shift and stay, we can then help him reprocess the specific traumatic event. We always stay with sensation while processing; we help the client's nervous system experi- ence regulation as he recounts the story of the trauma. The practitioner care- fully tracks the veteran and helps him come back to the resilient zone if the sensations become too much. When the veteran has the confidence that he can be "in charge" of the sensations connected to the experience, we can then help him restore survival responses that may have been blocked at the time of the traumatic war experience.

### Aggressor–Prey–Witness

The "aggressor, prey and/or witness" paradigm helps individuals understand the biology of their nervous system when in their different roles as a result of military service. Some individuals who experienced trauma as a result of their service may feel like there is danger everywhere. Simultaneously, the person can experience biological reactions connected to being the aggressor, the prey, or the witness. The biological responses happen automatically, without conscious thought.

An aggressor is the role a person can be in if he is actively engaged in finding and fighting a threat. Prey is the role a person can be in when he feels he is under attack. The role of a witness is when a person sees, hears, and smells all parts of the aftermath of being in combat. If a person is in all three roles at the same time, it can create the perfect storm within the human nervous system that heightens reactivity and can lead to his being always bumped out of the resilient zone. These roles may equate with survival in a combat zone. There is no magic "reset" button that is turned off when the service member returns home and is faced with the tasks of daily living. There are many triggers connected to being bumped out of the resilient zone that can cause a strong reaction. Helping the service member and his family understand this paradigm can reduce the shame and self-blame experienced when integrating back into family life. In addition, the wellness skills of both models teach the person to become aware of the sensations connected to the high and low zones and most importantly, to the resilient zone. As the client is able to differentiate between sensations connected to each zone, he then has a choice of using one of the wellness skills to return to his resilient zone.

### Traumatic Grief and Loss and Shock Trauma

Traumatic grief differs from normal grief and loss. It violates our understanding of how the world should be. If a soldier is talking with his buddy one minute about what video they will play after they get back from patrol, and the next minute they are hit by an IED and his buddy is killed, this is shock trauma. In order for the warrior to complete the mission, he needs to put his grief aside, as war leaves little space for grieving. There needs to be a degree of security from enemy attack in order for the grief process to begin.

> *One Iraq vet described having a nightmare almost every night in which his buddy appears and asks, "Why did you let me die? Why didn't you save me?" The veteran thought, "He had a wife and kids, it should have been me. He didn't deserve to die."*

Survivors may go over and over the incident, often thinking that there must have been something they could have done to save their buddy. They may experience rage toward the enemy and want revenge, and they may believe that if they let go of the grief, they will not be honoring the buddy who was killed.

Adaptations to resourcing are questions that encourage the veteran to think differently about the loss, for example:

*An Iraq veteran was stuck grieving for his buddy who was killed during a second deployment. He was consumed by the thought, "If I had been there, I could have helped him survive." The TRM practitioner, using the lens of resourcing, asked, "If it was you that died, how would you want your buddy to honor you? Would it be by staying stuck in the grief or living his best life?" The veteran said, "I would want him to live life to its fullest; that is how I would want him to honor me." The TRM practitioner then asked the veteran what he sensed on the inside when he said he would want him to live life to the fullest. The practitioner noted that the veteran took a deep breath, his body relaxed, and he came into his resilient zone.*

Rituals can be another way of building resources after deployment.

*One veteran lost a buddy in Afghanistan. To help him cope with his grief, the TRM practitioner asked the veteran in what ways would he like to memorialize his friend. The veteran created a ritual that he performed at a Memorial Day ceremony. As he discussed the ritual, the TRM practitioner asked him what he was noticing inside. He sat for a minute, sensing inside, and then said, "Maybe I can let it go a little bit." As he made this comment, he was invited to sense his body. The practitioner then reinforced that bringing this new, reframed perspective into sensation is like saving it to one's hard drive.*

When we work with traumatic grief and loss, we also ask questions like, "What is your favorite memory of your buddy? What was the best part of having him for a friend? What or who is helping you get through this?" We are using the skill of resourcing in ways that bring in more elements to the experience of loss. Often sensations of sadness emerge along with those of comfort. The TRM practitioner acknowledges the sadness and also invites the client to draw attention to the sensations of comfort. As the veteran senses into the good memories as well as the sad ones, the lens widens. The veteran often reports that he can sense the positive memories of his buddy and that these override the memories of sadness.

### Living with Guilt and Shame

Shame and guilt can be challenging for veterans as they try to integrate into civilian life. Many young men and woman who decide to enlist in the military do so out of a sense of duty and service to their country. One of the horrors of war is the killing of noncombatants. In the Vietnam, Iraq, and Afghanistan wars, it was not always possible to determine who the enemy was. Vietnam veterans have described having children run toward them and having to make a split-second decision whether to shoot or not. The child could have been booby trapped. If the soldiers did not shoot, they could endanger their entire unit.

*One Iraq veteran described being at the head of a convoy. A teenage boy ran toward their convoy and the veteran made the decision to keep going. Like the Vietnam vet, if he had stopped, he could have endangered the entire convoy. This veteran said, "I just kept driving. I will never know if I killed that kid, but I couldn't take the chance of us getting killed." For many veterans, this creates tremendous guilt and shame.*

When working with veterans and active-duty service members on these types of issues, clinicians must stay grounded and present. Inviting tracking and shifting back into one of the wellness skills is imperative. Asking survival resourcing questions like, "What or who is helping you get through this?" and "When did you know you were going to survive?" can help bring the person back to his resilient zone. As we have stated earlier, making sure the client is well-resourced and can get into his resilient zone and stay there for a period of time is important before starting any trauma reprocessing.

*A psychologist who served in the Marine Corps in Vietnam and treated combat veterans for many years described the concept of atonement. He related a story about an Iraq War vet who, in the heat of combat, ended up killing a small girl. She was around the same age as his daughter. He was unable to get that girl's face out of his mind. When he came back to see this psychologist, he discussed not being able to get past this issue and that every time he looked at his daughter, he saw the child he had killed. The psychologist talked to him about the Knights of the Round Table and how when they came back from battle in the crusades, they would sometimes be consumed with guilt. The priest required them to perform an act of service to atone for what they had done. This veteran took this advice to heart. He decided that although he could not make up for the child who was killed in combat, he could take another action that would help him come to terms with this issue. He decided that he would guard the playground in an inner-city neighborhood in his town of Philadelphia in order to protect those children from being harassed by gangbangers. So, every Saturday, he stood guard at that playground to protect those children (Silver & Rogers, 2002).*

### Violations of the Social Contract

Many veterans have great difficulty with what is called "violations of the social contract." For some, these violations can be more difficult to deal with than the combat and military trauma.

> A social contract is a voluntary agreement among individuals by which, according to any of various theories, as of Hobbes, Locke, or Rousseau, organized society is brought into being and invested with the right to secure mutual protection and welfare or to regulate the relations among its members.
>
> (Dictionary.com, 2014)

Service members are trained for combat and various military operations. They know that when they go into a combat zone, they may be shot at or might shoot at others. They prepare for that eventuality and know that it is part of deployment. However, the violations of the social contract are frequently more troubling because of a sense of betrayal.

*One Iraq vet who was part of the initial surge described an incident where they were expecting to be overrun by Iraqis. He said he was given just 10 rounds of ammunition. He expressed anger at not getting the equipment that he needed and that if they had been overrun, he and many other service members would have died unnecessarily. Strong feelings with regard to violations of the social contract can be amplified when a warrior has experienced childhood trauma and has been betrayed by primary caregivers.*

Before reprocessing a traumatic war incident, the TRM practitioner educates and teaches the veteran all six wellness skills. Then, the practitioner starts with what we call "Trauma plus one" (T + 1). Trauma plus one refers to going to the end of the story first—the survival story, which is often imbued with energy or life and relief. The therapist can ask, "Can you tell me about the moment you knew you were going to survive?" Next, the practitioner asks the veteran to sense into knowing that he survived. Once that experience of having survived is anchored in sensation, the therapist can invite the veteran or warrior to begin telling his story.

At that point, the three skills of trauma reprocessing are used: titration, pendulation, and completion of survival responses. The practitioner can also use a TRM pause to slow down the story and help the client titrate the distress. This pausing during the recounting of the trauma story helps the client begin to integrate the elements of the trauma story. In telling the story in this way, the veteran frequently is able to come to terms with the memory, and meaning frequently organically emerges. "I realized I did the best I could do," and "It's over and I am okay" are common themes.

### Working with Anger and Rage, Complex Trauma, and Being Stuck in the High or Low Zone

#### Anger and Rage

Among the most common reactions warriors experience after returning from deployment are anger and rage. In TRM terminology, this is being stuck in the high zone. Aggression and high levels of arousal can be advantageous and necessary in a war zone. When troops go through military training prior to deployment, they are taught to tap into their anger. This anger can help them overcome obstacles, override the fear response, and potentially increase their chances of survival. As one veteran shared, "If you think, you die." Unfortunately, this anger can become the default response, and what helped them survive in the combat zone can become a significant liability when they are trying to readjust after deployment or to civilian life. If the veteran is stuck in the fast system, he may take action that he would not take if he were in the slow system and could evaluate the consequences of his actions.

*A veteran gets cut off on the freeway. If he is in the fast system, he may become enraged, as someone cutting him off in Iraq could be a life-or-death situation. He begins to tailgate the guy who cut him off. He follows him off of the freeway, gets into a verbal and then physical altercation, and before he knows it, he has been arrested for felony assault. The whole trajectory of his life has now been altered in a profound way. However, if he got cut off on the freeway and was able to stay in the slow system and he had learned the TRM/CRM skills, he might immediately start grounding himself while driving. Once he got back into his resilient zone, he might say to himself, "I'm not in Iraq. I'm back home. That guy is a jerk, but I am not in immediate danger. If I get angry and go after him, I could get myself in trouble. He's not worth it. I'm just going to let him go on his way."*

When we work with the TRM model with veterans or warriors who are experiencing rage and anger, it is very important that prior to that work, they have learned the wellness skills so they are able to get themselves back into their resilient zones. Many veterans are fearful of how intense the rage can be and want to avoid working with it. They may be afraid of hurting the therapist. They may believe that if they let it out, they will lose control. Therefore, it is important to work very slowly, using titration and pendulation to enable the completion of defensive responses in a controlled manner that feels safer for the veteran. One Iraq veteran imagined a plate in the center of his core. He would only put the amount of anger on that plate that he felt he could manage. He was able to do his own titration and keep the level of activation at a manageable level.

Anger can come up for a variety of reasons. It can mask underlying feelings of helplessness, sadness, guilt, and grief. Those feelings could be a liability in a war zone, when one needs to complete a mission. However, the emotional numbing that is so essential in combat can interfere with intimacy and connections with loved ones. It is important for practitioners to explain how the nervous system works and the adaptive response of emotional numbing during combat.

*Complex Trauma*

When service members and veterans have complex trauma and have experienced childhood or developmental trauma, it can take longer for them to learn how to track their nervous systems and begin to find neutral or pleasant sensations inside. A female Iraq War veteran asked when learning about the concept of the resilient zone, "What if you have never been in your resilient zone?" She had experienced childhood sexual abuse as well as military sexual assault and sexual harassment. Initially, the Help Now! strategies helped her the most. She needed to make several attempts at finding a resource that didn't overwhelm her with distressing sensations, but over time, she was able to begin to notice neutral sensations inside and start to experience being in her resilient zone. When clients are not able to find positive sensations, they are encouraged to focus instead on the neutral sensations. With time, individuals are able to track and notice neutral sensations and the depth of the resilient zone widens. When someone's nervous system has been dysregulated his entire life, it can take longer for him to begin to experience neutral or pleasant sensations. He may experience a paradoxical reaction to calming down because of traumatic coupling with a past experience of his body being calm and being in danger.

> *This was the case for a woman vet who was sexually harassed by a senior officer. She had also been sexually assaulted at night as a child so initially when she started to calm down, she would get triggered into high arousal. The psychoeducation of this traumatic coupling was essential in explaining what was likely happening in her nervous system. Over time, she was able to begin uncoupling those experiences and to feel calmer on the inside when working with the wellness skills and the TRM for trauma reprocessing.*

*Stuck in the High Zone*

Warriors and veterans stuck in the high zone may take actions they would never take when in their resilient zones. When they are stuck in the high zone, they do not have the same access to their prefrontal cortex that helps them to problem solve and evaluate the consequences of their actions. A helpful metaphor is that it's easier to stop the train before it leaves the station than when it is going 100 miles an hour and is already 50 miles down the track. The goal for the veteran or service member is to learn to track his nervous system and intercede with one of the wellness skills so the nervous system does not leave the station.

*Stuck in the Low Zone*

Some veterans and service members are stuck in the low zone and still others bounce back and forth. For those stuck in the low zone, it can be like walking through molasses. Everything takes a huge amount of energy. Just as the Help Now! strategies can be helpful for the veteran who is stuck in the high zone, these tools can also be very helpful for those stuck in the low zone. When a veteran or service member is stuck in the low zone, the practitioner can ask him to get up and walk around, inviting him to sense the movement of his arms and legs and his feet making contact with the ground. The therapist can also invite the client to push against a wall or door. Anything that helps him to move major muscle groups and joints can help him get back into his resilient zone.

*During a TRM/CRM group session for women veterans, there were times that many of them were stuck in the low zone. The TRM practitioner invited them to get up and walk around the table and track their nervous systems. Soon, they were able to feel the movement in their arms and legs and started to notice sensations of release such as tingling and heat. After about five minutes of walking, most of them were able to get back into their resilient zones.*

### Working with the Freeze Response

If a veteran or service member experienced a freeze response during combat, he may be flooded with shame. Since he was trained to override fear, if fear overwhelmed him and he froze, it may have resulted in the injury or even death of others. Many individuals who have experienced this freeze response have also survived childhood trauma. There is a template already embedded within them that is triggered to freeze, so even with the best training, if the combat experience is life threatening, the freeze response may occur automatically. As has been discussed in previous chapters, working with the freeze response can be some of the most challenging work therapists do with clients and this can be especially so with veterans and service members.

The freeze response can be a common experience for female veterans and service members, particularly those who have experienced MST.

*A female veteran who was assaulted by someone in her unit while she was sleeping saw herself as someone who was very strong and had effectively handled many difficult situations in* her military career and in her life. She was very distressed about having this freeze response and saw it as a sign of weakness. The concept of freeze was explained to her, and the fact that she was sound asleep when the assault occurred was emphasized, as she did not have time to take any defensive action. After providing psychoeducation about the freeze response and being assured that the veteran had the TRM/CRM wellness skills well anchored in her body, the practitioner began to work with the client on this memory of the assault. The session began with questions about the moment of survival: "When did you know you were going to get through this? Who helped you survive?" Once her survival story was anchored in sensation, the veteran was invited to begin to tell her story. As the client began to tell the story, she reported feeling like she was trapped and could not move. She noticed sensations of cold and an eerie calm. She was invited to see if there was a place inside where she could move just a little bit. As she focused on where she could move just a little, she started to notice her body was heating up and there was more and more movement. TRM pauses were inserted frequently, giving her more time, pendulating and titrating the memory. As the practitioner and client slowly worked, the client continued to notice sensations of release such as tingling and heat. The practitioner drew the client's attention to the movement in her feet and invited her to sense into whatever motion her feet wanted to make. She said she wanted to run to safety. The client had a problem with that, because, as she said, "Soldiers don't run." The practitioner explained that it did not mean she would run in real life; she was just working on letting go of the stuck energy in her body. At one point, she was clutching her hands, and the practitioner asked what her hands wanted to do. She replied, "I just wanted to punch that guy." The client was invited to let her hands make whatever motion they wanted to do. As she made the movement of punching in the air, she continued to experience sensations of release. New meaning began to emerge, and she said, "This wasn't my fault. This guy was an aggressor and a coward for attacking me in my sleep." She was then asked to become aware of what she was sensing inside as she said those words, and she let out a big breath. "I think I can begin to put this behind me now," she said. This new meaning was then anchored in sensation. She continued to report *sensations of release. As the session came to a close, the practitioner invited her to notice all of the changes and what it was like to give those sensations the space they need inside. She took a deep breath and stated, "I survived!" and reported she could feel her strength to her core.*

### Fear of Harming and Killing

Lt. Col. Dave Grossman, a well-known author who has written extensively on the military, aggression, and combat, discusses the concept of sheep, sheepdogs, and wolves in his book *On Combat* (Grossman & Christensen, 2008). Quoting from a Vietnam veteran, he wrote:

> Most people in our society are sheep. They are kind, gentle productive creatures who can only hurt each other by accident. . . . Then there are the wolves who feed on the sheep without mercy. There are evil men in this world and they are capable of evil deeds. . . . Then there are the sheepdogs. They "live to protect the flock and confront the wolf."
>
> (Grossman & Christensen, 2008)

The sheepdog has the capacity for violence but its job is to protect the sheep. What happens when the sheepdog becomes the wolf? We believe that when a warrior stays stuck in the high zone, even after danger has passed (such as when he returns from deployment or leaves the military and is adjusting to civilian life), the capacity for violence and hurting the sheep becomes greater. We have seen a sharp increase in incidents of domestic violence, child abuse, assault, and murder in the military population.

It is not uncommon for active-duty service members and veterans to fear that they could kill or greatly harm a civilian when integrating into civilian life. One service member reported waking up in the middle night from a nightmare ready to pounce on his wife. Others report that even minor irritations can trigger an overly aggressive, hostile response. Another veteran shared that the very impulse that would have made him an excellent warrior could now land him in jail.

*George had been in prison and was trying to turn his life around. When learning the wellness skills, he noticed that when he practiced the skills he did not get as upset by some of the small things that would trigger his irritability and, in some instances, his rage. George wanted to share a trauma story that had haunted him since 2003, when he and his battle buddies were trapped and surrounded. Some of his buddies died in the incident. As he started to talk about the event, his legs began to move and he began to sweat. He was asked to track what his body wanted to do. He stopped and looked at his practitioner and said, "I have to stop, because I want to kill you." The practitioner knew that George's biggest fear was that he would be triggered into killing a civilian. The practitioner stated, "George, you can stop and notice what it is like inside to stop." George looked surprised and tracked his body and began to tremble and feel a lot of heat (release sensations). The practitioner brought his attention to the releases. George took a deep breath and began to softly cry. He then repeated, "I did stop and I can stop." As new meaning emerged in the present moment, George was invited to repeat the words and to sense his body. George stated, "This is the first time since 2003 that I have felt safe in my own skin."*

The State of California Mental Health Services Act with the County of San Bernardino funded a project to evaluate the efficacy of the CRM skills for veterans—the Veterans' Extension Project. The veterans who learned the CRM wellness skills had statistically significant reductions in their hostility scores, which continued in follow-up evaluations three to six months after they learned the skills. The most statistically significant factor was their ability to "amp down" and come back into their resilient zones (Citron, 2013).

## Ending a Session

When ending a session, practitioners should be aware that there may be more that needs to be processed. The wellness skills are brought in at the end of every session. Because self-regulation can be problematic for many veterans and active-duty service members, the ability to track sensations connected to resilience and well-being at the end of session gives the client confidence that the trauma can be reprocessed and the activities of daily living can be managed within the resilient zone. The iChill app was developed at the direct request of a group of women veterans at the VA who, when learning the wellness skills, wanted something that could help them in between sessions. iChill is available free of charge at www.iChillapp.com for personal computers and can be downloaded onto an Android or iPhone from their respective app stores. iChill guides the user in the wellness skills.

We have learned so much from our veterans and active-duty service members. As women who have never served and who had family members who served in World War I and II, we have not always known all the nuances of military service. Service members and veterans have educated us. We have sometimes been tested to see whether or not we could hold the story of war and killing. We have had the honor of helping men and women who have given so much to so many come back to their better selves. We have learned that the gentle approaches of the TRM can guide the nervous system back into regulation. As opposed to the "big bang" approach of many trauma treatment models, through the TRM we can help clients gently ease into beginning to experience sensations connected to well-being and resilience. As a result, we have seen men and women live their lives more fully again.

*A service member, Jennifer, had been deployed twice to Iraq. She had been harassed during her first deployment. This harassment triggered childhood memories of assault. After her second deployment she became suicidal. All her attempts to deal with her distress were not enough. She wrote a suicide note and had a suicide plan. She decided to try a therapist who had experience working with service members. She learned the CRM wellness skills and the neuroscience behind her symptoms. She discovered she was not aware of her resilient zone. She realized she had her darkest moments when she was in her high and low zones. As she practiced the skills, she slowly became aware that she could access her resilient zone. Slowly, the suicidal thoughts lessened and then stopped. She was able to understand her reactions as being common, rather than human weakness. Jennifer is no longer suicidal. She feels whole again and she has become a Community Resiliency Model Skills Trainer.*

## References

Alvarez, L. (2009, August 15). Women at arms: G.I. Jane breaks the combat barrier. *New York Times*. http://www.nytimes.com/2009/08/16/us/16women.html?pagewanted=all&_r=0

Citron, S. (2013). *Final veteran extension program report*. Claremont, CA: Trauma Resource Institute.

Department of Defense. (2014). *Department of Defense fact sheet: Secretary Hagel issues new initiatives to eliminate sexual assault, updates prevention strategy and releases 2013 annual report on sexual assault in the military*. http://www.sapr.mil/public/docs/reports/FY13_DoD_SAPRO_Annual_Report_Fact_Sheet.pdf

Dictionary.com. (2014). Social contract. http://dictionary.reference.com/browse/social+contract

Grossman, D., & Christensen, L.W. (2008). *On combat: The psychology and physiology of deadly conflict in war and in peace.* Millstadt, IL: Warrior Science Publications.

Halvorson, A. (2010). *Understanding the military: The institution, the culture, and the people* (Working draft). Rockville, MD: Substance Abuse and Mental Health Services Administration.

Hoge, C.W., McGurk, D., Thomas, J.L., Cox, A. L., Engel, C.C., & Castro, C.A. (2008). Mild traumatic brain injury in U.S. soldiers returning from Iraq. *New England Journal of Medicine, 358,* 453–463.

IOM (Institute of Medicine). (2014). Treatment for posttraumatic stress disorder in military and veteran populations: Final Assessment. Washington, DC: The National Academies Press.

Kessler, R.C., Heeringa, S. G., Stein, M.B., Colpe, L.J., Fullerton, C.S., Hwang, I., . . . Ursano, R.J. (2014). Thirty-day prevalence of DSM-IV mental disorders among nondeployed soldiers in the U.S. army. *JAMA Psychiatry, 71,* 504–513. doi:10.1001/jamapsychiatry.2014.28

Lew, H.L., Otis, J.D., Tun, C., Kerns, R.D., Clark, M.E., & Cifu, D.X. (2009). Prevalence of chronic pain, posttraumatic stress disorder, and persistent postconcussive symptoms in OIF/OEF veterans: Polytrauma clinical triad. *Journal of Rehabilitation Research & Development, 46*(6), 697–702.

Mansfield, A.J., Kaufman, J.S., Marshall, S.W., Gaynes, B.J., Morrissey, J.P., & Engel, C.C. (2010). Deployment and the use of mental health services among U.S. army wives. *New England Journal of Medicine, 362,* 101–109. doi:7710.1056/NEJMoa09001

McCarroll, J.E., Ursano, R.J., & Fullerton, C.S. (1995). Symptoms of PTSD following recovery of war dead: 13–15 month follow-up. *American Journal of Psychiatry, 152*(6), 939–941.

Middleton, K., & Craig, C.D. (2012). A systematic literature review of PTSD among female veterans from 1990 to 2010. *Social Work in Mental Health, 10,* 233–252. doi:10.1080/153329 85.2011.639929

Mulhall, Erin. (2009). *Women warriors: Supporting she "who has borne the battle."* Iraq and Afghanistan Veterans of America (IAVA) Issue Report. New York: IAVA.

Myers, S.L. (2009, August 16). Women at arms: Living and fighting alongside men, and fitting in. *New York Times.* http://www.nytimes.com/2009/08/17/us/17women.html?pagewanted=all

Nock, M.K., Stein, M.B., Heeringa, S.G., Ursano, R.J., Colpe, L.J., Fullerton, C.S., . . . Kessler, R.C. (2014). Prevalence and correlates of suicidal behavior among soldiers: Results from the Army Study to Assess Risk and Resilience in Servicemembers (Army STARRS). *JAMA Psychiatry, 71*(5), 514–522. doi:10.1001/jamapsychiatry.2014.30

Pincus, S.H., House, R., Christenson, J., & Alder, L.E. (2010). The emotional cycle of deployment: A military family perspective. Operation: Military Kids. United States Navy Reserve. http://4h.missouri.edu/programs/military/resources/manual/Deployment-Cycles.pdf

Reising, M.M. (2013). *The effects of chronic stress on executive function, coping, and prefrontal functioning in children of depressed parents* (Doctoral dissertation). Vanderbilt University, Nashville, TN. http://etd.library.vanderbilt.edu/available/etd-06192012–144801/unrestricted/Reising.pdf

Schoenbaum, M., Kessler, R.C., Gilman, S.E., Colpe, L.J., Heeringa, S.G., Stein, M.B., . . . Cox, K.L. (2013). Predictors of suicide and accident death in the army study to assess risk and resilience in servicemembers (Army STARRS). *JAMA Psychiatry, 71*(5), 493–503. doi:10.1001/jamapsychiatry.2013.4417

Seelig, A.D., Jacobson, I. G., Smith, B., Hooper, T.I., Gackstetter, G.D., Ryan, M.A.K. . . . Smith, T.C. (2012). Prospective evaluation of mental health and deployment experience among women in the U.S. military. *American Journal of Epidemiology, 176*(2), 135–145.

Silver, S.M., & Rogers, S. (2002). *Light in the heart of darkness: EMDR and the treatment of war and terrorism survivors.* New York: W.W. Norton & Company.

Stalsburg, B.L. (n.d.). *Military sexual trauma: The facts* (SWAN Fact Sheet). New York: Service Women's Action Network (SWAN).

Tick, E. (2005). *War and the soul: Healing our nation's veterans from post-traumatic stress disorder.* Wheaton, IL: Quest Books.

Ursano, R. J., Colpe, L. J., Heeringa, S. G., Kessler, R. C., Schoenbaum, M., & Stein, M. B., on Behalf of the Army STARRS Collaborators. (2014). The army study to assess risk and resilience in service members (Army STARRS). *Psychiatry: Interpersonal and Biological Processes, 77*(2), 107–119.

U.S. Army Surgeon General. (2008, February). *Mental Health Advisory Team (MHAT) V: Operation Iraqi Freedom 06–08: Iraq Operation Enduring Freedom 8: Afghanistan.* http://armymedicine.mil/Documents/Redacted1-MHATV-4-FEB-2008-Overview.pdf

# 7 The Community Resiliency Model (CRM)

*Elaine Miller-Karas*

It is hot and muggy as we travel through the broken streets of Haiti. Our driver negotiates around the rubble to bring us to our destination where more than 100 Haitians huddle underneath a corrugated metal roof in a makeshift camp waiting for our arrival. The camp emerged in one of the many neighborhoods in Port au Prince after the January 2010 earthquake. We ask to exchange a song, as sharing music and dance bring our two worlds together. A woman moves forward from the crowd and begins to sing and soon everyone joins in, rising from the wooden benches, gathering together in song and dance. The laughter and singing resounds through the camp and is contagious as more people join us—men, women, children, the old and the young. A moment of reprieve from the harsh realities . . . a reminder that joy can still exist. . . . In simple ways, we begin to teach the survivors about the biology of the human nervous system—the biology of traumatic stress reactions and resiliency. We share with the survivors the basic skills of the Community Resiliency Model (CRM) and demonstrate how they can help one another rebalance their nervous systems. They share with us physical symptoms—insomnia, palpitations, sensations of the earth moving when it is not, stomach aches and headaches, weakness in the limbs, and sadness. We share that we have seen these symptoms all over the world after catastrophes like the earthquake. . . . This is biology, not human weakness. We then ask, "What or who is helping you now?" The crowd shouts out, "Jesus, my family, my friends!" We demonstrate and practice the basic CRM skills. "Remember your resources," we say. There is chatter and agreement in *words. "Yes, yes, we will," we hear in Creole. As we get ready to leave, the Catholic nun who leads the camp comes toward us enthusiastically, and through our Creole translator, takes my hands in hers and says, "This is the first time since the earthquake that I have felt joy."*

In December 2006 the Trauma Resource Institute (TRI), a nonprofit corporation, was founded, dedicated to bringing culturally sensitive interventions to underserved communities worldwide. We have designed interventions that can be simply taught and learned. The experience from Haiti has now been replicated in many places around the world and throughout the United States. We are ambassadors of hope and even though we have seen great suffering, we have also seen the most awe-inspiring resiliency of the human spirit. We are exhilarated witnessing the adaptability and relevance of the CRM model across cultures, ethnicities, and developmental ages. CRM interventions can be delivered in individual and group formats. Both community members and professionals can be trained to teach the skills thereby providing resiliency training to a wider net of the populace. This chapter will explain the CRM skills training and will address some of the major themes in designing interventions for a global community. And as a widow from Tocloban, the Philippines, who lost her husband in Typhoon Yolanda, shared with our training team, "Thank you for reminding me what I already knew, and had forgotten." This is the wisdom of the nervous system, the elegant design as I often say, that is within us all—the potential to heal from the wounds of our past.

## The Need for Community-Based Interventions

### Global Inadequacy of Services (for Domestic Violence, Child Abuse, and Disaster-Related Trauma)

Globally, mental health services are inadequate and often nonexistent. If mental health services do exist, the staffs are often so small that they do not have the capacity to impact the throngs of community members who need help. For example, in Hinche, in the Central Plateau of Haiti, we met a young psychologist who had worked unpaid for over a year. She was the only psychologist for over 60,000 people. In the United States, there has been a waxing and waning of mental health services for the underserved and there are wide differences between the states. The services are often inadequate or nonexistent. If services do exist, they are often provided in larger group settings, as individual therapy is too costly or culturally inappropriate. Individuals in rural communities often have limited access to services, and the clinics in inner cities are often over-crowded and underfunded (Leitch & Miller-Karas, 2010).

### Veterans and Their Families

As we are now facing thousands of men and women returning from Iraq and Afghanistan who are attempting to reconstruct their lives after serving in our nation's armed forces, the limitations of individual therapy in response to war trauma becomes starkly apparent. There simply are not enough trained pro-fessionals to meet the numbers returning with traumatic stress reactions and depression. In addition, many of those suffering are not psychologically ori-ented and if they seek help, many will seek out a member of their social network rather than a therapist.

### Civilian War Trauma

There are lifelong repercussions to warfare and the numbers who need assis-tance are beyond the capacity of worldwide mental health systems. War is dev-astating to civilian populations. Essential services such as power and water are often compromised. Women and children are often the most vulnerable. Chil-dren may be orphaned, and women of all ages are exposed to war-related vio-lence, including rape and physical abuse. The health of women and children is greatly compromised in these situations.

### Climate Change

The world community is turning its attention toward the impact of climate change on the mental health of people throughout the world. Factors that increase a community's susceptibility to the psychological effects of climate change include large populations of older adults, children and infants, the disabled, recently arrived immigrants, migrants, and refugees. Also, coun-tries where there are high levels of poverty, social inequality, low education levels, and a lack of access to health care are also at risk. The American Psy-chological Association & EcoAmerica (Clayton, Manning, & Hodge, 2014) reported that the likely impacts of climate change on adults and children include PTSD; distress; depression and anxiety; hopelessness; increases in violence, aggression, and crime; and strains on social relationships. Our work in Haiti and the Philippines certainly brings light to the issues high-lighted in their report. When vast numbers of people are displaced and there is a great loss of life and decrease in physical well-being, the numbers over-whelm existing systems of help.

As a world community, we must look at innovative interventions that can be used with large numbers of people not only to build a prevention infrastructure for mental health challenges, but to create capacity. We must not only have models that can provide professionally guided individual and group therapies, but also community-based models that use group formats that are peer-to-peer, and are thereby more accessible. The CRM lifts up entire communities by creating interventions that support our innate healing systems to promote individual and community resiliency (Leitch & Miller-Karas, 2010).

## The CRM Train the Skills Trainer Program

The CRM Train the Skills Trainer program consists of 32 hours of training and a fifth day as the student teaching day (40 hours total). The training is a combination of lecture, discussion, practice, and student teaching. During the course, the trainees learn the key concepts of the CRM, the biology of traumatic/stressful reactions, the skills of the CRM (see Chapter 3; the first six skills of the TRM are the CRM skills), and teaching methods to enhance their training abilities. The trainees also practice the skills within a larger group and individually within small practice groups. CRM training also includes information about how to access one's community mental health system, if there is one. Trainees are educated about the warning signs of suicidal or homicidal risk and how to make referrals to a different level of care. The training sessions are lively and the teaching methods include the expressive arts. The CRM methods can be used for adults and children.

After each component of training, the trainees spend time creating teaching plans in pairs, and then teaching the material back to the master CRM trainers. This approach builds competency in teaching the skills and in explaining the CRM concepts. The fifth and final day of training is student teaching, during which the trainees break out into pairs and prepare a one-hour CRM orientation that can be delivered to their community. The student teaching is evaluated by the master CRM trainers based on objectives that have been previously handed out to the trainees. Individualized plans are created to help the motivated trainer if they need more time to develop competency. The master CRM trainers help the trainees identify places within their community where they can share the CRM skills. A statement of understanding is explained in the beginning of the training that outlines the program and indicates that attendance does not guarantee a person will be made a trainer. Competency in teaching the skills and concepts must be demonstrated before a person can graduate to the level of a CRM skills trainer (CST).

Follow-up sessions are incorporated into the training plan. The follow-ups are set up on an "as needed basis"—at least within three months and quarterly for a year after the last day of training. Technical assistance in implementing

CRM trainings is offered via phone, in-person consultation, and email. The website (www.communityresiliencymodel.org) is another tool to help CSTs and community recipients of the training reinforce their skills. The skills can also be reinforced through an app available for iPhone and Android devices, and personal computers, called iChill (www.iChillapp.com). The trainings are offered in many countries and in many languages. All training materials are translated in the commonly used dialect of the individuals being trained.

### Culture, Religion, and Language

A culture is expressed through religion, law, music, language, art, health beliefs, and customs. Culture is transmitted formally and informally to succeeding generations. Culture influences what we eat; how we work and play; how we raise our children; how we celebrate life events; and how we view traumatic events (Mead, 1928). When we embark on projects in the global community, learning about a people's culture is critical to increasing our cultural sensitivity when we deliver CRM trainings.

"Cultural sensitivity" is the ability to empathize with and understand the beliefs, customs, language, and rituals of a particular culture. Before embarking on a CRM project, to increase our cultural sensitivity, we require our training teams to perform a personal evaluation of attitudes and beliefs about working within cultures that may have divergent attitudes and beliefs from their own. Sensitivity includes designing culturally relevant training materials, which incorporate images of people who reflect the local training community. Our training materials are translated into the local dialects. For example, in preparation for our CRM trainings in the Philippines, we discovered there are over 171 dialects in the region. Our trainees helped identify the most pertinent dialects for our project in the typhoon-impacted area, and we translated our materials into four dialects.

Individuals, families, and communities interpret the aftermath of a traumatic event through a cultural screen. Culture and experience shape notions about causality. Learning about local dialects and common idioms used to describe suffering can help us craft CRM interventions incorporating the perceptions from each culture. New information can be introduced and can coexist with cultural views of health and illness. Each culture has a wide array of folk illnesses and remedies that guide perceptions of "why" traumatic stress symptoms occur. For example, the "evil eye" (one of the most widely held cultural beliefs across cultures) causes an imbalance inside the body, disrupting health. Many Latinos believe that a "susto" (sudden unexpected fright) or "coraje" (angry feelings) causes an imbalance within in the body that leads to illnesses. Many cultures believe that ghosts from people who died unexpectedly can invade the human body and cause illness and weakness. Each culture has its own array of folk remedies to ameliorate the effects of folk illnesses.

*After learning CRM skills, and feeling better in his body and mind, a villager inquired of one of our trainers if he could see the ghost of his dead brother leave his body. He believed his traumatic stress symptoms were caused by the spirit of his brother. The CRM trainer invited the villager to notice the change in his body. The villager smiled and took a deep breath.*

The astute CRM trainer supported both explanatory models—the villager's cultural beliefs of causation of the symptoms emanating from his dead brother's ghost, and the lens of the CRM—and brought in tracking to support the change in the villager's nervous system.

As a result of civil wars in neighboring countries and immigration, populations may face additional challenges due to the stress of migration or immigration. Minority groups from displaced communities may be experiencing prejudice from the dominant culture. Because of colonialism and slavery, people may be mistrustful and angry when interacting with humanitarian aid workers because of past negative encounters with a particular ethnic group or citizen of a particular country. If a governmental agency has brought our training to those who are suffering and the response has been delayed, people may justifiably feel that the lack of response is because of prejudice. Cultural attitudes towards women can shape help-seeking behaviors as well and whether women can even access trainings given by Westerners. Many countries do not have child protective laws or laws to protect women from intimate partner violence. There can be tremendous shame in revealing that one has been sexually assaulted or physically abused.

Regardless of cultural or ethnic background, people have a curiosity about how the human nervous system works. Respecting long-held cultural beliefs is how we join and make connections with individuals from different cultures. We introduce the biology of the human nervous system as a coexisting concept. Many of our trainers come from diverse cultural backgrounds and help us understand the cultural nuances that are important in cross-cultural information sharing. TRI's inclusivity has been helpful in bridging cross-cultural divides. We have also made cultural errors and have asked with humility how we could do or say something differently. We have often received a "cultural pass" when we have asked for forgiveness and respectfully asked how we could improve. We have witnessed an enthusiasm when we have an open mind and heart about learning about the customs of other cultures. We also have learned not to overgeneralize cultural information because within one culture, there can be many variations.

We have trained people who have a broad range of religious practices. Although there can be a "crisis of faith" after experiencing traumatic event, one's faith is often the only thing that sustains the human spirit. Asking open-ended resiliency questions like, "Who or what is helping you the most right now?" can trigger an abundance of responses. A Christian might say, "I have Jesus right here in my heart!" and immediately take a deep, relaxing breath and lay her hand on her chest. In China after the Sichuan earthquake, a woman responded to the same question, saying, "The teachings of Buddha are helping me now," as she took a deeper breath and her muscles relaxed. Thus, we have observed throughout the world as people describe deeply held spiritual beliefs, there is a universal response of a deep parasympathetic breath accompanied by muscle relaxation. When awareness is brought to the sensation connected to one's beliefs, the experience is strengthened and felt more deeply. Like cream rising to the top, individuals will then spontaneously generate new meanings like, "With God's help I will make it through this." The internal locus of control and empowerment that springs forth is remarkable when taking into consideration the hardship of people's lives. If a person has lost their faith as a result of their traumatic experiences, we ask additional resiliency questions like, "Who is helping you the most now?" and "Is there anyone you are able to help right now?" Often a spark of hope can be ignited when reminded of help received and given.

When orienting people within the African-American community to the CRM trainings, our team visited a dedicated group of ministers and deacons. The group decided that we could return and bring the CRM skills training to their community. After the first day, the size of the class doubled. I was curious about the overnight expansion. One of the leaders of the community approached me and said, "I wasn't too sure about what you were up to with the CRM. You know we will have none of that yoga or meditation in our churches here and we had to make sure you were not going to do anything like that with the CRM." I realized that she and others had decided that the CRM was not in opposition to their beliefs. I appreciated her candor. Accordingly, this underscores the need for designing interventions that take into consideration the "one size does not fit all" perspective. For example, although mindfulness practices are well researched to be beneficial, they will not always be well received no matter how one might try to secularize the practice because it can be perceived as being connected to Buddhism. The African-American community is very protective regarding what interventions are brought into their community. Accordingly, it was also clear that the ministers and deacons read scripture to make sure that CRM skills were in alignment with their Christian beliefs. For example, Loistine Herndon, one of the activists from the African-American Christian community contributed to our training materials by sharing scripture that supports the CRM skill of resourcing:

*"Finally, brothers and sisters, whatever is true, whatever is noble, whatever is right, whatever is pure, whatever is lovely, whatever is admirable—if anything is excellent or praiseworthy— think about such things. Whatever you have learned or received or heard from me, or seen in me—put it into practice. And the God of peace will be with you" (Philippians 4:8).*

As individuals learn the skills, trainees themselves make the CRM more relevant to their own community, inspired by their unique cultural lens. Ben Romero, who was then an active-duty marine at 29 Palms in California, asked me if he could "Marine-ize" the CRM slides. I said, "Go ahead Ben. Make them relevant to the women and men you are serving." A group of young Mayan women in Solala, Guatemala, redesigned the resilient zone using Lake Atitlan, which is a magnificent body of water, central to the villages and towns of this region. The lake when it is calm is the resilient zone; the lake on stormy days is the high zone and during times of drought, when the water recedes from the shore, it is the low zone. These young women are community trainers and they visit homes of the girls in their programs, helping the families understand how they can reduce stress and now stabilize their nervous system using Lake Atitlan as the metaphor for the resilient zone!

We have been inspired by two additional projects, one in El Paso, Texas, training counselors from Juarez and the other, mentioned above, in Solala, Guatemala, where a group called "Starfish One-by-One" is training indigenous Mayan women. Marina Compean, a Mexican-American bilingual social worker working within the inner city of Los Angeles, has traveled with TRI, bringing the CRM to our international communities in Mexico and Guatemala. She conducts the CRM trainings in her first language, Spanish. Marina expressed:

*"Disseminating the Community Resiliency Model to Spanish speaking/Latino organizations has been transformative and inspirational. In Guatemala we met with young women from indigenous villages whom despite subsisting in the informal economy, were so 'resource rich,' vibrant, and alive as they learned and practiced these skills. With counselors from Juarez, working against social conditions in which femicide thrives, we heard stories of how these skills helped thera-pists fill in the gaps for healing, allowing the 'senses to tell the*

*story' of unpunished crimes of gender violence. Most powerful in working on these projects, was witnessing how each group adapted the concepts, infusing the model with their unique culture, landscape, and local expertise. It fills me with great gratitude to speak in my native language, sharing neuroscience research-informed, resiliency-focused self-care skills. Across borders, in different languages and dialects, I have experienced and witnessed the immediacy and transformative power of this resiliency-focused, biological approach."*

### Communal Learning

In the West, many of our models of intervention are designed for emancipated, single individuals who live separately from their families. Mental health counseling is a foreign concept to many from the worldwide community, and seeing someone for an individual problem is not customary. In addition, there is great stigma for many who are perceived to have a mental health challenge. Often, individuals suffer in silence because of the shame. In some cultures, individuals are shunned if they appear to have a mental health challenge. The CRM can be presented in a group format and normalizes and de-stigmatizes the common reactions that result from cumulative "large-T" and "small-t" traumas. In addition, when members of a group bear witness to the whole group returning to its resilient zone like the beginning example from Haiti, each member of the group begins to have a changed nervous system. In our trainings, I track closely what is happening within the group, and when I notice deeper breaths, smiles, and muscle relaxation, I bring awareness to those changes so that each person can sense into his or her resiliency. Resiliency can be contagious because when we shift a whole group's awareness to the inherent wisdom of the body, there is an improvement in well-being, as is beginning to be evidenced in our research. We can also weave neuroscience nuggets into our trainings by discussing mirror neurons and the elegant design—that we are wired for empathy and resiliency. Bringing attention to our own resiliency not only impacts the individual, but the wider community. As one Haitian trainer shared with us, "These skills have helped me with people who surround me in my life, whether it's a co-worker, family, or friends. If they have a problem, they come to me and call me Mr. Get Well!"

### Resiliency-Informed Groups—Shifting Awareness to the Survival Story

The sheer numbers of individuals impacted after disasters calls for bringing CRM skills into group settings. CRM skills can be intertwined into group settings by incorporating the expressive arts of song, movement, and art. Community sharing in this way can enliven the survivors and propel community members to begin to work for the reconstruction of their communities. Energies can then be focused on rebuilding. Chapter 4 highlights some of the activities we use for children, and many of the activities can be adapted to working with adults. The "resiliency questions" can also be interwoven into group settings to expand resiliency and nervous system regulation rather than to amplify the retelling of the trauma story that often results in nervous system dysregulation. Another example of the group format follows:

*After the Boston Marathon bombing of 2013, I flew to Boston to work with a group of humanitarian aid workers. Their office was a block from the bombing site. The staff lived in the neighborhoods surrounding the bombing site as well as in the areas of Boston that were in lockdown after the bombing. After brief introductions, we began by asking an "open-ended" question, encouraging expression of what was on people's minds. A few individuals spoke up and talked about an increase in fear and anger for a myriad of reasons. I then shifted the conversation to the "resiliency questions." I asked, "How are you getting through this? What is helping right now as Boston recovers?" A vibrant stream of heartwarming reflections came forth of neighborhood generosity, faith, and profound love and admiration for the spirit of Bostonians. As the group leader, I tracked and noticed deeper breaths, smiles, and laughter. I oriented the group briefly to the importance of sensing the change inside as the resiliency reflections were shared. After working with the group in this way, group members began offering powerful solutions of community organization and family and individual support. One of the group members had attended previous trainings with me and suggested that each person think about a personal resource so when things became difficult in the days and weeks ahead, awareness could not only be brought to the individual's personal resource, but to the memory of this group sharing. The group's energy was shifted from the trauma story to the resiliency survival story. The shift was palpable.*

## CRM Innovation Project and the Veterans' Extension Project, Funded by the State of California Mental Health Services Act and the Department of Behavioral Health (DBH), San Bernardino County (Citron, 2013)

The Community Resiliency Training (CRM) Innovation Project and the Veterans' Extension Project were initiated in December 2010 and February 2012 through the California Mental Health Services Act through the Department of Behavioral Health (DBH) in San Bernardino County, California. The DBH serves the underserved population of the largest county in the United States. Their constituents are the chronically mentally ill and community stakeholders with mental health challenges. Implemented by DBH and the TRI, the goals of the projects were to bring the CRM training to marginalized groups in San Bernardino County who have limited access to mental health resources. The intent was to expand the community's capacity to meet mental health challenges by offering training in CRM skills. The CRM skills training would address the needs of community members needing mental health education and coping skills. The groups were chosen because they were likely experiencing the effects of the cumulative trauma that is associated with racism, homophobia, poverty, and untreated post-traumatic stress from military service, including combat.

The DBH has a long-standing TRM program (which include the skills of the CRM) in which it has its own cadre of TRM trainers, and over 600 of its professional and case management staff have been trained in the TRM. The DBH conducted a survey in 2012 to determine its professional staff's perceptions of the usefulness and effectiveness of the TRM. At that time, the department had 500 TRM-trained staff with 242 responding to the survey. The survey found that TRM skills were versatile in that 83% of the respondents use the TRM skills they learned, with 76.5% using the skills at work and 61% using the wellness skills outside of work. When the respondents were asked if they found the TRM useful, 85.5% of the respondents found the TRM effective (Ruffalo, 2012). Their experience with the effectiveness of the TRM propelled them to suggest the CRM Innovation Project to the State of California to determine whether some of the TRM skills could be transferable as a peer-to-peer community training model.

### CRM Innovation Project, 2010–2013

Trainees representing marginalized groups were recruited and trained. The six groups were Latino, African-American, GLBTQ (Gay, Lesbian, Bisexual, Transgender, Questioning), API (Asian Pacific Islander), veterans, and at-risk youth. There were 109 participants: 60% of the participants were female and 40% were male, and the age of the participants ranged from 22 to 75 years, with an average age of 53. Eighty-six percent of the participants were non-Caucasian. The participants reported an array of physical and emotional symptoms, reflecting the extensive impact on the mind-body system when one is a member of a vulnerable group in a high-poverty county. Participants reported an average of six physical distress symptoms and an average of five emotional distress symptoms. Three data points were analyzed: pre-training, immediately post-training, and a three- to six-month follow-up.

Results of training evaluations received immediately after the last training session indicated the following:

- 96% of the respondents believed that the CRM skill training would be very to moderately relevant or useful for their work with people in their community.
- 90% said they thought they would use the skills very to moderately frequently during the month following the training.
- 94% of the trainees reported that they would be able to use the skills learned from the training for their own self-care.

When asked to report on other specific ways they thought the CRM training would help their work with people in the community, at the end of the training, they reported the CRM skills would be useful in the following ways:

- to help reduce distress (82%) and anxiety (81%)
- when facing a challenge (75%)
- in building hope (73%)
- to help reduce anger (67%)
- to help reduce depression (64%)
- to help reduce physical pain (60%)

Pre- to post-comparison analyses showed statistically significant decreases in the average number of depression, hostility, anxiety, and somatic symptoms, and statistically significant increases in the average number of symptoms related to relaxed, contented, somatic well-being, and friendly indicators. The most significant area of improvement was related to the depression indicator.

Our analysis showed that the positive distress and well-being findings were not quite as strong three to six months after the training as immediately post-training; however, comparison analyses between the pre-training and follow-up data showed positive trends in the desired direction of improvement in every distress and well-being indicator, with statistically significant decreases in anxiety, depression, and hostility symptoms in the follow-up period as compared with the pre-training period.

Additional three- to six-month follow-up data received across the six groups indicated that over 90% of the respondents believed that the CRM skills helped them in managing stress, maintaining better self-control, and getting through hard times. A high percentage (84%) used the skills frequently (30% used the skills daily and 54% used the skills several times per week).

*Veterans' Extension Project Initiated in 2012*

There were 46 participants; approximately 58% of the participants were female and 42% were male, and the age of the participants was 28–74 years, with an average age of 53. The participants reported an array of physical and emotional symptoms, reflecting the extensive impact of high stress on the mind-body system when one is a veteran in a high-poverty county. Participants reported an average of six emotional distress symptoms and five physical distress symptoms.

Results of training evaluations received immediately after the last training session indicated that all of the respondents believed that the CRM skill training would be very to moderately relevant or useful for their community, and all said they thought they would use the skills very to moderately frequently during the month following the training. One hundred percent of the trainees also reported satisfaction with their understanding of the CRM skills and said they would be able to use the skills learned from the training for their own self-care. When asked to report on other specific ways they thought the CRM training would help their work with people in the community, at the end of the training, they answered as follows:

- 97% said it would help reduce someone's distress
- 94% said it would be useful with anxiety and depression
- 88% said it would be useful with anger
- 85% said it would be useful to build hope
- 82% said it would be helpful for someone facing a challenge
- 79% said it would helpful with physical pain

In order to assess effectiveness of treatment, trainees were assessed immediately after training was completed, and again three to six months later. Results indicated that immediately after training, symptoms of distress improved at the level of significance in the areas of anxiety, depression, and hostility. Combined, the three groups reported positive improvement in the distress indicators of anxiety (74% reporting fewer anxiety symptoms post-training), depression (69%), somatic (52%), and hostility (65%). The most significant areas of improvement were related to hostility and depression symptoms.

Participants also reported improvements in their daily functioning after participating in the trainings. The largest improvements were related to participants' ability to self-regulate emotions of agitation, anger, impulsivity, and proclivity toward self-medication through substances. The ability of participants to note when they are getting amped up (hyperarousal), and then being able to settle themselves down, was the most significant and sustained measure reported. This change of increased emotional regulation was statistically significant immediately following the training and remained constant at follow-up three to six months later.

Additional results of follow-up data three to six months after the training indicated that over 90% of the respondents either completely or somewhat agreed that the CRM skills were useful in managing stress (100%), maintaining better self-control (94%), and getting through hard times (91%). At follow-up, 82% said they used the skills daily (21%) or few times a week (61%).

The results of the Veterans' Extension Project suggest that continuing to provide CRM trainings to veterans and their families within San Bernardino County, with adequate follow-up support, could have a powerful impact by reducing agitation, anger, impulsivity, and behaviors related to substance abuse within a wider veteran population. Most importantly, the ability to regulate these emotions could impact the community in reducing behaviors linked to hyperarousal and impulsivity including child abuse, domestic violence, road rage, and other highly destructive behaviors that have a great cost to society. The fact that at the three-month follow-up, 82% of the trainees reported that they were using the skills daily to a few times per week suggests that the CRM skills may have a lasting effect on reducing behaviors that result from being either stuck in the low or high zone.

The results of the research suggest that offering CRM trainings to the underserved within San Bernardino County, and providing adequate support networks following the initial training, could have a potentially powerful impact in reducing the symptoms of depression and anxiety within a wider population. In this Train the Trainer model, most of the trainees reached the level of competency to become CSTs. The fact that so many lay people across all of these marginalized groups have been able to learn the CRM skills well enough to become CSTs who can then teach the skills to others in their cohort speaks to the ease of learning of the CRM model, as well as its simplicity, accessibility, and cultural sensitivity. It is important to underscore that 86% of the trainees were nonwhite, and that each cohort trained, representing different ethnicities, was equally enthusiastic about the effects of the training. Citron (2013) emphasized the importance of evaluating the effectiveness of the first-tier CSTs when they teach the skills to groups in their own cohort. When it can be demonstrated that they can indeed impact a second tier of the underserved within San Bernardino County, there will be evidence that the CRM model can help create stronger, healthier, more resilient communities. We will continue to pursue this research, and we can now with confidence say that we are "research informed." For copies of the full reports, go to www.traumaresourceinstitute.com. Stephanie Citron,

PhD, is TRI's research consultant, and she is the author of both the "CRM Innovation Final Report" and the "Veteran Extension Project Final Report."

DBH conducted community stakeholder meetings on the innovation projects in the summer of 2013. From the stakeholder meetings and the preliminary research conducted on the CRM Innovation Project, DBH decided for the fiscal year beginning July 2014 to make CRM an official county program. TRI is conducting refresher trainings for approximately 40 of the CSTs originally trained. This will enhance the CSTs' skills and provide the CSTs with closer follow-up and support. The CSTs began providing CRM skills training in the outpatient mental health clinics in August of 2014. DBH will conduct an outcome evaluation on the effectiveness of the CSTs' CRM skills classes.

## In Their Own Words

Randy Imhoff was an active-duty chaplain and the head of the chaplains at Fort Drum, New York, when I first met him at one of our trainings many years ago. Randy has now retired from the army and is a psychotherapist and a CRM and TRM master trainer. He expressed the following in relationship to working with veterans, active-duty service members, and their families:

> *"I like CRM because it is simple to teach, simple to use, and it works. I like it because the explanations make sense to the average person. I like it because people can see immediate results even when learning the skills. It gives them something to take with them that they can use right away to help manage anxiety and depression. Mostly, it provides hope for those struggling with the biological reactions that occur because of traumas, stresses, and triggers."*

This testimonial and those that follow propel us forward and we have now trained a wide variety of individuals including ministers, priests, chaplains, teachers, police officers, firefighters, community leaders, veterans, doctors, nurses, and therapists. Participants who attend our CRM trainings share with us the profound personal impact of learning the wellness skills. We highlight the impressions of individuals trained in the CRM from two countries—one the richest in the Western Hemisphere (the United States), and the other, Haiti—the most economically challenged in the Western Hemisphere. Our project has spanned four years in Haiti. The majority of our work took place between 2010 and 2012. A follow-up team left for Haiti in July 2014. Fifty-two of the 61 original CRM trainers returned for follow-up. The Haitian CSTs were given updated information and we learned that the majority were actively teaching and sharing the wellness skills in many parts of Haiti. The reflections from both groups reveal how learning a simple set of skills can be transformative and empowering.

From the United States:

*"This is the first time in 40 years that I understand my symptoms, and you taught me that in two days." (Vietnam War veteran)*

*"I've had all kinds of therapy, and this model is the first time I've been able to share something with my wife and feel that she understands me better." (Vietnam War veteran)*

*"Learning about the freeze response is the first time I felt that the slowing down of time I experienced was explained." (First Gulf War veteran)*

*"I'm kind of a hot head, and these skills helped me when I was disappointed about not having dinner with my grandson. I was able to have good conservations with my son and daughter about it." (Veteran)*

*"This class has been a million times more valuable than I ever imagined. I've read a lot about PTSD and this is the first new material I've heard in a long time. While in a massage class I became stuck on high but I was able to go outside and ground and resource myself and go back to class. In the past I would have left angry and never completed the training. I have a history of not completing things due to my PTSD symptoms." (A woman who suffers from PTSD)*

*"I went into a panic at a meeting but was able to pull a fellow CRM class member outside of the room to help me. I got back in my resilient zone in a few minutes where before my symptoms would have put me in bed for days. My husband was shocked at how fast it worked." (A woman with PTSD)*

*"Before this class started, I was feeling really burned out and thinking that I needed to take a break from the work and people in general. Now I can use tracking, grounding, and resourcing to help myself so I no longer carry the burden from work to the car to home. I had forgotten what feelings should be like toward others. I take more time for me now, and the skills help me with self-awareness. I found that the skills help me to maintain a healthy distance from clients so that I can continue to help people." (Social worker with vicarious trauma)*

From Haiti (each quote is from a different CRM Skills Trainer):

> *"Before learning these skills when I'd be facing a difficult situation, I could not find a way out nor could I help someone else in the same situations. Thanks to these skills, I no longer have this problem."*
>
> *"Learning this model has helped me set goals, something that was hard for me to do before. I am a calmer person now because I use the skills for myself. I am less shy now and I don't underestimate myself anymore."*
>
> *"I have more love for others now. I have more respect and understand others better now. I have more self assurance and I am proud of myself."*
>
> *"Learning this model has brought equilibrium to my life: at work, school and in my everyday activities. The skills have helped me recognize different sensations in my body and I am able to help myself in times of need."*
>
> *"I have helped people in my community who have lost loved ones, get back into their resiliency zone. I use the skills to help people cope with rape, deaths, and conflicts."*
>
> *"I have learned that no matter your social rank, we are all humans and we can learn to live together. I have learned not to make fun of handicapped people or anyone else with a disability. We all need one another to make life more beautiful."*

## The Past, the Present, and the Future

> *"I hope that when TRI leaves Haiti they will continue to teach people these skills worldwide. I would like to encourage the team to train around the world. I believe that with these skills, we can change the world"* (Haitian trainee, 2012).

The truth is that since Haiti, TRI has been teaching the CRM skills worldwide. The Haitian people in so many ways were our teachers for refining our thoughts and concepts so that they would and could expand to other parts of the world. DBH in the County of San Bernardino gave TRI the opportunity to see if the wellness skills of the TRM could be effectively brought to community members who are categorized "at risk." Every country we have been welcomed into has taught us so much about how to bring the CRM to more populations. I often say at our trainings, "My goal is to be obsolete and my hope is that we will share with you everything we know and you can decide what is relevant for yourself, your family, and your community and adapt the trainings using your cultural screen." We are building an international network. Our CSTs are expanding CRM skills to their families, neighborhoods, and wider communities. Some of the people and places that CSTs have brought CRM skills to are elementary, middle, and high schools; prisons; churches; veterans' centers; domestic violence recovery support groups; alcohol and drug treatment programs; neighborhood groups; holistic centers; university counseling centers; rape crisis centers; domestic violence shelters; child welfare workers; human rights attorneys; crisis response teams; and outpatient mental health centers. In the Philippines, our group of CSTs have incorporated a non-governmental organization, PHILACTS, which stands for the Philippine Association of Community Resiliency Model Skills Trainers. They have now trained over 600 individuals in CRM skills since January 2014. The list continues to grow.

We have learned that economic challenge does not mean resiliency challenged. When you make "sense" of something, it feels right. Sensation awareness is what holds CRM apart from other models, and that awareness changes people worldwide. . . . We are all part of that elegant design. Ellen Elgart, one of TRI's master trainers who headed up the Haiti project, describes the ripple effects of CRM trainings, "From body to resiliency to compassion to hopefully more peace and justice." This is our hope and our dream. As one of our funders, the Unitarian Universalist Committee, recently stated in one of their newsletters addressing the CRM's impact, "People who have the skills to heal themselves from trauma are more likely to connect, to endure the struggles they face, and to effect real change in their communities. This bodes well for all invested in the vision of a world where all people can realize their human rights" (Atcheson, 2014).

Haiti, the Philippines, Washington, DC, Maryland, Kenya, Japan, China, Darfur, Somalia, Uganda, the Congo, Guatemala, Mexico, Texas, Germany, New Mexico, Idaho, California, New York, North Carolina, Montana, Oregon, Canada—the list grows. We have now taught people CRM skills at domestic violence programs like Peace over Violence in Los Angeles and the Vera House in Syracuse, New York. We have presented the skills to the Peer Counselor Police Officers of the Syracuse Police Department; to Head Start workers in New York; to WIC workers in California. We have CSTs at Children's Hospital in Los Angeles and at Mountain Area Health Education Center (MAHEC), in Asheville, North Carolina. We have been asked to go to Lebanon; to the Western Balkans; Istanbul, Turkey; Rwanda; and to the Ukraine. We will see what is in store for our growing troop of "CRMers" as they are now calling themselves. I have been reluctant to call our CRM trainings the beginning of a worldwide movement, but maybe it is just that! Stay tuned!

We have discovered that in the face of great suffering, tragedy and horror, the human spirit can be awakened back to resiliency and health and wellness by simply paying attention to the wisdom of the body.

(Elaine Miller-Karas, 2014)

## References

Atcheson, J. (2014, Winter/Spring). Starting to live again: Healing trauma after disaster. *Rights Now: The Newsletter of the Unitarian Universalist Service Committee.*

Citron, S. & Miller-Karas (2013). Final CRM innovation evaluation report: Community resiliency training innovation project.

Clayton, S., Manning, C.M., & Hodge, C. (2014). *Beyond storms and droughts: The psychological impacts of climate change.* Washington, DC: American Psychological Association and EcoAmerica.

Leitch, M.L. & Miller-Karas, E. (2010). *It takes a Community*, Psychotherapy Networker, November, December 2010 Issue.

Mead, M. (1928). *Coming of age in Samoa: A psychological study of primitive youth for western civilization.* New York: William Morrow & Company.

Ruffalo, M. (2012). *Department of Behavioral Health WET Center TRM survey 2012.* Department of Behavioral Health, County of San Bernardino, California.

# 8    Assessment and Interviewing

*Elaine Miller-Karas*

This chapter will define retraumatization, as well as vicarious and secondary traumatization, and discuss ways to conduct assessments and interviews that can minimize the effects of these kinds of traumatization.

> *In January of 2005, a researcher sat on a bamboo mat in a makeshift hut in Thailand, collecting information regarding a man's reaction to the tsunami of 2004. When the researcher began asking questions, the wife of the man began to weep, and she raced out of the hut; the man, visibly disturbed by the questions, fell silent. Witnessing this scene in which the researcher was unintentionally causing harm by her questions helped us crystalize our ideas about how best to collect information so as to reduce retraumatizing the interviewee.*

Duckworth and Follette (2012) describe retraumatization as traumatic stress reactions occurring in the aftermath of subsequent traumatic events after an initial experienced trauma. In addition to the questions posed in research, many governmental and non-governmental agencies, mental health programs, and legal proceedings require detailed information about a person's trauma history. Interweaving wellness skills into the interview can help reduce the risk of retraumatization for the interviewee. In addition, when the interviewer learns the wellness skills for self-care, he has the potential to reduce the secondary and vicarious traumatization that can occur when one bears witness to another's trauma story.

For clarity, we will use "interviewer" to refer to the role of the person conducting the interview or assessment, and "interviewee" for the person being questioned.

Interviewers from the fields of mental health, health, law, research, and emergency response recount stories of stopping the information gathering about traumatic events because the questions were too distressing for not only the interviewee but also for themselves (Figley (1995), Jaffe (2003), Levin (2003), McCann (1990), Saakvitne (1996)). A judge at The Hague was asked about his personal impressions of asking questions and listening to the testimony of witnesses. He began to speak and suddenly stopped, choking back tears; he then eloquently described the difficulty of witnessing video testimonies of atrocities. He described the secondary and vicarious trauma that can occur from witnessing a story even if the situation was not personally experienced.

Baird and Kracen (2006) differentiate vicarious traumatization and secondary traumatic stress. Vicarious traumatization consists of harmful changes that occur in the professionals' views of themselves, others, and the world as a result of exposure to the graphic and/or traumatic material of others. Secondary traumatic stress refers to a set of psychological symptoms consistent with PTSD and is acquired through exposure to persons suffering the effects of trauma. Boscarino, Adams, and Figley (2010) stated that therapists who work with traumatized patients also demonstrate psychological distress reactions, including symptoms of PTSD.

Numerous studies have reported the distress caused by asking questions about traumatic experiences. Murphy (2014) suggests that children endure an extra risk of harm when testifying about their own victimization because testifying exposes them to at least some fear of reprisal, which could be a significant contributor to their psychological suffering in the aftermath of violence. She further addresses the issue of sexual abuse and that these victims endure even more harm because they are disproportionately exposed to harsh and intimate questions. Delays in legal proceedings are common and have been highly associated with retraumatization as is having to testify for an extended period of time.

Galecki (2004) addresses the issues faced by individuals seeking asylum. She describes cases in which victims with PTSD were completely paralyzed with fear when asked to describe their experiences of torture. Many of them were unable to tell their stories and were then denied asylum. Additionally, she highlights two major factors that are important in asylum cases—coherence and details. Both of these factors are a challenge for torture victims who suffer from PTSD or other psychological disorders and may compromise their chances of getting asylum. Bögner, Brewin, and Herlihy (2010) found that those with a history of sexual violence reported more difficulties in disclosing personal information during asylum interviews, were more likely to dissociate during these interviews, and scored significantly higher on measures of PTSD symptoms and shame than those with a history of non-sexual violence. Feelings of shame and traumatic stress reactions can make it difficult for individuals to disclose personal details in interviews.

Newman (2008), however, states that evidence suggests that there is a low probability of significant emotional harm from participating in trauma-focused studies. She goes on to state that unexpected distress may occur for some participants, and that this distress appears tolerable and is linked with positive outcomes for most. To us, the statements "distress appears tolerable" and "positive outcomes for most" minimize the experience of those, however small in number, who are retraumatized. In addition, individuals who experience trauma are often so used to the physiological arousal and distress in recounting their stories that they may not report the experience as being intolerable because it is so customary.

Collecting information from trauma survivors can trigger a "memory capsule." A memory capsule contains the multisensory experience of the traumatic event as discussed in Chapter 2. A memory capsule can occur suddenly, unexpectedly, and steal away the safety of the present moment. Memory capsules can be triggered by a variety of internal and external triggers and can vary in intensity from mild physiological arousal to a full-blown traumatic flashback that is experienced as if the traumatic event was happening in the present moment (Scaer, 2007). Thus, information gathering about the traumatic event has the potential of triggering psychological distress. Shin (2006) reports that amygdala hyper-responsivity in PTSD has been reported during the presentation of personalized traumatic narratives and cues, combat sounds, combat photographs, and trauma-related words. So, when a person is asked to recount his trauma story, the amygdala is driving the bus, and the prefrontal cortex's ability to dampen the fear response triggered by the amygdala is compromised. Thus, a person being questioned, regardless of the reason, may respond with hyperarousal, distress, and avoidance behaviors. Incorporating the lens of neuroscience and interweaving the wellness skills into the information-gathering interview can reduce retraumatization and result in a more cogent narrative about the traumatic experience. As the nervous system stabilizes during the interview and the interviewee is able to come back to his resilient zone throughout the interview, the prefrontal cortex is more available to the client to recount the narrative of the experience. The interviewee will have a greater internal locus of control and does not have to feel like he is again swept away by the trauma story.

*A social worker and advocate from a rape crisis center shared that after learning the wellness skills, she was able to help women in the emergency room recount the details of the rape in a more modulated way without retraumatizing the survivors. She was surprised to find out that the survivors could recount more detailed, clearer narratives of what happened when they were helped to stay within their resilient zones. She also noted that as individuals were guided back to their resilient zones, new meanings about the experience would spontaneously emerge, such as "I survived," and "I had more strength than I imagined."*

The vitality of human existence and survival can be overridden by the existential experience of torture and horror. When one learns to track the well-being that also existed, and exists in the present moment, the person can begin to sense his own strength and power of having survived. This kind of approach has far-reaching implications for the fields of human rights and restorative justice.

Secondary and vicarious traumatization can be reduced when the interviewer learns the wellness skills and is able to stay within her resilient zone when asking provocative informational questions.

*After a training session for human rights attorneys in San Francisco, many of the attorneys shared stories of their clients' distress during asylum interviews. One attorney shared that she had integrated "resourcing questions" into her interviews after the training. She reported experiencing fewer symptoms of vicarious trauma and that her clients experienced less distress during the interviews.*

The human nervous system is elegantly designed, and when we use the lens of neuroscience in crafting our interventions, resiliency abounds. When individuals strengthen and widen the bandwidth of their resilient zones, there is a corresponding increase in well-being that spans the entire gamut of human existence (behaviorally, emotionally, cognitively, physically, and spiritually). Individuals make better decisions for themselves, their families, and their wider community. When we educate individuals about the possible pitfalls of repeating the trauma story without safeguards of self-regulation skills, we can help the interviewee learn there is a gentler, more humane way of gathering information.

## Interview Protocol

### Step 1: Psychoeducation and Beginning with the End

Explaining to the interviewee how the nervous system works can help him understand his reactions to recounting the trauma history. Explaining how multisensory cues can trigger the release of a memory capsule can help underscore the physiological and psychological impact of sharing information about traumatic events. Helping the interviewee understand the amygdala and its function (as a personal appraisal system that triggers an alarm when there is danger) also provides him with insight into his reactions as the story is told. Understanding the biology behind reactions can be another way of helping the nervous system come back into balance. The interviewer can introduce the concepts of CRM/TRM by briefly introducing simple information about the nervous system and the importance of taking resiliency pauses so that the nervous system can come back to the resilient zone if bumped into the high or low zones while telling the story. The following italicized paragraphs are an example of how to introduce the concepts.

*"The trauma story is a highly emotionally and physically charged experience. The challenge of collecting information is that for some people the body and mind can react as if the traumatic experience that occurred yesterday or years ago is happening in the present moment. It can be more difficult to recount the important elements of the trauma story because the physical and emotional reactions can be very strong. It can then be hard to think clearly. This is a common reaction and has to do with the human nervous system. The nervous system can get out of balance when we recall traumatic events. It is important for you to know that this reaction is not about personal weakness but is about the biology of the human nervous system.*

*When a person has the opportunity to pause during a difficult part of an interview, the nervous system can return to a more balanced state. Thus, the sharing of the story can be less stressful emotionally and physically. So, if recounting the details of your experience becomes too difficult, you can pause and take break or, with your permission, I will invite a 'resiliency pause' into the interview. A 'resiliency pause' gives your body and mind a break from the intensity of your story. A 'resiliency pause' can include asking you to describe peaceful or comforting experiences in your life that become your personal resources. I can also introduce a few other skills called grounding and Help Now! that may be helpful too."* (The interviewer can explain the two skills at this juncture if they are needed or wait until a later part of the interview.)

The interviewer can use "resiliency pauses" to weave in and out of the trauma story, to give the interviewee time for his nervous system to come back into balance before proceeding to the next part of the interview. So, as the person is invited to recall the traumatic memory, interweaving skills that focus on resiliency and nervous system stabilization is essential. Memory is not just "thinking" about something, but it is also all the sensory ingredients. The sensory ingredients of the traumatic experience can plague individuals who do not have a cogent narrative of what happened. When individuals understand that implicit memories (memory capsules) are triggered without intention and can occur underneath consciousness, the web of physical and emotional reactions can make sense to the interviewee and move him from a negative self-view to looking at his symptoms as common reactions to an extraordinary event. This cognitive shift can be an additional resource as the person shares his trauma history.

*"As we begin the interview, I would like to talk first about the part of the story that is about your survival—the part of the story that is about how you helped yourself and how others may have helped you get through this traumatic event. So, to begin with, I would like to ask you some questions that we call 'resiliency questions.'*

- *Can you tell me when you knew it was over?*
- *Can you remember the moment of survival?*

- *Who else survived?*
- *If children, other family members, or friends were involved and survived, can you remember the moment you knew that they had survived?*
- *Who helped you?*
- *Who is helping you now?*
- *Who did you help survive?*
- *How did you get to a safer place?"*

The "resiliency questions" above give direction as to how to begin building resources into the survival story. The interviewer may not need to ask every question. In asking about the ending first, the interviewer is building a survival resource as the person begins to tell the story. Often, survivors are so stuck in the trauma story that they do not realize there are other elements of the story, too. In addition, some individuals are surprised at the questions about survival because they have never thought of the fact that they, indeed, did survive. This approach also integrates into the story's narrative, the survival story. The survival story is often empowering and fills the person with energy and vitality. In some instances, a person may express that he does not feel like he survived. If this is the case, you can ask about who is helping him now. Asking the interviewee about his personal resources is another way to preload resiliency skills into the encounter before starting to interview about the trauma story. After the client learns about the resources, the interviewer can reinforce that she will at times remind the interviewee of his resources.

*"If I notice that the elements of the story are becoming too distressing to you, at times I will ask you to pause the recounting and to bring to mind one of the resources we have identified."*

Many interviewees have had difficulty with unpleasant feelings and sensations when relating their story, or they have spent a lifetime avoiding discussing the traumatic event for fear of being too overwhelmed. Thus, they may want to hurry and get the story out as fast as possible, even if it is at great cost to their emotional and physical well-being. Reminding the interviewee of the rationale behind "resiliency pauses" can be interwoven into the interview and can be helpful to the interviewee who thinks it will be less stressful to pour the story out. Knowing that there is a way, with intention, to help the nervous system regulate, can be very empowering for individuals who live daily with the haunting multisensory experience of trauma.

### Step 2: Beginning to Recount the Traumatic Event

After finding out about survival and other resources, the interviewer can then invite the client to go back to the beginning and share the trauma story.

*"We have discovered that you have many personal resources. Keeping this in mind, let us now go back to the story of what happened to you. So, where would you like to start?"*

As the person begins to recount the story, the interviewer not only pays attention to the content but also uses the first skill of tracking to pay attention to reactions that the interviewee may or may not be aware of (e.g., noticing more rapid, shallower breath; muscles tightening; changes in skin color, etc.). The interviewer can integrate a "resiliency pause" into the interview at any time. The "resiliency pause" can be explicit:

*"I wonder if this would be a good time to pause and remember the people who came to your aid that night."*

Or the pause can be simply woven in as the interviewer shifts the person's awareness to a survival resource in a conversational manner. For example:

*"Even though you thought you were going to die with your children, you managed to get your children out safely."*

As the person pauses, the interviewer will track the changes. As the interviewee takes a deeper breath and is visibly less agitated, the interviewer can say:

*"I noticed as you remembered how you survived, you took a deeper breath."* After allowing the person time to sense his body returning to greater balance, the interviewer can ask, *"Are you ready to go back to the story now? If so, what is the next part that you would like to talk about?"*

The interviewer has two important tracking tasks during the interview:

1. To monitor her own nervous system throughout and, if noticing sensations connected to being bumped out of her resilient zone, to use the wellness skills to bring her nervous system back into balance, and

2. To monitor the interviewee's nervous system through observation and periodically checking in to determine if he is in his resilient zone. A person can appear calm on the outside when he may be in a high state of arousal, so checking in with questions periodically is critical when gathering information. A question such as, *"As you have said this much, what are you aware of on the inside?"* helps the interviewee track and also become aware if sensations are too much. Since many people who experience trauma are used to overriding their awareness of sensations to just keep moving through the story, periodic check-ins are critical for greater self-awareness. Greater self-awareness by the interviewee, along with the interviewer's careful observation, can help the interviewer to determine when to shift into a "resiliency pause" and use one of the wellness skills to help regulate the interviewee's nervous system. This process continues throughout the interview.

In some cases, the interviewee may get extremely agitated and it may be more helpful to invite the client to walk with you around the room and pay attention as his feet are making contact with the floor. This is a "walking grounding" exercise that has proven to be effective when there is high activation of the nervous system. In addition to "walking grounding," some of the Help Now!

strategies, such as naming the colors in the room, counting backwards slowly from 20, or pushing one's hands against the wall slowly, can be interjected for nervous system stabilization. It is reassuring for the interviewee and the interviewer to know that the wellness skills are very concrete and can be integrated into the information gathering to help the nervous system calm down if in the high zone or amp up if in the low zone.

These strategies do not take much time and can actually help the interview move faster, as the person learns to regulate his nervous system throughout the information gathering.

### Step 3: Ending the Interview

As the interviewer guides the session to a close, she can help the interviewee by reinforcing the survival story and also by asking open-ended questions to determine if there are any new thoughts, feelings, or meanings that emerged since the interview began.

*"As we are getting ready to end today, are there any thoughts, feelings, beliefs, or new meanings about the experience that come to mind?"*

If more positive changes are present, suggesting that the interviewee notice the changes on the inside can help anchor these changes in sensation. This can be done in a conversational way that can help the interviewee expand his sensed internal resources. So, the interview can be of therapeutic value regardless of the reason for the information gathering. If there are no new positive changes, bring the interviewee's awareness to the survival aspects of his narrative as you bring the interview to an end.

*"As we come to a close, I am struck by your story of survival and what you shared with me today. There is a wisdom in remembering those parts as you go forward with your day."* (Depending on the story shared, you can highlight the elements of the survival story and add whatever words you would want to say as you bring the interview to a close.)

It is not uncommon for the interviewee to make comments in closing such as,

"This is the first time I have told this story without feeling like I would lose my mind," or

"I did not think I could handle saying out loud what had happened to me, and I did not want to affect another person with my horror. Thank you for helping me tell my story."

Interviewers repeatedly share that information gathering in the manner suggested in this chapter has brought a new awareness as to how to help the interviewee throughout this process. Many have stated that there is a new sense of shared hope about the present and the future. In addition, interviewers have been pleasantly surprised at the details that can be remembered when the interviewee relates his trauma story while in his resilient zone. There is a broader stroke of awareness as a person's lens expands about this often-defining life experience when he is not trapped in the high or low zone of dysregulation.

## References

Baird, K., & Kracen, A.C. (2006). Vicarious traumatization and secondary traumatic stress: A research synthesis. *Counselling Psychology Quarterly, 19*(2), 181–188.

Bögner, D., Brewin, C., & Herlihy, J. (2010). Refugees' experiences of home office interviews: A qualitative study on the disclosure of sensitive personal information. *Journal of Ethnic and Migration Studies, 36*(3), 519–535.

Boscarino, J.A., Adams, R.E., & Figley, C.R. (2010). Secondary trauma issues for psychiatrists. *Psychiatric Times, 27,* 24–26.

Duckworth, M.P., & Follette, M.V. (2012). Conclusions and future directions in the assessment, treatment, and prevention of retraumatization. In M.P. Duckworth & M.V. Follette (Eds.), *Retraumatization—Assessment, treatment, prevention.* New York: Routledge.

Figley, C.R. (Ed.). (1995). *Compassion fatigue: Coping with secondary traumatic stress disorder in those who treat the traumatized.* New York: Routledge.

Galecki, M. (2004). The victim's vicious cycle: The trauma and torture of seeking asylum in Germany. Humanity in Action. http://www.humanityinaction.org/knowledgebase/238-the-victim-s-vicious-cycle-the-trauma-of-torture-and-seeking-asylum-in-germany

Jaffe, P.G., Crooks, C.V., Dunford-Jackson, B.L., & Town, M. (2003). Vicarious trauma in judges: The personal challenge of dispensing justice. *Juvenile and Family Court Journal, 54*(4), 1–10.

Levin, A.P., & Greisberg, S. (2003). Vicarious trauma in attorneys. *Pace Law Review, 24*(1), 245–252.

McCann, L., & Pearlman, L.A. (1990). Vicarious traumatization: A framework for understanding psychological effects of working with victims. *Journal of Traumatic Stress, 3*(1), 131–149.

Murphy, W. (2014). Traumatized children who participate in legal proceedings are entitled to testimonial and participatory accommodations under the Americans with Disabilities Act. *Roger Williams University Law Review, 19*(2), 361. http://rogerwilliamslawreview.org/files/2013/12/murphypdf.pdf

Newman, E. (2008). Assessing trauma and its effects without distress: A guide to working with IRBs. *The Observer, 21*(5).

Saakvitne, K.W., & Pearlman, L.A. (1996). *Transforming the pain: A workbook on vicarious traumatization.* New York: W. W. Norton & Company.

Scaer, R. (2007). *The body bears the burden: Trauma, dissociation, and disease* (2nd ed.). Binghamton, NY: Haworth Medical Press.

Shin, L. M., Rauch, S. L., and Pitman, R. K. (2006). Amygdala, Medial Prefrontal Cortex, and Hippocampal Function in PTSD. *Annals N. Y. Academy of Sciences, 1071,* 67–79.

# 9 Integration of CRM/TRM Wellness Skills into Group Settings

*Elaine Miller-Karas*

The wellness skills of the CRM and TRM can be easily taught and practiced within a group format. The group format can be an adjunct to individual psychotherapy or a stand-alone group offering. The group format can be used across cultures and can be taught to adolescents as well as adults. CRM/TRM wellness groups have been especially well received by veterans and active-duty service members. Clinicians working at Walter Reed Medical Center and the VA have initiated such groups. The basic CRM/TRM Wellness Skills Group is a 10–14 hour program where participants learn the six wellness skills in order to increase individual, familial, and community functioning.

When deciding to put a CRM/TRM wellness group together to teach the six skills, practitioners should consider the following factors:

1. **Membership.** We recommend a closed group. Depending on the setting where the group will be offered, it is important to think about whether to have a mixed gender group or whether to separate men and women. When CRM/TRM wellness groups were introduced at the Veterans Administration, the clinician learned that the women wanted a gender-specific group because of the high incidence of military sexual trauma. Prescreening participants is suggested as a way for clinicians to give a brief description of the group along with information about sensations by introducing tracking and resourcing. If a person has difficulty with tracking and resourcing, a CRM/TRM wellness group may not be the best fit, as being able to sense pleasant and/or neutral sensations is fundamental for participation in the group.

2. **Structure.** There are seven group modules that follow. The group modules can be broken down for more than seven sessions depending on the time allotted for the group. The modules are designed for a 1.5-hour format. It is important to practice skill development in each module. The skills need to be experienced. Homework is assigned to enhance skill development. The iChill app can be suggested as one way to practice the skills outside of the group.

3.    **Content.** The content of the modules is divided into four phases:

- An overview of the key concepts to be covered in each module
- The objectives of each module
- The step-by-step script to be used in each module
- Homework

4.    **Size.** We recommend a group of no more than 10 members. The group leader must be very well versed in the CRM/TRM wellness skills. The leader must use her tracking skills to be aware of each member of the group. She must watch for nervous system activation and help the individual group members pause and come back to the resilient zone if they are getting bumped out. Thus, a smaller group is encouraged.

5.    **Schedule.** Some groups meet regularly on a specific day and time for the seven weeks or longer if the modules are divided into shorter sessions. Some groups want to continue meeting after learning the skills, as practicing in the group has increased their abilities with the skills. Some agencies have had open groups that continue with the wellness skills as part of their format.

6.    **CRM/TRM Group Leader.** The group leader must be well versed in the wellness skills. She must be able to track and sense her own body and be able to return to her resilient zone if she gets bumped out. Tracking the whole group as wellness skills are introduced is essential in order to be aware of individuals who are having difficulty. A co-leader of the group is suggested if possible. Some people who participate in groups want to tell every detail of their trauma story. CRM/TRM wellness groups discourage the retelling of the trauma story without inserting "resiliency pauses." Thus, if a group member begins to dive into a trauma story and the group leader tracks that other members are getting bumped out of their resilient zones, the leader can insert a "resiliency pause" in order to bring stabilization back to the group by using one or a combination of the skills.

7.    **Group Rules.** Each agency tends to have its own guidelines about confidentiality. The group leader must set the ground rules from the beginning and also clearly state that the CRM/TRM groups are confidential. Some individuals do not appreciate the importance of confidentiality. In addition, the concept of respect is introduced to encourage constructive feedback among the group members. It is important to underscore that CRM/TRM is not psychotherapy and is not designed to take the place of a mental health counselor.

8.    **Group Leader Availability.** When you begin a group with community members, some individuals may not like working with sensation. Be respectful and help them problem solve whether this is the right modality for their learning. The wellness skills are not for everyone. However, some individuals who want to continue working with CRM/TRM may be surprised by their response. Make sure that the participants have a way to contact you after the

session, as working with the body can bring up many questions. Some sensations can be distressing and some group members will need additional support.

## Module One

### *Overview*

1. Introduction
2. Introduction to the Community Resiliency Model (CRM)
3. A brief and simple introduction to:

    a. Resilient zone
    b. Stuck in the low/high zones
    c. Autonomic nervous system

4. The resilient zone scale
5. The CRM/TRM skills of tracking, resourcing, and resource intensification will be defined and practiced.

### *Objectives*

The participant will be able to describe the following:

1. The resilient zone
2. Being stuck in high/low zones
3. The accelerator and brake of the nervous system
4. One or more ways to track the nervous system
5. Resourcing and resource intensification
6. One objective of the CRM

### *Module One: Step-by-Step*

1. Introduce yourself and explain why you are presenting this model. Share with the participant a bit about yourself and how you became interested in CRM/TRM. To engage the participant, use one of the following resourcing questions:

    a. What or who helps you the most now?
    b. What or who is helping you get through?

2. Introduce CRM/TRM.

    *Script: What is CRM/TRM?*

    • CRM/TRM is based upon current research about the brain.
    • CRM/TRM is a method that will help you understand why you may feel anxious all the time or why you may feel depressed and disconnected or why you may feel both.

- You will learn the CRM/TRM skills and how to apply them to your daily life. The skills of CRM/TRM will help you interrupt reactions that may be troubling to you and which may have developed since

  _____.

- It is important for you to know that our nervous systems are designed to be reset and to come back to balance.
- CRM/TRM skills can help your body and mind return to balance. I will help you learn the skills and teach you how to track sensations that can help you feel more calm and resourced.

3. Explain the resilient zone.

   *Script*

   - It is important for you to know that no matter what your symptoms were as you walked in today, you have the capability to learn skills that will help you feel better in both body and mind. The human body and mind have an amazing capacity to heal.
   - The nervous system can be likened to a computer. It receives information and then processes that information and produces a result. It regulates the activities of the body and mind. There are some terms I want you to become familiar with today—the first is your resilient zone.
   - Every person has a resilient zone. When we are in our resilient zones, we can handle the daily life stresses without getting bumped out of our resilient zones.
   - People say that they feel like themselves again when they are in their resilient zone. Some people, after a traumatic experience like being in combat, may not be able to sense their resilient zone.
   - One of our goals is to help you find your resilient zone again or to expand the existing capacity of your resilient zone.

As you describe the normal wave of the resilient zone, you can draw it on a white board or poster paper.

4. Explain the resilient zone scale.

   *Script*

   - The resilient zone scale can be used to track whether you are in your resilient zone or whether you are stuck in the high or low zone. One of the goals is to expand or deepen your resilient zone so that you experience it more often. Your ability to handle life stresses and the triggers that may occur because of past traumas increases as you expand your resilient zone.
   - Paying attention to whether you are in your resilient zone or bumped out into the high or low zone is one way to gain greater awareness.

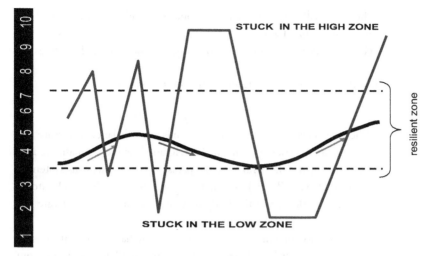

*Figure 9.1* The Resilient Zone Scale

Once you start regularly tracking your nervous system, you can be more aware of when you are in your resilient zone and also start paying attention to what knocks you out and, most importantly, learn the wellness skills to help you bounce back into your resilient zone.

- On a scale of 1–10, write down the number that describes whether you are in your resilient zone. The red yardstick shows that 1–3 represents stuck in the low zone, 4–7 represents your resilient zone, and 8–10 represents stuck in the high zone. As you learn the skills, the goal is to be within your resilient zone more often.

5.   Explain being "stuck in the high or low zone."

*Script*

- Many experiences can bump us out of our resilient zones (e.g., traffic, waiting for appointments, family members). When you get bumped out of your resilient zone by stressful or traumatic life events or reminders of those events (the thunderbolt), look at what happens to your resilient zone.
- You can get stuck in the high or low zone or go back and forth between the two. Let's look at the symptoms that go along with being stuck in the high and low zones.
- The good news is that CRM/TRM skills will help you get back into your resilient zone when you get bumped out.
- In CRM/TRM, we believe that your reactions are common reactions to extraordinary life experiences that happen after a traumatic event.

The skills will help you rebalance your body and mind and come back into your resilient zone.
- These reactions are about your biology, not about mental weakness.

6. Explain the brake and accelerator of the nervous system.

*Script*

- When we get stuck, our nervous system is not in balance. There are two parts of the nervous system: the "accelerator" or the sympathetic nervous system, and the "brake" or the parasympathetic nervous system.
- Being what we call "stuck in the high zone" is when the accelerator is down to the floor, and the body may react with a fast heart rate and rapid, shallow breathing.
- When we are in our resilient zone we can have different sensory experiences—our breathing may slow down and become deeper, our heart rate may slow down, and our muscles relax. Or our heart rate and breathing may be faster like when we experience joy, but the sensation is pleasant. The resilient zone is about our vitality and both biological reactions could occur and you are still within the zone.
- It is important to remember this is a system that is hard-wired in all of us. CRM/TRM skills can help you get this system back into balance. The nervous system can be reset.

7. Introduce the CRM/TRM skills of tracking, resourcing, and resource intensification.

*Script: For tracking*

- The first three skills we will learn today are tracking, resourcing, and resource intensification.
- In order to begin to bring your nervous system back into balance, you must first learn how to track your inner sensations. It is not uncommon for people to be very aware of discomfort and pain. However, many do not pay attention to the comfortable or neutral sensations within the body and mind.
- To reestablish your inner balance, it is necessary to pay attention to sensations of comfort and/or neutrality within your body. This stimulates the part of your nervous system that helps you rest and digest (the parasympathetic nervous system), which helps you get back into your resilient zone.
- Paying attention means bringing your awareness to the sensations associated with comfort (deeper breathing, slower heart rate, muscle relaxation, spaciousness).
- One of CRM/TRM's goals is to help you be the best tracker of your own nervous system.

- As we start, I will help you observe by bringing your attention to a deeper breath and any changes in body posture that may indicate you are bouncing back into your resilient zone.
- I will also ask you questions like "What are you noticing now?" to bring your attention to sensation change.

*Script: Explaining resourcing and resource intensification*

- A resource can be anything that helps a person feel better.
- It can be something the person likes about himself; a positive memory; a person, place, animal, or spiritual guide; faith; or anything that provides peace, joy, or calm.
- Can you tell me one resource that comes to mind?
- Resource intensification means providing more detail about your resource. We need to have more descriptions of your resource to override the sensations connected to discomfort. Can you tell me three or more details about the resource?
- Now I would like to invite you to notice what is happening inside as you think about the resource and your descriptions of the resource.
- Draw your attention to sensations that are pleasant or neutral to you.
- Notice what is happening to your breath, heart rate, and muscle tension. Stay with that for a few moments.
- What did you notice?

*CRM/TRM Alert: What if someone becomes distressed or cannot feel anything? If this happens, you can try one of the following:*

1. *Ask the person if he can touch the chair and ask him if he can feel the texture of the chair.*
2. *Ask for permission to touch the person's shoulder or hand and ask him if he can track the sensations.*
3. *Resources can have many natures. One example is if an individual's resource is his mother and she has died. The person can remember her fondly but also experience sadness at her passing. After honoring the sadness, the practitioner can gently shift the group member's attention back to his mother as a resource by asking him what qualities he loved about his mother and then tracking the sensations connected to those memories.*

### Homework—Module One

1. Practice sensing into your resource.
2. Make a list of other resources in your life. Tell one friend or family member about the resilient zone.
3. Familiarize yourself with the iChill app available on smart phones and accessible from website (http://www.ichillapp.com) via PC/Mac.

The information in module one can be delivered in one to two sessions.

## Module Two

### Overview

1.  Review the key concepts:

    a.  Resilient zone
    b.  Stuck in low/high zones
    c.  Autonomic nervous system

2.  Review the resilient zone scale.
3.  Review the CRM/TRM skills of tracking, resourcing, and resource intensification.
4.  Introduce grounding.

### Objectives

The group member will be able to describe the following:

1.  The autonomic nervous system
2.  Grounding and how to apply this skill to activities of daily living
3.  The resilient zone scale and its relationship to the resilient zone

### Module Two: Step-by-Step

1.  Ask the group to bring to mind one of their resources, to describe the resource to themselves, and notice what happens on the inside.
2.  Briefly check in with group members.
3.  Debrief homework from module one.

    a.  Were you were able to use resourcing skills during the past week?
    b.  Were you able to explain the resilient zone to anyone?
    c.  Were you able to make a list of other resources?
    d.  Did you download the iChill app?

    If the group members have not done their homework, you can do it with them at the beginning of the session.
    Use the resilient zone scale. Show the scale and have each group member rate himself.

4.  Review the autonomic nervous system and the concept of being stuck in the low/high zones.
5.  Introduce grounding.

As you read the script, make sure to give your group enough time between each bullet point, as it takes time for sensations to develop.

*Script:*

- Grounding is the direct contact of the body with something that provides support to the body. You can ground by sitting in a chair, standing against a wall, walking and paying attention to how your feet make contact to the ground, or lying down on the floor or on a bed.
- Grounding can help you stay in the present moment to experience physical and emotional safety. When you are grounding, you are in the present moment and you will not be thinking about or sensing things in the past or the future.

    - Find a comfortable position; take your time. As you find a comfortable position, bring your attention to a part of your body that feels more comfortable or neutral.
    - Notice how that part of your body is making contact with the chair, sofa, wall, floor.
    - Now bring your attention to how your back is making contact with the chair, sofa, wall. Slowly guide yourself down your body and notice how each part is making contact with a solid surface, and lastly, notice your feet making contact with the ground.
    - Notice the sensations that are more pleasant to you or neutral within your body. Take your time.
    - If you become aware of uncomfortable sensations, bring your attention to places that feel neutral or better. Take your time.
    - As you bring your attention to the contact of your body to the chair/floor/wall/bed, notice your breathing, heart rate, and muscle relaxation.
    - As we get ready to end, slowly scan your body and bring your attention to all sensations that are pleasant or neutral.

### Homework—Module Two

1. Practice the skill of grounding at least once when you are already feeling calm, just to remind yourself where the resource sensations are in your body. You may want to try resourcing and/or grounding as you are about to go to sleep. Using these skills at bedtime may help you sleep better.
2. When experiencing tension during the week, bring your attention to one of the resources you identified or practice grounding and track the sensations associated with the resource or with grounding.

3. The more you practice, the more you help your body move back into your resilient zone.
4. Use the iChill app at least once during the week.

*CRM/TRM Alert: For some individuals who have experienced high-intensity physical trauma, bringing attention to sensations in the present moment through grounding can trigger trauma sensations. If this is the case, you can shift the person's attention back to a resource or to the Help Now! strategies.*

## Module Three

### Overview

1. Discuss the organizing principles of the brain, highlighting the survival brain and the importance of sensation.
2. Discuss the defensive responses of "tend and befriend" and "fight, flight, and freeze."
3. Discuss sensations of release.
4. Review the resilient zone scale.
5. Review the CRM/TRM skills of tracking, resourcing, resource intensification, and grounding.

### Objectives

The group member will be able to describe/review the following:

1. The three parts of the brain ("thinking," "feeling," "survival")
2. The survival responses and the 1000-yard stare (freeze response)
3. Nervous system release
4. The CRM/TRM skills of tracking, resourcing, resource intensification, and grounding

### Module Three: Step-by-Step

1. Bring to mind one of your resources, describe your resource to yourself, and then notice what happens on the inside.
2. Briefly check in with group members.
3. Debrief homework from module two. Ask for situations since last module in which group members used the skill of grounding or when they could in the future.

    a. Did you use the skill of grounding during the week?
    b. Using the resilient zone scale, track where you are on the scale.

4.  Explain the organizing principles of the brain.

    *Script:*

    - The brain is part of the nervous system. There are many complex ways to describe the brain. For our purposes, we will talk about the brain having three parts. The three parts are the "thinking" brain, the "emotional" or "feeling" brain, and the "survival" brain.
    - The "thinking" brain is your center for executive functioning and when you are using your "thinking" brain you can make better decisions. The "emotional" brain assesses risk and sounds an alarm when you are in danger, and the "survival" brain triggers the defensive responses that can help you survive if you are threatened.
    - When faced with danger that is perceived as life threatening, the human body goes into automatic defensive response. This happens without thinking, and comes from the survival brain. This part of the brain does not respond to "talking." It is about keeping us alive, as the brain is designed to help us live if threatened.
    - The survival brain responds to sensation. This is why many of our skills will help you "sense" changes in your body in order to reset your nervous system so that your body and mind can come back into balance.

5.  Explain the survival responses.

    *Script:*

    - The survival responses can be triggered by traumatic experiences. The body has a natural defensive system. It first may try to "tend and befriend"—to reach out to the threat (women use this strategy more than men). If the threat is great enough, "tend and befriend" may be bypassed and a person may go into fight or flight when perceiving an "inescapable attack."
    - When the body goes into fight or flight, the accelerator of the body is activated (the sympathetic nervous system). Sometimes people get stuck there. They can get stuck in the high zone. What are the physical reactions of being stuck in the high zone?
    - If a person gets stuck in the high zone, his body does not know the threat is over. It can feel like the traumatic event is happening all the time. (The practitioner may want to give an example.) Watch for activation and shift to resourcing or grounding as needed.
    - CRM/TRM skills help the body know the threat is over by putting on the brakes (the parasympathetic nervous system). What are the physical reactions when the brake is on?

6. Explain the survival response of "freeze," also known as the 1000-yard stare.

   *Script:*

   - When the traumatic experience overwhelms the nervous system and the person cannot get away or fight, and at the same time is terrified, the freeze response can result. In the military, the freeze response is known as the "1000-yard stare." People who experience a freeze response have a greater chance of developing more serious reactions as time goes by. The freeze response is hard-wired within the body. It is not a choice. It happens without thinking and it can result in either decreasing or increasing one's chances of survival. Without understanding the automatic nature of the freeze response, people can make faulty assumptions. The faulty assumptions can include thoughts such as, "I am weak," or "I am a coward."
   - A history of traumatic experiences increases the chance of a freeze response. If a person was abused as a child, he has a greater chance of experiencing a freeze response as an adult when experiencing something traumatic. The reason for this is that children, when abused, often respond by freezing. A history of freezing increases the risk of that automatic defensive response being activated during subsequent traumatic experiences.

7. Explain what release sensations are.

   *Script:*

   - As you track your nervous system, you will notice your resilient zone more often. As your body comes into balance, you may notice what is called nervous system release.
   - Nervous system release is a biological process that happens automatically when your body releases stuck energy. This can cause sensations that can be unsettling unless you understand their purpose. If you notice any of the sensations of release, just let them happen.
   - Release sensations are a way that your nervous system rebalances itself even though the sensations may feel strange. If the release sensations are too strong, you can consciously stop them and notice the urge to release, without allowing all the energy to discharge at once. This can be a way of slowly letting the body release.
   - Release sensations include tingling, trembling, warmth, cooling down, burping, yawning, clearing of the throat, and more.

8. Family members. Explain to the group that it can be helpful for significant supportive family members to learn about CRM/TRM and to learn about the biological perspective of their symptoms.

Depending on how your group is put together, you can invite the family member for an educational session with regard to the model. You could say, if you would like to bring a family member to the next session, it can be very helpful for her to learn about the concepts we will be discussing next week.

### Homework—Module Three

1. Practice the skills of grounding and resourcing at least once when you are already feeling calm, just to remind yourself where the resource sensations are in your body. You may want to try resourcing and grounding as you are about to go to sleep. Using these skills at bedtime may help you sleep better.
2. When experiencing tension during the week, bring your attention to one of the resources you identified and track the sensations associated with the resource. Remember to think about details of your resource to strengthen the sensations. The more you practice, the more you help your body move back into your resilient zone.
3. Use the iChill app at least once during the week.

## Module Four

### Overview

1. Introduce the "fast" versus "slow" system.
2. Discuss the appraisal system of the body and brain.
3. Review the resilient zone scale.
4. Introduce the Help Now! skill.
5. Review the CRM/TRM skills of tracking, resourcing, resource intensification, and grounding.

Note: Family member may or may not be present. Spend time orienting the family member to CRM/TRM. Spend time developing rapport.

### Objectives

The group member will be able to describe/review the following:

1. The fast and slow systems of reaction
2. The purpose of the appraisal system of the body
3. The gesturing and Help Now! skills
4. Nervous System Release
5. The CRM/TRM skills of tracking, resourcing, resource intensification, and grounding

*Module Four: Step-by-Step*

1. Bring to mind one of your resources, describe your resource to yourself, and then notice what happens on the inside or use the skill of grounding.
2. Briefly check in with group members.
3. Debrief homework from module three.

    a.  Did you use the skill of grounding and/or resourcing during the week?
    b.  Using the Resilient Zone Scale, track where you are on the scale.

4. Introduce the body's appraisal system and the fast and slow systems; review the resilient zone.

*Script:*

- We will talk about a part of your brain called the amygdala. The amygdala is part of your body's appraisal system—it scans the environment for anything that is different or new. The amygdala remembers negative experiences so that it can warn you if there is danger based on your life experience. Some people call it your personal "alarm system."
- The amygdala decides whether something in the environment is safe or dangerous and it determines whether to trigger two different systems in your body: the fast system or the slow system. The fast system reacts quickly and triggers the fight or flight response when it detects danger. It is automatic and it helps you survive dangerous or life-threatening situations. When the appraisal system does not detect threat, the slow system is triggered and then your brain can take its time to respond to a situation and make plans.
- The problem is when someone has experienced trauma, the appraisal system can lose its ability to tell the difference between situations that are dangerous and those that are safe. In this case, the fast system is always triggered; the slow system is not as available. I want to help you with the CRM/TRM skills that can help your appraisal system tell the difference between a match and a forest fire. If there are many triggers in the environment, it can be a real problem and your reactions may be much bigger and potentially lead to all sorts of problems with family, friends, and the law.
- The good news is that the CRM/TRM skills can help reduce the power of the triggers and in some cases, the triggers may go away altogether. As you apply the CRM/TRM skills in your daily life, you will find that you are more often in your resilient zone. When we are in our resilient zone, we think better and also can manage our emotions better.
- As we have discussed these new concepts, do you have questions? Can you think of times that your body has been in the fast system? The slow system?

5. Introduce gesturing and spontaneous movements.

   *Script:*

   - Gesturing refers to:
     - A movement, usually of the body or limbs, that expresses or emphasizes an idea, sentiment, or attitude.
     - The use of motions of the limbs or body as a means of expression and the practice of focusing on those that are self-soothing.
   - There are different kinds of movements and they are usually just below your conscious awareness. If you start paying attention to gestures that are self-calming, your gestures can help you stay within your resilient zone.
   - The following represent the types of gestures that others have found helpful to pay attention to:
     - Self-calming: bring comfort and safety
     - Release: represent the body releasing sensations of stress or trauma
     - Universal: represent wholeness, spiritual beliefs, or deep personal meaning
     - Joyful and powerful: represent well-being
     - Protective: movements of the hand, leg, and whole body that we do spontaneously to protect ourselves
   - Exercise:
     - Take five seconds to think about a self-soothing gesture . . . count 1, 2, 3, and then make the gesture.
     - Take five seconds to think about a gesture of joy or confidence . . . count 1, 2, 3, and then make the gesture.
     - As you make your gesture of joy, notice what happens inside. . . .
     - You can begin bringing awareness to gestures that are self-calming and even intentionally make a gesture that helps you as you move through your daily activities.

6. Introduce Help Now!

   *Script:*

   - When people have experienced challenging events such as combat zone trauma, sexual abuse, or other difficult situations, triggers can happen "out of the blue" and suddenly you can get stuck in the high zone or low zone.
   - Help Now! strategies can help. It can also be helpful to educate your close friends and family members on these strategies because sometimes we need help if we get really stuck.

- Anyone who has experienced trauma or stress can get bumped out of his resilient zone. If the bodily sensation is too overwhelming, the following suggestions may help a person get back into his resilient zone.
  - Open your eyes if they have a tendency to shut.
  - Drink a glass of water or juice.
  - Look around the room and pay attention to anything that attracts your attention.
  - Name six colors you see in the room or outside.
  - Notice the temperature in the room.
  - Notice the sounds around you.
  - Count backwards from 20 to 0.
  - Walk and pay attention to the movement in your arms and legs and how your feet are making contact with the ground.
  - Push your hands against the wall or door slowly and notice your muscles pushing. While leaning against the wall face-forward, slowly push your back against the wall.
  - Think of a sound or smell that is pleasant to you.

- Not every one of the strategies will help if you are way out of your resilient zone. You may find one more helpful than others. The more you practice, the better you will be able to manage these sensations. It is also okay to ask for help if you are being knocked out a lot.

### Homework: Module Four

1. Practice CRM/TRM skills each day. This can be especially helpful right before you go to sleep at night.
2. Practice the skill of resourcing at least once when you are already feeling calm, just to remind yourself where the resource sensations are in your body. Resourcing can also be helpful as you are about to go to sleep. The grounding, tracking, and resourcing skills at bedtime may help you sleep better.
3. Bring self-calming gestures to mind when bumped out of your resilient zone.
4. When experiencing distress during the week, practice either grounding, resourcing, or Help Now! strategies, and bring your attention to the places in your body that feel calmer or at least neutral.
5. The more you practice, the more you help your body move back into your resilient zone.
6. If a family member participated, discuss how you could help each other with the skills.

## Module Five

*Overview*

1.  Module five introduces the concept of "memory capsules" as a way to understand how memory can be stored as a multisensory experience and how easily it can be triggered by external or internal sensations. The scaffolding for the learning of the CRM continues with the learning of shift and stay.

*Objectives*

The group member will be able to describe the following:

1.  How he is incorporating resourcing and grounding into his activities of daily living
2.  The concept of memory capsules
3.  Shift and stay

*Module Five: Step-by-Step*

1.  Briefly check in with group members and review the resilient zone scale. Then start the session with a grounding or resourcing exercise.
2.  Debrief homework. Ask about the continued experiences using resourcing.

    a.  Are you using the skill before sleep? At other times?
    b.  Did you use any of the skills when bumped out of your resilient zone?

3.  Introduce the concept of memory capsules.

    *Script:*
    *   When people have experienced challenging events, including being in a combat zone where a person may have seen, heard, smelled, and felt difficult things, the brain may not remember the experience as a "story."
    *   The various parts of the experience can be stored as pieces of sensations and images, and when triggered, it can feel as if the experience is happening in the present moment. Dr. Robert Scaer refers to this form of memory as "memory capsules."
    *   Memory capsules are triggered by a whole variety of cues or triggers that can unexpectedly result in a memory capsule releasing some of the contents into your body and mind.
    *   You may not have any idea why you are experiencing sensations of distress. Since the contents are not all neatly connected, they can emerge

as emotion, a sensation like nausea or shaking, or other sensory images like sounds and smells or intrusive thoughts. There may not be a memory connected with the sensations.

- By using the CRM/TRM skills, you can help to reduce the power of the memory capsule and the triggers that cause unexpected and unpleasant sensations that make you feel uneasy, fearful, or out of control.

4. Discuss content introduced.

   *Script:*

   - As we have discussed the concept of memory capsules, do you have questions?
   - Have you had experiences that you think might be a memory capsule being triggered?
   - As we talk about this, it will be important to track your sensations.
   - If you notice that you are starting to be bumped out of your resilient zone, you can ground and resource to restore balance to your nervous system.
   - I also may suggest that we pause while you relate an experience and bring your awareness to the present moment through a grounding or resourcing exercise.

5. Introduce shift and stay.

   *Script:*

   - Shift and stay means shifting your attention away from something unpleasant to something pleasant or at least neutral, and then staying there.
   - If you feel distressed, you can:
     - Move your attention to a place in the body that is more comfortable, calmer, or neutral, or
     - Use one of your resources, and then notice the places inside that are calmer or neutral, or
     - Bring attention to how your body is making contact with the chair, sofa, ground, and notice the places that are more pleasant or neutral inside, or
     - Make a self-calming gesture and notice the sensations, or
     - Bring your attention to one of the Help Now! strategies, or
     - Track what happens inside as you stay focused on the more positive or neutral sensations, or
     - Bring your attention to the whole body and track all the changes. Stay with that for a few minutes.

- We'll practice shift and stay now.
  - Choose a resource from your list.
  - You can open or close your eyes, whichever is more comfortable for you.
  - Now bring the resource to mind and bring in the details of the resource.
  - Notice the sensations.
  - Now think about a future daily routine or incident that is mildly upsetting to you.
  - As you think about that mildly upsetting daily routine, shift your awareness to the image of the resource and notice the sensations associated with the resource. Stay with the sensations that you notice when you focus on your resource.
  - As you bring in the resource, notice the changes that happen inside.
  - Do the best you can. If you notice tension arising or uncomfortable feelings or sensations, let me know so I can help you shift back by staying with resource sensations.

*Note to practitioners: As you did in previous sessions, track your group closely so that you can help if you see any signs of difficulty. Help group members shift out of traumatic sensations by intensifying their resource by asking sensory and image-oriented questions (example: Let yourself take in all the details of your resource . . . notice all the parts that attract your attention. . . . Is there a pleasant sound or smell? What is the temperature?)*

6. Discuss exercise and close the session.

   *Script:*

   - We've got to wrap up for today but I want to emphasize again the importance of practicing the CRM/TRM skills you are learning in order to spend more time sensing your resilient zone.
   - The more that you practice the CRM/TRM skills, the more you will experience your resilient zone.
   - This can make a very big difference in managing yourself when you get very agitated.
   - The skill of shift and stay will help you return to your resilient zone. People often say that they feel more in charge of their sensations rather than the sensations being in charge of them.

### Homework—Module Five

1. Practice the skill of resourcing at least once when you are already feeling calm, just to remind yourself where the resource sensations are in your body. Again this week try resourcing as you are about to go to sleep. Using this skill at bedtime may help you sleep better.

2.  As you go through each day, periodically check in to see how resilient you feel. If you are on the low end of the resilient zone scale, bring one of your TRM skills in to help.
3.  If you notice frustration, tension, or any other unpleasant symptoms during the week, use the skill of shift and stay to bring your attention to one of the resources you identified, to grounding, to a self-soothing gesture, or to a place in the body that feels neutral or more pleasant, and track the sensations associated with the skill you are using. Pay particular attention to where in your body you notice these sensations. Stay with the pleasant or neutral sensations until you come back into your resilient zone.

## Module Six

### Overview

The wellness skills continue with Help Now! as a way the group member can help himself get back into his resilient zone if stuck in the low or high zone.

1.  Review Help Now!, shift and stay, and gesturing.
2.  Review the concept of memory capsules.

### Objectives

The group member will be able to describe how he is incorporating all six skills into his activities of daily living

### Module Six: Step-by-Step

1.  Briefly check in with group members about using the resilient zone scale; then start the session with a grounding or resourcing exercise.
2.  Debrief homework. Ask about the group's continued experiences using resourcing and whether shift and stay was used during the previous week.

    a.  Are you using the skills before sleep? If so, which ones? At other times?
    b.  Did you use any of the skills when bumped out of your resilient zone?
    c.  What is a memory capsule?

3.  Guide the group in a CRM/TRM skills exercise by suggesting that each member think about a potentially stressful reoccurring event that could happen in the future. As they think of the event, think about one or more of the skills that could help deal with the event.

    *Script:*

    •   Choose a resource from your resource list.
    •   As you bring the resource to mind, think about three descriptors of your resource.

- Notice all the sensations that are pleasant or neutral.
- Now, think about a future daily routine that is mildly upsetting to you.
- As you think about that mildly upsetting daily routine, shift your awareness to one of the following:
    - The resource
    - Grounding
    - A pleasant or neutral sensation within the body
    - A self-calming gesture
    - Help Now! strategies

4.  Help Now! strategies

    *Script:*

    - Did you use Help Now! strategies?
    - If so, did they help? If not, can you imagine situations in which the Help Now! strategies would be helpful? Are there any friends or family members who may want to know about Help Now! strategies who can help you if you get bumped out of your resilient zone?

5.  Discuss exercise and close the session.

    *Script:*

    - I want to emphasize again the importance of practicing the CRM/ TRM skills you are learning in order to reset your nervous system and be aware of your resilient zone.
    - The more that you practice the CRM/TRM skills, the more you will experience your resilient zone. This can make a very big difference in managing yourself when you get very agitated.
    - The skill of Help Now! will help you come back into your resilient zone. This is another skill that can help you be in charge of your symptoms.

**Homework—Module 6**

1.  Practice the skill of resourcing at least once when you are already feeling calm, just to remind yourself where the resource sensations are in your body. Again this week, try resourcing as you are about to go to sleep. Using this skill at bedtime may help you sleep better.
2.  As you go through each day, periodically check in to see how resilient you feel.
3.  If you notice frustration, tension, or any other unpleasant symptoms during the week, use the skill of shift and stay and stay with the pleasant or neutral sensations until you come back into your resilient zone.
4.  Use Help Now! strategies if you need to.

## Module Seven—Closure

*Overview*

All of the key concepts and CRM/TRM skills will be reviewed.

*Objectives*

The group member will be able to describe how he is incorporating all six skills into his activities of daily living.

*Module Seven: Step-by-Step*

1. Briefly check in with group members, ask about the resilient zone scale, and then start the session with a grounding or resourcing exercise.
2. Debrief: Ask about how the CRM/TRM skills are helping the group members. Discuss any challenges that may be occurring.

    a.   Are you using the skills before sleep? At other times?

    b.   Did you use any of the skills when bumped out of your resilient zone?

3. Let's brainstorm ways that you can remind yourself to use the CRM/TRM skills now that class is ending.

    *Script:*

    • Choose a resource from your resource list.
    • As you bring the resource to mind, think about three descriptors of your resource.
    • Notice all the sensations that are pleasant or neutral.
    • Now, think about a future daily routine that is mildly upsetting to you.
    • As you think about that mildly upsetting daily routine, shift your awareness to one of the following:
        • The resource
        • Grounding
        • A pleasant or neutral sensation within the body
        • A self-calming gesture
        • Help Now! strategies

Ask group members for any feedback about the experience.

This group session will also reinforce how the group members will use the skills once the group disbands.

*As we close, it would be helpful to hear how each one of you are using the skills now and how will you interweave the wellness skills into your life.*

Make sure the group members know how they can follow up if they need a tune-up. You can let the group know about iChill and the TRI website.

Invite the participants to give verbal or written feedback about the group. Group members may want to keep in touch with each other. Thus, having a list of participants and their email addresses and phone numbers can be a helpful support.

*If you would like to keep in touch with each other, sign the contact list and we will email each of you a roster.*

*As we get ready to close, I want to give each of you an opportunity to express your thoughts and/or feelings about the group.*

Invite open expression at the end. Some group members can be very creative and bring poetry, a song, or a personal statement to share.

### Note

Elaine Miller-Karas and Laurie Leitch wrote the first derivation of the group model. The group format has been further refined and expanded by Elaine Miller-Karas, LCSW; Lois Clinton, LCSW, at Walter Reed Medical Center; Jennifer Burton, LMFT, at Sherman Oaks Hospital; and Jan Click, formerly at the Veterans Administration.

# 10 Research Best Practices for International Environments

*Beverly J. Buckles with Elaine Miller-Karas*

The last few decades have brought increased realization that exposure to trauma is much more prevalent throughout the world than once thought (World Health Organization [WHO], 2013; Straussner & Calnan, 2014). With this recognition also comes an acknowledgement that one of the most neglected, and one of the most needed, interventions in global health is the provision of appropriate and timely trauma-focused mental health services. Finally, the importance of mental health interventions in mitigating the chronic effects produced by acute and complex trauma experiences is better understood. However, as a knowledge transformation is still in process, much more needs to occur if the relationships between trauma experiences, trauma-informed care, the impact on human capacity and resiliency, and social and economic recovery and redevelopment are to be fully understood and effectively addressed with appropriate intervention malleable enough to meet the needs of international environments. The Community Resiliency Model (CRM) and Trauma Resiliency Model (TRM) are research-informed and have great promise in expanding our global capacity to expand mental health interventions. This chapter will explore salient issues in researching innovative interventions and provide a brief overview of best practices. We also highlight diffusion of innovation research as an effective way to research interventions suitable for transfer to international environments.

## Expanding Global Involvement and the Importance of Mental Health Interventions

More than at any prior time in history the United Nations (UN), its development partners, and the whole of the international community of humanitarian non-governmental organizations (NGOs) now see the infusion of trauma-informed mental health services as an integral part of the development needs and issues that must be addressed if the UN is to be successful in achieving its Millennium Development Goals (MDGs).[1] Consequently, the international focus on the centrality of trauma-informed services, along with realistic and appropriate measures to infuse these into high-risk and at-risk global environments is greater than ever before. As a reflection of this change, all development projects funded by the UN and the United States Agency for International Development (USAID)[2] must now not only give evidence of the infusion of mental health services, but also demonstrate the inclusion of effective sustainable programming that can be assessed for positive community impact (World Health Organization [WHO], 2010).

WHO recognizes that much more is needed to underscore the centrality of mental health services in global health interventions. As such, at the convening of the Sixty-fifth World Health Assembly, a resolution was adopted to address the global burden of mental health disorders and the WHO's 2013 Mental Health Action Plan (WHO, 2013) was established as a comprehensive and coordinated response to mental health services as a global health emergency. As part of the launching of this initiative, Dr. Margaret Chan, director general of WHO, recognized mental well-being as a fundamental component in WHO's definition of health and endorsed the four major objectives to be achieved through the 2013 action plan (see http://apps.who.int/iris/bitstream/10665/89966/1/9789241506021_eng.pdf).

## Trauma-Informed Interventions: Evidence and Research

Up until recently, the selection of treatment approaches to address trauma symptoms was guided by client variables such as age and gender, the type of trauma, and cultural relevance. Therapist training, preference, and standard of practice considerations have also been primary factors influencing the selection of specific interventions (Straussner & Calnan, 2014). However, the global mental health initiative set forth in WHO's 2013 Mental Health Action Plan has brought new attention to the identification and selection of interventions appropriate for trauma-informed care. This increased focus on trauma-informed services has given way to a beneficial resurgence in the debate over which interventions should be used to prevent and address the consequential symptoms associated with trauma.

One of the benefits of this revived dialogue is the distinction between levels of intervention commonly referred to as basic and advanced (Bisson et al., 2007). These designations distinguish the preventative tools (e.g., psychological first aid [PFA]) that can be appropriately implemented in non-specialized health-care and service settings by persons other than advanced mental health professionals, from clinical interventions—which are designed to address chronic and/or complex trauma symptoms, which follow standard of practice time requirements, and which (when applied appropriately) are used only by professionals who have advanced degree preparation (WHO, 2010).

Clinical research is available that demonstrates support for the full range of intervention options from basic to advanced (e.g., Vernberg et al., 2008; Bisson et al., 2007, *2010*; Ponniah & Hollon, 2009; Albright & Thyer, 2010; Kleim et al., 2013; Gartlehner et al., 2013; Straussner & Calnan, 2014). Whereas most of the research examining the effectiveness of basic levels of intervention emphasizes the importance of these approaches as preventive in nature, the focus of research on advanced interventions has been to examine the effectiveness of specific psychological treatments in mitigating trauma-related symptoms. However, the number of studies that have provided comparative analyses between interventions is limited—with the results being the preferential selection of one clinical technique over another. What is useful, however albeit also infrequent, are studies that engage in meta-analysis, such as the meta-analysis conducted by Bradley, Greene, Russ, Dutra, and Westen (2005) that examined PTSD protocols and treatments and concluded that cognitive behavior therapy, exposure therapy, and eye movement desensitization and reprocessing (EMDR) were efficacious therapies. A more recent meta-analysis conducted by Bisson et al. (2007), completed in support of establishing PTSD guidelines for the National Institute of Health and Clinical Excellence (NICE), examined the results of randomized controlled trials (including comparative studies). Using rigorous inclusion-exclusion criteria, this meta-analysis reviewed 98 potential studies, which resulted in the inclusion of 38 randomized controlled studies. Five psychological treatment categories were used (clinician-rated; PTSD diagnosis; self-rated PTSD symptoms; anxiety; and depression) based upon advanced direction provide by NICE and review of the literature (Schnurr et al., 2003; Bisson et al., 2007). Among the benefits of the Bisson et al. (2007) study are the identified study limitations outlined. As such, considerable clinical diversity/heterogeneity was found within the studies examined (e.g., trauma types, individual vs. group treatment, and differences in what constituted trauma-focused interventions— basic vs. advanced). Additionally, none of the studies examined reported any adverse effects—leaving the question about possible negative effects unanswered. Small sample size was also a challenge of most of the studies examined, raising the possibility that baseline differences before treatment affected scores after treatment. The inclusion-exclusion criteria used by Bisson et al. (2007) also provides an important template for consideration when conceptualizing high-quality vs. low-quality clinical trials on psychological treatments for PTSD.

## Interventions with Traumatized Individuals: Best Practices

There is general, but varied consensus regarding the effectiveness of specific psychological interventions for the treatment of PTSD. For example, Gartlehner et al. (2013) identified trauma-focused cognitive behavioral therapy (TFCBT); eye movement desensitization and reprocessing (EMDR); and exposure therapy all as effective in the intervention of adult PTSD. Still others conclude that because of the highly subjective and widely varied experiences and consequences of trauma, no single treatment approach is preferable (Straussner & Calnan, 2014).

Using the categories of basic and advanced levels of interventions, a summary examination of the research that addresses the effectiveness of specific interventions used to prevent and/or treat the chronic effects of PTSD is presented below:

## Basic (Preventive) Interventions

### Psychological First Aid

Developed by World Vision International, the War Trauma Foundation, and WHO (Vernberg et al., 2008), Psychological First Aid (PFA) is a framework used in post-crisis settings for individuals who are experiencing acute distress to reduce their likelihood of developing PTSD. PFA supports resiliency by focusing on practical needs, basic comfort, and connection of people to necessary supports—all elements needed to assist individuals in developing adaptive functioning and returning to normalcy as soon as possible. As such, the primary merits of PFA are as follows: (1) its appropriateness for use by all responders—specialized and non-specialized; (2) its application in diverse non-specialized clinical and field settings; (3) its application for working with individuals across the lifespan; and (4) its cultural relevance and adaptability. Research on the effectiveness of PFA is ongoing, but it is generally considered a preventative measure, and is not considered effective if applied alone or when addressing chronic or complex trauma symptoms (Vernberg et al., 2008).

### Critical Incident Stress Debriefing (CISD)

CISD was developed for use within 24 hours of a crisis event to support small, homogeneous staff groups (such as firefighters, police officers, military and emergency services personnel—not trauma survivors) to process information and mitigate the onset of stress reactions. Further, the guidelines established for the use of CISD emphasize its use only with staff groups whose individual members demonstrate normal positive resiliency, and show no signs of abnormal or extreme stress reactions (Everly & Mitchell, 1999; Mitchell, 2003).

Data regarding the effectiveness of CISD has been the subject of serious debate. Studies (Bisson et al., 2007; Carlier, Lamberts, van Uchelen, & Gersons, 1998; Mayou, Ehlers, & Hobbs, 2000; Rose, Bisson, & Weesely, 2001) have suggested overwhelmingly negative intervention outcomes for CISD (i.e., no improvement or significantly worse systems at follow-up). However, according to Mitchell (2003) research on the effectiveness of CISD is positive when personnel have been properly trained in Critical Incident Stress Management (CISM; i.e., through certified training), and when providers adhere to the published and international standards and guidelines of CISM and CISD practice. Mitchell (2003) also reports that without exception, negative research outcomes on CISD have been associated with studies where personnel were not trained and/or the core CISM standards of practice were violated. As such, Mitchell (2003) points out that 100% of the negative research results on CISD have occurred when the intervention was inappropriately used to treat primary victims—instead of the intended target populations (i.e., firefighters, police officers, military and emergency services personnel, etc.).

### Advanced Interventions for Addressing Trauma Symptoms

#### Cognitive Behavioral Therapy (CBT)

Often referred to as trauma-focused cognitive behavioral therapy (TFCBT) when used in the context of addressing chronic and complex trauma-related symptoms, CBT is a type of talk therapy that focuses on restructuring ways of thinking (cognitive patterns) that sabotage the resiliency of survivors of trauma. The cognitive patterns that are addressed are considered inaccurate and negative ways of interpreting or perceiving normal situations. These inaccurate and negative ways of thinking may not only keep the survivor from improving, but have the potential to produce downward spiraling ways of thinking and emotional responses—and are thus the focus of intervention (Ponniah & Hollon, 2009).

Research on trauma-informed CBT (TFCBT) provides substantial consensus on its effectiveness for treating PTSD symptoms (Bisson et al., 2007; Stein et al., 2009; Stewart & Chambless, 2009; Department of Veterans Affairs and Department of Defense, 2010; Ehlers et al., 2010; Kleim et al., 2013) as well as secondary psychosocial and behavioral benefits that improve overall quality of life (Schnurr et al., 2007). The National Institute for Health and Clinical Excellence (National Institute for Health and Clinical Excellence, 2005) and the American Psychiatric Association (American Psychiatric Association Work Group on ASD and PTSD, 2004) have identified TFCBT as one of the most effective first treatment choices when working with individuals with PTSD. CBT is listed as one of the evidenced-based practices for trauma intervention supported by the WHO (2010). A normal course of CBT treatment is administered through weekly sessions over several months (Ehlers et al., 2010).

When CBT is found to be ineffective, standard of practice supports alternative and/or the addition of pharmacological treatment (e.g., for individuals declining or not responding well to this approach; for individuals considered at serious risk for continuing threat of additional traumas; and for individuals with co-morbid or cognitive issues that affect treatment engagement) (National Collaborating Centre for Primary Care, 2004, in Bisson et al., 2007).

*Eye Movement Desensitization and Reprocessing (EMDR)*

Introduced over 20 years ago (Shapiro, 1989), EMDR combines trauma memory reprocessing (a form of exposure therapy) with guided dual attention stimulation tasks (e.g., eye movements, hand tapping, or tones) to assist trauma survivors in processing negative trauma-related memories, emotions, and thoughts. This process is continued/repeated until trauma-related distress is reduced and the survivor's belief in more positive trauma-related thoughts has increased (Ponniah & Hollon, 2009; Albright & Thyer, 2010). However, among the criticisms about the use this technique is concern that recalling a traumatic incident may retraumatize rather than desensitize the trauma survivor (Church, 2010). For this reason, it is recommended that therapies such as EMDR be used only in clinical settings by individuals who have been certified in their use so that if extreme cathartic experiences occur, they can be immediately addressed. With these quality assurances in mind, clinical research (Rogers & Silver, 2002; Bisson et al., 2007) supports EMDR as an effective evidenced-based treatment for PTSD, and suggests that EMDR may be a more efficient treatment option than other exposure therapy approaches (Ironson, Freund, Strauss, & Williams, 2002; Lee et al., 2002). According to Salvatore (2009), studies comparing EMDR to other recognized treatment approaches for trauma found the effectiveness of EMDR equal to or better than other PTSD treatments. Other studies also found EMDR to generally work faster (Van der Kolk et al., 2007). However, contradictory evidence also exists, which concludes that the benefits of EMDR are moderate and secondary to CBT (Rogers & Silver, 2002; Bisson et al., 2007). According to Rogers and Silver (2002), dismantling studies have focused on the eye movement component of the EMDR, noting that research failed to clearly demonstrate differences in treatment outcomes when eye movements or other stimulus were omitted, thus raising the question of whether the primary mechanism at work in EMDR is the imaginal exposure— an observation that points again to the advanced clinical and professional quality assurances that must be in place if this treatment technique is to be appropriately administered (Church, 2010).

However, given EMDR's apparent usefulness with PTSD as a general diagnostic category, it is currently being used to treat redeploying soldiers and returning combat veterans (Department of Veterans Affairs, 2004). It is also recognized by WHO as an evidenced-based intervention appropriate for use with trauma survivors (WHO, 2010). Like CBT, EMDR is normally provided to individuals on an outpatient basis over 8–12 sessions.

Despite the general support for EMDR, variable clinical research results suggest that not all chronic PTSD sufferers will benefit from this treatment. When this occurs, modification to the treatment regime as well as other treatment approaches are recommended, including extending the number of sessions to extend beyond the normal 8–12, and adding pharmacological aids as a secondary clinical support (National Collaborating Centre for Primary Care, 2004, in Bisson et al., 2007).

*Community Resiliency Model (CRM)[3] and Trauma Resiliency Model (TRM)*

Until recently, most mental health professionals engaged in the treatment of PTSD have focused on modalities that address the cognitive, psychological, and emotional needs of trauma survivors instead of emphasizing the biological results of trauma, which are now understood to be central to human resiliency and wellness (Adams, Marlotte, Douroux, & Kane, 2009). As such, emerging evidence suggests that CRM and TRM may be a more effective means of treating traumatized individuals as compared to other established methods. The CRM and TRM employ skills to balance the autonomic nervous system by addressing the dysregulation of the physiological response experienced by trauma survivors, dysregulation which, if not addressed, can result in the onset or continuation of PTSD-related symptoms (Adams et al., 2009).

Unique from other interventions used to address trauma-related symptoms, CRM and TRM methods are taught to trauma survivors as a set of self-stabilization skills that help reregulate the central nervous system in the wake of upsetting and traumatic experiences. These techniques are easily learned by most individuals in non-clinical settings within one to a few sessions. The learned techniques have been found to support self-care and subsequently instill a sense of personal mastery and self-management over intense physical and emotional states. This focus on the mastery of the biological responses to the extraordinary events normalizes the experience of trauma as a pliable health condition, rather than focusing on the survivor's suffering as a form of mental illness. As such, the CRM and TRM appear to be the only trauma-focused interventions that may have the added impact of de-stigmatizing PSTD as a mental health condition. Further, CRM and TRM skills are reported by survivors as sustainable, and with continued use they are associated with the development of a renewed sense of hope. Survivors also report that as they continue to use these skills their efficacy in completing activities of daily living improves, and that they incorporate CRM and TRM skills into their lives as part of a personal wellness practice (Citron, Dust, & Miller-Karas, 2013). Also reported (and notable) is the ease and frequency with which survivors report sharing these self-care skills with family, friends, and members of their community (Adams et al., 2009).

Now regarded as research-informed, the CRM was put into practice on a widespread scale to help survivors after the 2010 Haitian earthquake in both Port au Prince and the Central Plateau of Haiti. A joint project between the Unitarian Universalist Service Committee and HelpAge evaluated the effectivenss of the CRM two years after the earthquake. Seniors in one of the displaced persons camp were taught the skills in three 20-minute sessions during one week by

Haitian providers trained in CRM skills. The Hopkins 25 was used and administered pre- and post-treatment. CRM skills training led to significantly greater reductions on the Hopkins 25 in depression scores as compared to beneficiaries who did not receive TRM training (Citron et al., 2013).

More recently, the CRM Innovation Project was conducted in 2010 to support the health, education, and coping skills of residents living in a severely impoverished community marginalized by severe and persistent violence. See Chapter 6 for the details of this project.

The transferability of the CRM and TRM to support trauma-related symptom reduction is becoming increasingly evident. Since 2006, the CRM and TRM have successfully been used in a variety of settings around the world (including Guatemala, China, Haiti, Kenya, Darfur, Uganda, Somalia, Rwanda, the Ivory Coast, the Philippines, and the United States) following natural or man-made disasters, and they have been found to be efficacious and innovative cross-cultural interventions (Adams et al., 2009). Because of the observable effectiveness of the CRM and TRM, both are being rapidly disseminated around the world. Associated with this dissemination is the expansion of research, including impact studies, to move the CRM and TRM from research-informed to that of evidenced-based practice.

## Identifying and Selecting Appropriate Techniques for International Environments

Research provides support for multiple interventions as effective in preventing and/or addressing the effects of trauma (Gartlehner et al., 2013). However, noticeably absent from the majority of studies and literature on the effectiveness of PTSD treatment methods is the assessment of the suitability and/or transferability of prevalent approaches for use in international environments. Although the considerable heterogeneity among the populations studied could suggest that some interventions are suitable for transfer into diverse global environments, the majority of the evidence was derived from controlled clinical treatment sites, unlike what is found in international post-disaster environments. This huge difference raises the question about determining the effectiveness of interventions for use in third-world and developing countries where (1) established mental health systems do not exist and (2) there is a substantial shortage of mental health professionals with the advanced training needed to implement the treatment regime required to produce optimal effects. In addition, the research reviewed did not address transferability across cultures or significant socio-economic barriers. Also, shockingly absent is the lack of attention given to the impact of various treatments on the mental health stigma (positive or negative) that may be experienced by treatment recipients. The impact of such stigma, if not fully examined and understood, can lead to devastating if not deadly effects in countries where the treatment of persons with mental illness appears to have not progressed past the 1600s (WHO, 2010). Finally, although the highest priority for improved mental health services internationally is the expansion of interventions that promote sustainable self-care (personal communication with Dr. Saxena, director of Mental and Substance Abuse, July 11, 2014), remarkably little, if any, consideration is given to the ability of service recipients to use recognized PTSD treatments without the presence of highly trained mental health professionals. Sustainability through self-care, supporting normalization and anti-stigma, is a seriously lacking attribute of most of the recognized PTSD treatments.

These apparent gaps in the appropriateness of PTSD treatment approaches for international use underscore the need to find a better way to identify and select trauma-informed interventions. WHO has substantial influence in determining the criteria for the selection and use of treatments to prevent or address the effects of PTSD. Currently, interventions are endorsed only if they are evidenced-based and in the public domain (personal communication with Dr. Saxena, director of Mental and Substance Abuse, July 11, 2014). As such, WHO endorses the use of PFA for prevention and early intervention, and the use of CBT and EMDR as advanced treatments for PTSD (WHO, 2013). However, with regard to endorsing CBT and EMDR, WHO leadership also recognizes that dissemination of these interventions is challenged by the lack of available advanced professionals needed to train individuals and provide supervision in the appropriate use of these techniques. WHO also recognizes that these issues must be resolved (or the techniques must be modified) before the use of these approaches can be made widely available.[4]

One method that was developed to resolve some of the issues about appropriate interventions in international settings was reported in a study conducted by Bisson et al. (2010). In this effort, Bisson et al. (2010) used the Delphi process to engage an independent group of 106 experts from 25 countries to reach consensus regarding protocols for psychosocial care following disasters. As a result, the group reached strong consensus against the early application of formal universal interventions for all individuals (psychological and pharmacological). Support was shared for the identification of individuals who might have been affected by a traumatic event for possible symptoms, albeit this did not suggest universal screening, rather methods by which individuals with special needs could be triaged. In addition, consensus was reached that the limited and selective use of pharmacological interventions could be provided, but only as a secondary line of intervention in emergency situations. Experts also agreed that psychoeducation information should be disseminated regarding the consequences of trauma—with the emphasis on an understanding of resiliency rather than the onset of potentially negative and possibly frightening symptoms. Agreement was also reached on the relevance of social support, and that the perceived lack thereof should be used as a possible indicator of the presence of PTSD. And finally, consensus was reached that the provision of stepped care using interventions designed to treat PTSD (i.e., trauma-focused CBT or evidenced-based alternatives such as EMDR) should be used only for those individuals who develop symptoms within the first three months.

While this process and the recommendations reached by these experts strengthen a unified perspective on post-disaster interventions, the consensus supports well-known positions and does nothing to advance the challenge of identifying and implementing trauma-focused interventions that are transferable to international environments. The problem of assisting individuals who urgently need symptom relief from chronic and complex trauma without being further stigmatized has risen to the level of a global health crisis. The review did not address biological interventions like the CRM and TRM that have demonstrated effectiveness in reducing and, in some cases, ameliorating the impact of shock trauma (i.e., trauma caused by a sudden and unexpected traumatic event).

Other methods need to be developed to identify effective PTSD interventions suitable for transfer to international environments. One approach that draws on the rich tradition of research about dissemination of new ideas (innovation) into international environments is diffusion of innovation research (Rogers, 1995; Mendel, Meredith, Schoenbaum, Sherbourne, & Well, 2007). As such, diffusion of innovation research not only helps us to understand the process by which an innovation is communicated through members of a social system over time, but also helps practitioners gain insights about how the members of the social system develop mutual understanding about the new idea (innovation)—which in this case is treatment for trauma-related symptoms. Within this process, attention is given to identifying and understanding individual, organizational, community, and innovation attributes and barriers that can affect the adoption or rejection of the new idea (innovation). This examination allows us to assess a population's readiness to implement the new idea, and depending on where individuals may be at in their conceptualization, actualization, and/or current utilization of similar ideas, strategies can be implemented to assist in moving their decision making forward (Buckles, 1989).

Even if an idea is not implemented in its entirety as a full diffusion study, the criteria used to evaluate the suitability of an innovation in a new environment have merit for providing a better way to identify and select PTSD treatments that are best suited for use in an international post mass disaster environment. As such, the comparative merits of all of the recommended PTSD treatments can be examined by assessing a recipient population's or comparative designee's perception of the characteristics of each option. As such, potential treatment audiences would evaluate the suitability of options by comparing each on the following criteria:

1. Relative advantage (e.g., of one option over another or current ways of feeling better)
2. Compatibility (e.g., with beliefs, values, and current ways of engaging, knowing, and doing)

3.  Complexity (i.e., how hard is it to learn or do?)
4.  Trialability (i.e., can it be tested without the requirement of a long-term commitment?)
5.  Observability (i.e., does it do what it is supposed to and are the benefits quickly apparent?)

Using this framework in a quick examination of already endorsed PTSD treatments, one can easily see that any approach that employs techniques that might be considered intrusive or strange (e.g., tracking eye movements, or tapping) could be suspect. Likewise, treatment options that require multiple sessions or months to realize benefits would not be favored over an approach that could be learned in one or a few interactions. But, perhaps the most glaring comparison would result if a group perceived the possibility that multiple treatment sessions with an advanced mental health professional would result in being labeled mentally ill. Undoubtedly, recipient evaluators would select almost any comparative option that provided them with observable self-care tools that could be shared with others to support individual and collective community wellness and empowerment. As one can readily begin to see, based on our working knowledge of international treatment environments in post-disaster situations, optimal treatments, and those strongly preferred by the populations being helped, support self-care and do not further marginalize those receiving assistance.

## Conclusion

As the WHO and its global affiliates give increased recognition to the importance of trauma-focused mental health services, our understanding of how to identify appropriate sustainable interventions needs to be expanded. Leaders in trauma-focused mental health need to move beyond the standard answers about what works in most cases in highly specialized environments, and begin to recognize that in international post mass disaster environments, people require interventions that trigger resiliency and self-care without any added burden of ostracism or potentially lethal mental health stigma. We need openness to innovations such as the CRM and TRM, which demystify trauma responses through a safe and effective lens of human physiology.

## Notes

1.  The eight UN Millennium Development Goals are as follows: (1) Eradicate extreme poverty and hunger; (2) Achieve universal primary education; (3) Promote gender equality and empower women; (4) Reduce child mortality; (5) Improve maternal health; (6) Combat HIV/AIDS, malaria, and other diseases; (7) Ensure environmental sustainability; and (8) Develop a global partnership for development (www.undp.org).
2.  USAID has provided humanitarian aid in Africa, Asia, Latin America, and Europe (www.usaid.gov).

3. Referred to in previous publications as TRM-C (Citron et al., 2013).
4. Along with the new guidelines, WHO now advises against the use of previously popular medical interventions (e.g., the use of anti-anxiety medication for stress and sleep issues during the first month following a traumatic event) (WHO, 2013).

# References

Adams, L. L., Marlotte, L., Douroux, A. N., & Kane, L. (2009). *Trauma Resiliency Model: A mind-body treatment modality for trauma survivors.* Division 27 of the American Psychological Association Society for Community Research and Action 12th Biennial Conference: Realizing Our New Vision: Values and Principles for Practice, Research And Policy, June 18–21, Montclair, NJ [Abstracts], 143. doi:10.1037/e628592012–402

Albright, D. L., & Thyer, B. (2010). Does EMDR reduce post-traumatic stress disorder symptomatology in combat veterans? *Behavioral Interventions, 25*(1), 1–19.

American Psychiatric Association Work Group on ASD and PTSD. (2004). *Practice guideline for the treatment of patients with acute stress disorder and posttraumatic stress disorder.* Washington, DC: American Psychiatric Association.

Bisson, J. I., Ehlers, A., Matthews, R., Pilling, S., Richards, D., & Turner, S. (2007). Psychological treatments for chronic post-traumatic stress disorder: Systematic review and meta-analysis. *The British Journal of Psychiatry, 190*(2), 97–104. doi:10.1192/bjp.bp.106.021402

Bisson, J. I., Tavakoly, B., Witteveen, A. B., Ajdukovic, D., Jehel, L., Johansen, V. J., . . . Olff, M. (2010). TENT guidelines: Development of post-disaster psychosocial care guidelines through a Delphi process. *The British Journal of Psychiatry, 196*(1), 69–74. doi:10.1192/bjp.bp.109.066266

Bradley, R., Greene, J., Russ, E., Dutra, L., & Westen, D. (2005). A multidimensional meta-analysis of psychotherapy for PTSD. *American Journal of Psychiatry, 162*(2), 214–227. doi:10.1176/appi.ajp.162.2.214

Buckles, B. J. (1989). *Identification of variables influencing the readiness-to-implement information technology by social work faculty* [e-book]. New York: Adelphi University, Abstracts.

Carlier, I. V. E., Lamberts, R. D., van Uchelen, A. J., & Gersons, B. P. R. (1998). Disaster-related post-traumatic stress in police officers: A field study of the impact of debriefing. *Stress Medicine, 14*(3), 143–148. doi:10.1002/(SICI)1099–1700(199807)14:3<143::AID-SMI770>3.0.CO;2-S

Church, D. (2010). The treatment of combat trauma in veterans using EFT (emotional freedom techniques): A pilot protocol. *Traumatology, 16*(1), 55–65. doi:10.1177/1534765609347549

Citron, S. (2013). Final CRM innovation evaluation report. Claremont: Trauma Resource Institute.

Citron, S., Dust, M., & Miller-Karas, E. (2013). *The effectiveness of trauma resiliency skills with older adult HelpAge IDP camp residents in post-earthquake Haiti: A randomized controlled trial.* Unpublished manuscript, Trauma Resource Institute, Claremont, CA.

Department of Veterans Affairs & Department of Defense. (2004). VA/DoD Clinical Practice Guideline for the Management of Post-Traumatic Stress. Washington, DC: Veterans Health Administration, Department of Veterans Affairs and Health Affairs, Department of Defense. Office of Quality and Performance publication 10Q-CPG/PT.

Department of Veterans Affairs and Department of Defense. (2010). *Management of post-traumatic stress.* Washington, DC: Department of Veterans Affairs. http://www.healthquality.va.gov/Post_Traumatic_Stress_Disorder_PTSD.asp

Ehlers, A., Clark, D. M., Hackmann, A., Grey, N., Liness, S., Wild, J., . . . McManus, F. (2010). Intensive cognitive therapy for PTSD: A feasibility study. *Behavioural and Cognitive Psychotherapy, 38*(4), 383–398. http://oxcadat.psy.ox.ac.uk/downloads/CT-PTSD%20Treatment%20Procedures.pdf/view

Everly, G. S., & Mitchell, J.T. (1999). *Critical Incident Stress Management (CISM): A new era and standard of care in crisis intervention.* Ellicott City, MD: Chevron.

Gartlehner, G., Forneris, C.A., Brownley, K.A., Gaynes, B.N., Sonis, J., Coker-Schwimmer, E., & . . . Lohr, K.N. (2013). Interventions for the prevention of posttraumatic stress disorder (PTSD) in adults after exposure to psychological trauma. *Comparative Effectiveness Reviews, 109.* doi:10.1037/e553852013–001

International Civil Defense Organization. (2014, March). www.icdo.org

Ironson, G.I., Freund, B., Strauss, J.L., & Williams, J. (2002). Comparison of two treatments for traumatic stress: A community-based study of EMDR and prolonged exposure. *Journal of Clinical Psychology, 58*(1), 113–128.

Kleim, B., Grey, N., Wild, J., Nussbeck, F.W., Stott, R., Hackmann, A., . . . Ehlers, A. (2013). Cognitive change predicts symptom reduction with cognitive therapy for posttraumatic stress disorder. *Journal of Consulting and Clinical Psychology, 81*(3), 383–393. doi:10.1037/a00311290

Kulig, J. C., Edge, D. S., Townshend, I. I., Lightfoot, N. N., & Reimer, W.W. (2013). Community resiliency: Emerging theoretical insights. Journal of Community Psychology, 41(6), 758–775.

Lee, G., Gavriel, H., Drummond, P., Lee, C., Gavriel, H., Drummond, P. . . . Greenwald, R. (2002). Treatment of post-traumatic stress disorder: A comparison of stress inoculation training with prolonged exposure and eye movement desensitization and reprocessing. *Journal of Clinical Psychology, 58*(9), 1071–1089.

Mayou, R.A., Ehlers, A., & Hobbs, M. (2000). Psychological debriefing for road traffic accident victims. *British Journal of Psychiatry, 176,* 589–593.

Mendel, P., Meredith, L. S., Schoenbaum, M., Sherbourne, C. D., & Well, K. B. (2007). *Interventions in organizational and community context: A framework for building evidence on dissemination and implementation in health services research.* RAND Corporation and NIMH Division of Services and Innovation Research. Administration and Policy in Mental Health and Mental Health Services Research, Springer Science & Business Media, LLC. 10.1007/s10488–007–0144–9.

Mitchell, J. (2003). *Crisis intervention and CISM: A research summary.* http://www.cism.cap.gov/files/articles/CISM%20Research%20Summary.pdf

National Collaborating Center for Primary Care. (2004). Clinical guideline 22. Anxiety: Management of anxiety (panic disorder, with or without agoraphobia, and generalized anxiety disorder) in adults in primary, secondary and community care. National Institute for Clinical Excellence.

National Institute for Health and Clinical Excellence. (2005). *Posttraumatic stress disorder (PTSD): The management of PTSD in adults and children in primary and secondary care* (NICE Clinical Guideline 26). http://guidance.nice.org.uk/CG26

Ponniah, K., & Hollon, S.D. (2009). Empirically supported psychological treatments for adult acute stress disorder and posttraumatic stress disorder: A review. *Depression and Anxiety, 26*(12), 1086–1109. doi:10.1002/da.20635

Rogers, E.M. (1995). *Diffusion of innovations.* New York: The Free Press.

Rogers, S., & Silver, S.M. (2002). Is EMDR an exposure therapy? A review of trauma protocols. *Journal of Clinical Psychology, 58*(1), 43–59. doi:10.1002/jclp.1128

Rose, S., Bisson, J., & Weesely, S. (2001). Psychological debriefing for preventing post-traumatic stress disorder (PTSD). Cochrane Database, *Syst Rev.,* 3.

Salvatore, R. (2009). Posttraumatic stress disorder: A treatable public health problem. *Health & Social Work, 34*(2), 153–155.

Schnurr, P. P., Friedman, M. J., Engel, C. C., Foa, E. B., Shea, M.T., Chow, B. K., . . . Bernardy, N. (2007). Cognitive behavioral therapy for posttraumatic stress disorder in women: A randomized controlled trial. *JAMA: The Journal of the American Medical Association, 297*(8), 820–830. doi:10.1001/jama.297.8.820

Schnurr, P. P., Friedman, M. J., Foy, D.W., Shea, M.T., Hsieh, F.Y., Lavori, P.W. . . . Bernardy, N. C. (2003). Randomized trial of trauma-focused group therapy for posttraumatic stress disorder:

Results from a Department of Veterans' Affairs cooperative study. *Archives of General Psychiatry, 60*(5), 481–489.

Shapiro, F. (1989). Efficacy of the eye movement desensitization procedure in the treatment of traumatic memories. *Journal of Traumatic Stress Studies, 2,* 199–223.

Stein, D. J., Cloitre, M., Nemeroff, C. B., Nutt, D. J., Seedat, S., Shalev, A.Y., & Zohar, J. (2009). Cape Town consensus on posttraumatic stress disorder. *CNS Spectrums, 14*(Suppl. 1), 52–58.

Stewart, R. E., & Chambless, D. L. (2009). Cognitive-behavioral therapy for adult anxiety disorders in clinical practice: A meta-analysis of effectiveness studies. *Journal of Consulting and Clinical Psychology, 77*(44), 595–606. doi:10.1037/a0016032

Straussner, S.L.A., & Calnan, A. J. (2014). Trauma through the life cycle: A review of current literature. *Clinical Social Work Journal,* doi:10.1007/s10615–014–0496-z

United Nations Development Project. (2014). www.undp.org

Van der Kolk, B., Spinazzola, J., Blaustein, M., Hopper, J., Hopper, E., Korn, D., & Simpson, W. (2007). A randomized clinical trial of EMDR, fluoxetine and pill placebo in the treatment of PTSD: Treatment effects and long-term maintenance. *Journal of Clinical Psychiatry, 68*(1), 37–46.

Vernberg, E.M., Steinberg, A.M., Jacobs, A.K., Brymer, M.J., Watson, P.J., Osofsky, J.D., & Ruzek, J.I. (2008). Innovations in disaster mental health: Psychological first aid.

World Health Organization. (2008). Mental Health Gap Action Programme (mhGAP). http://www.who.int/mental_health/mhgap/en/ World Health Organization

World Health Organization. (2010). *Mental health and development.* http://www.who.int/mental_health/policy/mhtargeting/en/

World Health Organization. (2013). *Mental health action plan 2013–2020.* http://apps.who.int/iris/bitstream/10665/89966/1/9789241506021_eng.pdf

# Index